COMMODITY
FUTURES TRADING

COMMODITY FUTURES TRADING
A Bibliographic Guide

JAMES B. WOY
Head, Mercantile Library
Free Library of Philadelphia

R. R. Bowker Company
A Xerox Publishing Company
New York & London, 1976

Published by R. R. Bowker Co. (A Xerox Publishing Company)
1180 Avenue of the Americas, New York, N.Y. 10036
Copyright © 1976 by Xerox Corporation
All rights reserved
Printed and bound in the United States of America

Library of Congress Cataloging in Publication Data

Woy, James B
   Commodity futures trading.

   Includes indexes.
   1. Commodity exchanges—Bibliography.
2. Commodity exchanges—Dictionaries. I. Title.
Z7164.C83W69 [HG6046] 016.3326'44 76-23430
ISBN 0-8352-0899-0

A speculator who dies rich has died before his time.
                                                —Anon

The surest way to end up with a small fortune in the commodity market is to start with a large fortune.
                                                —Anon

CONTENTS

Preface ix
Commodity Futures Trading 1
Bibliography 191
Government Reports and Periodicals of Interest to
    Commodity Traders 196
Directory of Publishers 201
Author Index 203
Subject Index 205

PREFACE

Back in 1960, an article in *Business Week* (June 11) took a dim view of the commodity markets, telling about "a steady decline in futures trading. . . . Over-all trading volume dropped to its lowest point since World War II. . . . Many commodity traders cry that within a few years only a shell will be left of several among the 15 major U.S. exchanges. . . . Individual speculation is clearly on the wane." Any broker, for example, who took the *Business Week* article too seriously, and got out of the commodity field in 1960, had a view from the sidelines of the greatest expansion of futures trading in history. Thirteen years later, on September 17, 1973, *Industry Week* was estimating that 500,000 commodity traders were active in the United States and that the number might grow to 5,000,000 by 1980! Whether the five million traders materialize or not, the fact remains that a record trading volume of over 30 million futures contracts was established in 1975. The lesson to be learned here, no doubt, is that information on commodity futures should always be viewed objectively and even with a certain amount of skepticism. This is certainly true in the case of information about how to actually speculate with success in commodities—the subject of this bibliographic guide.

To aid the growing number of commodity traders, especially amateurs, in their search for advice about how to operate profitably, this book defines various commodity trading methods, as well as related topics, and describes information available on each subject in leading textbooks, popular works, and selected magazine articles. Most of the material was published recently, but some goes back as far as 1920. All issues of *Commodity Year Book*, from the original 1939 volume to 1975 (not published during the years 1943–1947), were examined for trading method articles believed to be still of interest to present-day speculators. (For a valuable collection of reprints and new versions of *Commodity Year Book* articles of recent years, see the Commodity Research Bureau's 1975 volume, *Forecasting Commodity Prices*.)

Users of this guide are reminded that publishers and prices, where available, are included in the "Bibliography" section following the main body of this volume. Also, a separate, handy list of important government reports and periodicals has been included, with complete ordering information given for each item.

Finally, the reader should be aware that commodity futures trading, as usually practiced, is an extremely risky game. It is perhaps ominous for the small speculator that many books on the subject emphasize the same two words: good luck.

JAMES B. WOY
Head, Mercantile Library
Free Library of Philadelphia

COMMODITY FUTURES TRADING

ACTION AND REACTION THEORY
The theory that an interim drop in the price of a commodity that has been rising should retrace about half of the previous rise. The opposite should also apply; that is, a temporary rise in the price of a commodity that has been falling will often recoup about 50 percent of the previous loss. Unfortunately, the theory states only that these reactions are likely to occur; there is no clue given as to just *when* they will occur. The action and reaction theory is a "technical" rather than a "fundamental" theory.

Keltner, Chester W. "The Theory of Action and Reaction." In his *How to Make Money in Commodities*, pp. 114–117. 1960.

> The theory is illustrated by means of a chart entitled "A Theoretical Market Demonstrating the Theory of Action and Reaction." The various price actions and reactions are first identified by letters of the alphabet (A through L) and are then explained in the text.

ACTUALS. *See* Cash Commodity

ADAGES. *See* Trading Rules

ADVISORY SERVICES (*See also* Bibliographies; Periodicals; Statistics Sources)
Published advice or information about commodity markets and price trends, typically published in loose-leaf or newsletter form. Some services recommend specific trades, while others merely suggest the direction of future price movements.

Angrist, Stanley W. "Advisory Services." In his *Sensible Speculating in Commodities*, pp. 174–182. 1972.

> A general, intelligently written discussion of published advisory services and market letters for commodity traders. Specific services are not named in this particular chapter of Angrist's book (28 of them are described in an appendix), but there is a review of the merits of so-called "Technical

Services" versus "Fundamental Services." The author states that following the advice of fundamental services sometimes requires a strong stomach, because of the tendency of these services to stay with a losing position in the belief that the fundamental aspects of the position will eventually assert themselves profitably. On the other hand, as Angrist makes clear, being whipsawed (taking losses in opposite directions in rapid succession because of the failure of trends to establish themselves) a few times can put a strain on the nerves when following technical or chart advice.

Angrist, Stanely W. "Annotated List of Advisory Services." In his *Sensible Speculating in Commodities*, pp. 210–214. 1972.

Angrist does not claim to have compiled a comprehensive list of commodity advisory services, but he does list and describe briefly 28 of them that have come to his attention. Complete addresses and subscription rates are given.

"Directory of Futures Trading." Published annually in January as a special issue of *Commodities* magazine (1000 Century Plaza, Columbia, Md. 21044).

This special directory issue of *Commodities* lists names, addresses, and telephone numbers of about 60 commodity advisory services. Descriptions, chief personnel, and subscription prices are given for about 30 of the services. Also given are separate lists of about 20 commodity charting services and about 20 computer data services. Educational, investment management, and research services in the commodity area are also listed. (It has been announced that the special directory edition of *Commodities* will henceforth be published as the May issue. Coverage will be expanded to include statistical data, futures contract details, and other material. The new title will be "Reference Guide to Futures Markets.")

Sophisticated Investor. Published semiannually by Select Information Exchange (2095 Broadway, New York, N.Y. 10023).

About 50 commodity advisory services are listed and described in each semiannual issue. Subscription prices are given, ranging up to $750 per year, but addresses of individual services are not indicated. The services are available through Select Information Exchange, which acts as a subscription agent or clearinghouse. Special trial subscriptions are available at reasonable cost. For example, samples of 35 different commodity services were recently offered for a total fee of $21. Each issue of *Sophisticated Investor* is about 100 pages long, and describes many publications in various business and financial areas.

Williams, Larry R. "My List of Superior Advisory Services." In his *How I Made One Million Dollars in the Commodity Market Last Year*, pp. 22–24. 1973.

Advisory services are said to run hot and cold—each one has profitable periods and losing periods. Williams gives names, addresses, and short descriptions of nine services that he specifically recommends, including his own *Commodity Timing*.

AMATEUR SPECULATION (See also Commodity Futures in General; Losses; Psychology)

Speculation in commodity futures by the general public, as opposed to trading by commercial interests or large, professional speculators.

Angrist, Stanley W. "The Commodity Market: Is It for You?" *Investing*, vol. 2, October 1974, pp. 6–8, 13–14, 19.

>A brief, elementary review of commodity futures trading, including contract specifications for 11 actively traded commodities. Angrist refers to a U.S. Department of Agriculture study of about 50 years ago, which states that 75 percent of speculators lose money, and to a 1969 survey by T. A. Hieronymus in which 65 percent of the traders were losers. Nevertheless, one can make money in commodities by being right only four times out of ten, providing that one has the intestinal fortitude to cut losses short and let profits run. Commodity speculation is not recommended without a preliminary, careful evaluation of personality and goals.

Forbes, Inc. "Don't Phone Your Broker; Go To Aqueduct!" *Forbes*, vol. 104, August 1, 1969, pp. 54–55.

>Adrian C. Israel of the A. C. Israel Commodity Co. warns amateur investors that they will do better at the race track or dice table than in the commodity futures markets. Israel stated in an interview that he knows hundreds of men who became wealthy through real estate speculation, but not one who has been successful over the long run as a commodity futures speculator. In Israel's opinion, amateur commodity speculators disturb the markets unnecessarily because of lack of knowledge. "Take it from me," he said, "you have a lot of people speculating in commodities who don't know the first thing about them."

Gould, Bruce G. "The Public Speculator." In his *Dow Jones-Irwin Guide to Commodities Trading*, pp. 40–45. 1973.

>Describes a study by the Chicago Mercantile Exchange relating to the characteristics of the "average commodity speculator." Four thousand speculators were selected at random during the fall of 1970 and were found to be well above the national average in education and income.

Hieronymus, Thomas A. "The Results of Speculation." In his *Economics of Futures Trading*, pp. 249–258. 1971.

>According to Hieronymus, the consensus of informed opinion on commodity futures trading is that "big winners are relatively few in number and . . . the great majority of the speculators in the public sector are losers." After summarizing the Blair Stewart study published in 1949, Hieronymus gives the results of his own study of the "summary records of some customers of a major commission house for the calendar year 1969." All of the 462 accounts that were examined were speculative in nature, as opposed to trade accounts, and amounted to all of the accounts identified as speculative from three major offices of the broker. Losing accounts were

65 percent of the total number, but dollar amounts lost were relatively small ($1,439 average). Only 41 percent of the money put into the game by the losers went to the winners; 59 percent went to the broker and the clearinghouse. Hieronymus arrived at the conclusions that (1) there were only a few big winners and a few big losers and that (2) regular traders did much better than one-time traders. Regular traders were 193 in number, losing an average of $2,497 per account. Large commission expenses are what turned the regular traders into losers, on average. Only about 5 percent of all the traders profited handsomely, leading Hieronymus to make the discouraging statement that "in all fields of endeavor . . . it takes a lot of losers and also-rans to support a few champions."

Kroll, Stanley, and Shishko, Irwin. "CEA Study of Grain Trading." In their *Commodity Futures Market Guide*, pp. 84–86. 1973.

An analysis of Blair Stewart's famous study of amateur commodity futures speculation that was published in 1949 by the Commodity Exchange Authority (USDA Technical Bulletin No. 1001). Kroll and Shishko state that one of the most significant conclusions to be derived from the CEA study is that most amateur traders become reluctant to liquidate positions when the market begins to act unfavorably. This appears to be true regardless of whether traders are in profit or loss situations. That is, profits are allowed to fade or losses are allowed to accumulate.

Roscow, James P. "Commodities: For Gamblers or Investors?" *Financial World*, vol. 139, May 30, 1973, pp. 27–34.

States that commodity futures speculation by small investors is a "hot" alternative to the stock market, mainly because the 5 to 10 percent margin requirement provides very high leverage. Roscow points out, however, that more than half of the public speculators in silver futures lost money in 1967–1968, while the price of silver rose from $1.29 to $2.60 an ounce—and all of the public speculators were buyers! One professional skeptic commented that the small investor gets burned in the stock market, but electrocuted in commodity futures. Roscow mentions some of the restrictions placed by brokers on amateur commodity trading accounts. Merrill Lynch, for example, usually requires a minimum net worth of $50,000 exclusive of home equity and life insurance. Most brokers prefer that commodity speculators have at least $3,000 to $5,000 in high-risk capital available for trading. The president of the Association of Commodity Exchange Firms is quoted as saying, "I personally tell people that if you don't understand this market and haven't got the stomach for it, stay out with a capital O-U-T."

Rukeyser, Louis. "Should You Go Against the Grain?" In his *How to Make Money in Wall Street*, pp. 202–208. 1974.

According to Rukeyser, the interest that the average small investor should take in commodity futures trading is as follows: "none whatsoever." The chances of coming out ahead of the game are said to be *minimal*. "Those with scared money, or little money, should certainly look elsewhere...." However, a few people do make money in commodities, and these fortunate few generally have strong temperaments, adequate resources, a well-developed game plan, and a willingness to work hard at what they are doing. Rukeyser gives the standard advice to commodity speculators: don't fight the trend, let profits run, "add to successful positions in ever-smaller amounts," do not add to unsuccessful positions at all, don't be afraid to sell short if the trend is down, and use stop loss orders. Bernard Baruch (*My Own Story*) is quoted by Rukeyser on the subject of speculation: "Even being right three or four times out of ten should yield a person a fortune if he has the sense to cut his losses quickly on the ventures where he has been wrong."

Smidt, Seymour. *Amateur Speculators.* 1965. 53 pp.

A study of nonprofessional commodity traders based on 101 personal interviews and 248 mail responses. The amateur traders were categorized as "chartists" (53 percent) and "others" (47 percent). The latter group was further classified as "movement traders" (speculators looking for sustained, major price moves), "information specialists" (those who trade on inside information or the special interpretation of information), and "norm traders" (fundamentalists). Of course, these categories are not mutually exclusive—a chartist may be a movement trader, for example. Chartists, in comparison with others, tended to diversify, to close out positions before receiving margin calls, to look for actively traded commodities with large price fluctuations, and to be willing to trade on the short side as well as the long. About 26 percent of both chartists and others regarded themselves as successful in trading, and about 26 percent of both groups regarded themselves as not very successful. About 48 percent considered themselves as being someplace in between—breaking even, perhaps. Based only on an analysis of his own limited sample, Smidt suggests the hypothesis that during the initial four or five years of trading experience, "the annual rate of permanent exit from trading is on the order of 50 percent." In other words, the drop-out rate for beginning commodity speculators is very high. Smidt mentions the social status of futures trading in a footnote: "Investing in securities is socially acceptable; speculating in commodity futures frequently is not."

Smyth, David, and Stuntz, Laurance F. "How to Speculate and Win." In their *The Speculator's Handbook,* pp. 168–191. 1974.

A general review of commodity futures trading for the amateur speculator. The usual statements are made about three out of four speculators losing money, novice traders being expected to last no more than 18 months before being wiped out, and exbrokers admitting they never had a commodity futures customer who ended up with an overall profit. In addition to amateur losses, Smyth and Stuntz point out that professional commodity traders sometimes run up sensational losses, especially when dealing in cocoa. The authors emphasize the importance for amateurs of limiting losses and letting profits run. "This rule is absolutely essential for your success as a trader." Unfortunately for overall results, human nature dictates that it is much easier to engage in the happy procedure of taking a profit than to have to resort to the unhappy procedure of closing out a trade at a loss. Smyth and Stuntz discuss the specific markets for many different commodities.

Stewart, Blair, *An Analysis of Speculative Trading in Grain Futures.* 1949. 134 pp.

This analysis by a consulting economist to the Commodity Exchange Authority points out that "people from all walks of life participate" in futures trading. Stewart had access to the records of about 9,000 commodity speculators, made available in the 1930s "when one of the largest brokerage firms in Chicago retired from business." Trading data from a nine-year period (1924–32) were transferred to punched cards and analysis was made of about 400,000 individual trades. "The first obvious conclusion from the analysis is that the great majority of small speculators lost money in the grain futures market." There were 6,598 losers, who parted with a total of about $12 million, but there were only 2,184 winners, who managed to gain a total of about $2 million during the period covered. Primarily responsible for this state of affairs, according to Stewart, was the traders' habit of cutting profits short and letting losses run. Other conclusions: amateur speculators prefer to buy, not sell short; both profits and losses were individually rather small (trading was on a small scale); consistent bears did better than consistent bulls; the few large speculators included in the sample lost money; trading "against the current movement of prices was the dominant pattern" (buying "on dips," no doubt). The long period of declining prices from 1929 to 1932 "stimulated speculative buying by small speculators" (!).

Teweles, Richard J., and others. "Distribution of Profits and Losses." In their *The Commodity Futures Game,* pp. 296–307. 1974.

The Blair Stewart, Thomas A. Hieronymus, and Charles Rockwell studies of amateur trading are described. Teweles and co-authors state that they "have been able to confirm that the average expectation of a trader making net profits in any given year will be one in four." These would appear to be rather dismal odds.

Thackray, John. "The Perilous Present for Commodity Futures." *Money,* vol. 2, August 1973, pp. 28–31.

States that commodity speculators tend to lose money even in big bull markets, because nervousness causes them to sell out prematurely at a loss during temporary reversals of the major trend. "In their more candid moments, some brokers and traders estimate that nine out of ten speculators lose money." Stanley Kroll is quoted as saying that in all his years as a commodity broker he never had one single customer who came out with an overall profit from trading futures, nor did the customers of other brokers do any better. (However, Kroll has been successful in his own commodity trading.) A vice president at Merrill Lynch regarded the commodity futures markets as a potential "mine field for the neophyte." Eight "golden rules for survival" are given for those who insist on speculating in futures.

Train, John. "Commodity Speculation." In his *Dance of the Money Bees*, pp. 213–215. 1974.

> Gamblers are drawn irresistibly to speculation in commodity futures, "like dogs to a dogfight," but about the only people who consistently make money in commodity trading are the brokers. The main problems for public speculators are said to be excessive commission expenditures in overactive accounts and the lack of the information "edge" that large, commercial interests have.

Warden, Paul S. "Kiss Your Money Good-by, if You Start to Gamble in the Grain Market." *American Magazine*, vol. 90, October, 1920, pp. 54–56, 184–191.

> An early article outlining the perils of speculation in grain futures. Warden states that the futures-speculating public did better than usual after the war (1918–1919) because of generally rising commodity prices, but 1920–1921 is characterized as "a time for you to watch your step. . . ." Furthermore, "More people are yielding to the mania for speculation now than ever before." Warden's cheerful thoughts on the grain futures speculative market are as follows: "It is the graveyard where are buried the savings of countless people, an abyss that has swallowed hundreds of fortunes, a cemetery of dead hopes, a rag-bag of tattered reputations." An estimate is made in Warden's article that 99 out of 100 amateur commodity speculators lose money!

ANALYSIS OF COMMODITY PRICES. See Fundamental Analysis; Technical Analysis

AUTOMATIC TRADING SYSTEMS. See Mechanical Trading Systems

AVERAGING DOWN

The technique of buying additional amounts of a commodity as the price declines. Generally regarded as a dangerous method of trading, because the speculator may run out of margin capital before the price reverses. (Averaging up would be equally dangerous for a short seller.)

Belveal, L. Dee. "Adding to a Loss." In his *Commodity Speculation with Profits in Mind*, p. 268–270. 1967.

> Adding to losing positions multiplies negative risk exposure and can turn a reasonably small loss into a financial disaster. Positions should always be closed out when prices are going the "wrong way." Belveal uses the phrase "speculative madness" when referring to averaging down.

8 COMMODITY FUTURES TRADING

AVERAGING UP. See Pyramiding

BAR CHARTS. See Charts

BASIS (See also Hedging; Inverted Market; Spreads)
Usually defined as the difference between the cash (spot) price of a particular commodity and a specified futures contract price for the same commodity.

Arthur, Henry B. "Note: What Is Basis?" In his *Commodity Futures as a Business Management Tool*, pp. 64–69. 1971.

> Speaking of the word "basis" as used in the commodity business, Arthur says: "Trying to get traders to give a sharp definition of the term is a frustrating experience." To illustrate, a conversation between two grain exchange members is quoted, in which "basis" is used to mean several different things, as in "the basis," "my basis," and "close-out basis." These are all variations on the main theme of basis as the difference between cash price and futures contract price. The vartiations are explained in some detail.

Chicago Board of Trade. "The Basis: Relationship Between Cash and Futures Prices." In *Commodity Trading Manual*, pp. 66–67. 1973.

> The basis is clearly explained. Differences in cash and futures prices are said to be caused primarily by transportation costs, supply and demand conditions, variations in quality, availability of storage space, and supply and demand factors for substitutable commodities. Changes in the basis are what cause hedging operations to work out in a relatively profitable or unprofitable manner.

Clifton, Frederick T. "The 'Basis' Clarified." In *Commodity Year Book 1970*, pp. 35–37. 1970.

> Nine concepts of "the basis" are presented, as viewed by farmers, commodity users, and commodity merchants. Clifton states that there are situations in which the basis itself is subject to hedging, contrary to what may be found in some textbooks. Schematics of basis models are shown.

Cox, Houston A. "Basis as Aid to Fundamental Analysis." In his *Concepts on Profits in Commodity Futures Trading*, pp. 50–53. 1972.

> "Speculators would be . . . well advised to consider basis in designing their trading strategy." There are three tendencies that should be taken into consideration: (1) the tendency for expiring futures prices to converge with cash prices; (2) the tendency, if supplies are "normal," for distant futures to reflect carrying charges by being higher in price; and (3) the tendency, if supplies are scarce, for nearer futures to be higher in price than distant contracts. Cox uses a unique graph in conjunction with his textual material to develop a clear explanation of how variations in basis affect hedging and speculative opportunities.

Hieronymus, Thomas A. "Basis in Storage Markets." In his *Economics of Futures Trading*, pp. 150-164. 1971.

> "The essence of hedging is speculation in basis," Hieronymus says. He discusses both the theory of basis and what happens in real life. Charts show "Ten Years of Corn Basis" (1959-1960 through 1968-1969) and soybean basis and spreads for 1965-1966 and 1966-1967. The concept of carrying charges is explained in an unusually clear manner.

Kroll, Stanley, and Shishko, Irwin. "Price Variations Between Cash and Futures Market: The Basis," "Merchandising Profits and Risks and the Basis," "The Nature and Causes of Basis Changes," "Anticipating Changes in the Basis," and "Basis Trading." In their *Commodity Futures Market Guide*, pp. 284-291. 1973.

> An unusually complete exposition of the practical aspects of basis. The authors point out that, in practice, commercial commodity dealers or producers substitute the basis risks of hedging for the more severe, speculative price risks of outright positions. Also, the dealers attempt to profit through correct analysis of changes in basis.

Kroll, Stanley, and Shishko, Irwin. "The Relationship Between the Cash and Futures Markets." In their *Commodity Futures Market Guide*, pp. 67-71. 1973.

> The "basis" may reflect cash price for a particular grade, the particular futures price, time of shipment, and shipment destination. Changes in basis determine whether profits or losses will be made from hedging operations. The basis makes it possible to have three types of futures markets, classified as to price structure. In the carrying charge or premium market, "each future sells at a premium over the previous future," in the inverse or discount market, each future sells at a lower price than the previous future, and in the "flat" market, all futures for a particular commodity have the same price (a rare situation). Kroll and Shishko explain each type of market in some detail.

Powers, Mark J. "Hedging: The Basis." In his *Getting Started in Commodity Futures Trading*, pp. 115-120. 1973.

> The story is told of Bob Thompson, cattle rancher, who sold cattle futures as a hedge and wound up with a loss of one dollar per hundredweight on the transaction, when closed out. He lost because of failure to "calculate the basis." Powers gives an unusually clear explanation of just how "the basis" works in real life.

Teweles, Richard J., and others. "Basis." In their *The Commodity Futures Game*, pp. 34-42. 1974.

> A detailed definition of basis is given, followed by a discussion of basis as a vital factor in hedging operations ("hedging carried out to profit from movements in the basis"). A table shows "Variations in Gains or Losses Resulting from Differences in Cash and Future Price Movements." Unhedged and hedged, profit and loss results are given for various combinations of cash and futures price movements.

BEEF CATTLE. See Cattle

BEHAVIOR OF TRADERS. See Amateur Speculation; Psychology

BELLIES. See Pork Bellies, Frozen

BIBLIOGRAPHIES (See also Advisory Services; Periodicals; Statistics Sources)
Many books about commodities contain notable bibliographies. Some of these are listed here.

Arthur, Henry B. "Bibliography." In his *Commodity Futures as a Business Management Tool*, pp. 379–385. 1971.

> A wide-ranging bibliography of about 100 items relating to commodity futures, commercial hedging, and commodities in general.

Brealey, Richard A., and Pyle, Connie. "Commodities, Futures Markets and Hedging." In their *A Bibliography of Finance and Investment*, pp. 159–162. 1973.

> A chronological listing of about 100 books, journal articles, and dissertations from 1895 to 1972. Scholarly subjects are prominent, such as tests of market efficiency and the theory of normal backwardation.

Carabini, Louis E., ed. "Bibliography." In his *Everything You Need to Know Now About Gold and Silver*, pp. 159–176. 1974.

> A listing of books and articles in three separate categories: economics, gold, and silver.

Chicago Board of Trade. "Books on Futures Trading." In *Commodity Trading Manual*, pp. 265–267. 1973.

> Twelve general books on commodity futures are listed, five volumes on the history of futures trading, seven items on charting commodity prices (including five on the point-and-figure method), sixteen books on charting stocks (five on point-and-figure), and twelve "Additional Sources of Statistical Data" (mainly U.S. government publications).

Chicago Board of Trade. *Commodity Futures Trading: A Bibliography 1967–1974.* 1975. 85 pp.

> An annual compilation intended to serve as a cumulative supplement to the extensive bibliography published in 1966 by the University of Illinois College of Agriculture (see Heater, Nancy L. *Commodity Futures Trading, a Bibliography*). The Chicago Board of Trade's annual list is arranged according to 28 subject headings, covering all phases of commodity futures trading. There are no annotations, but the bibliography is unusually complete—over 1,000 books, pamphlets, and periodical articles are listed in this edition covering the years 1967 through 1974.

Chicago Board of Trade. "Selected sources of Information." In *Commodity Trading Manual*, pp. 154, 170, 183, 191, 209, 216, 226, 250, 263. 1973.

> These are short, specialized bibliographies covering the following topics: grain commodities, oil and meal commodities, livestock commodities; poultry commodities, metals, forest products, textiles, foodstuffs, and foreign currencies. Books, U.S. government reports, and some specialized services are listed, with the number of items for each commodity group being on the order of 15 to 30. These concise bibliographies are excellent for informing the commodity trader about practical sources of information on individual products.

"Directory of Futures Trading." Published annually in January as a special issue of *Commodities* magazine.

> This special directory issue of *Commodities* contains an alphabetical list by title of about 90 books dealing mainly with commodity futures trading (a few volumes having to do with the technical analysis of the stock market are also listed). Also listed are the names and addresses of specialty publishers in the commodity field, with monograph titles and prices given in some cases. A special list of free literature is provided, available upon requet from various brokerage firms, commodity exchanges, and other sources. (It has been announced that the special directory edition of *Commodities* will henceforth be published as the May issue. Coverage will be expanded to include statistical data, futures contract details, and other material. The new title will be "Reference Guide to Futures Markets.")

Goldberg, Ray A. "Bibliography." In his *The Soybean Industry*, pp. 177–183. 1952.

> Outdated, of course, but may still be of interest as a source of background material for those who are engaged in serious study of the soybean complex. Thirteen books, 15 unpublished theses, and about 130 pamphlets and periodical articles are listed.

Goss, B. A. "Further Reading." In his *Theory of Futures Trading*, pp. 114–116. 1972.

> A specialized bibliography featuring authors who take an econometric view of commodity futures. Much of the material listed is concerned with hedging.

Heater, Nancy L. *Commodity Futures Trading, a Bibliography.* 1966. unpaged.

> This list from the Department of Agricultural Economics of the University of Illinois College of Agriculture contains just about everything that was available in English on the subject of futures trading in December 1966. The 904 items are listed alphabetically by author. Books, periodical articles, pamphlets, and government reports are included.

Kallard, Thomas. "Bibliography." In his *Make Money in Commodity Spreads!*, pp. 161–177. 1974.

> About 130 books, 55 periodicals, 30 government reports, and miscellaneous other sources are listed. Commodity spreads are emphasized.

Kroll, Stanley, and Shishko, Irwin. "Bibliography." In their *Commodity Futures Market Guide*, pp. 355–357. 1973.

>A general bibliography of 37 items. Both scholarly and popular works are included.

Labys, Walter C., and Granger, C. W. J. "Bibliography." In their *Speculation, Hedging and Commodity Price Forecasts*, pp. 297–314. 1970.

>Price behavior, price forecasting, price effects of speculation, futures trading in general, price agreements, expectations, individual commodity studies, commodity market history, time series methods, and price data are the ten subjects covered by this classified bibliography. Over 300 items are listed.

Shaw, John E. B. "Basic Sources of Information." In his *A Professional Guide to Commodity Speculation*, p. 165. 1972.

>About 20 publications or information sources are listed.

Teweles, Richard J., and others. "Bibliograpy." In their *The Commodity Futures Game*, pp. 611–630. 1974.

>An excellent bibliography of over 500 items, in 11 sections: commodity exchanges, history, economic theory, behavior of traders, speculation effects, studies of individual commodities, behavior of prices, forecasting, money management, hedging, and price compilations.

Watling, T. F., and Morley, J. "Bibliography." In their *Successful Commodity Futures Trading*, pp. 217–219. 1974.

>Twenty-six books and four periodical articles are listed. While the articles are entirely British, the books are a mixture of American and British.

Zieg, Kermit C., and Zieg, Susannah H. "Bibliography." In their *Commodity Options*, pp. 157–158. 1974.

>A specialized bibliography of 18 items, mainly on the topic of commodity options (puts and calls).

BOOKS. See Bibliographies

BOTTOMS, DOUBLE. See Double Tops and Bottoms

BRITISH COMMODITY MARKETS. See London Commodity Markets

BROILERS. See Iced Broilers

BROKERS (See also Commissions; Orders to Brokers)
Agents who collect commissions for executing commodity trading orders. There are customers' brokers (representatives), who deal with the general pub-

lic, as well as floor brokers, who execute orders on the floors of commodity exchanges. Many stock brokerage firms also serve as commodity brokers.

Belveal, L. Dee "What a Broker Can and Can't Do for You." In his *Commodity Speculation with Profits in Mind*, pp. 249–261. 1967.

> States that advice from brokers relative to commodity price trends may be good, bad, or indifferent. Belveal says that, "there is no consistent authority on prices except the market." He mentions that some speculators look to their brokers for reassurance, companionship, and conversation, but these items are said to be no substitute for cutting losses short and letting profits run.

"Directory of Futures Trading." Published annually in January as a special issue of *Commodities* magazine.

> This special directory issue of *Commodities* lists the names, addresses, and telephone numbers of over 50 brokerage firms that make commodities their specialty. Listed separately are about 20 stock brokerage firms with commodity departments. Also included are over 50 commodity management firms that take individual accounts on a discretionary basis. Over 40 commodity consultants are also listed. (The directory issue of *Commodities* will be published in May in the future and will have the title "Reference Guide to Futures Markets.")

Kroll, Stanley. "The Broker 'Tells' You—but Who 'Tells' the Broker?" In his *The Professional Commodity Trader*, pp. 86–94. 1974.

> A report on Kroll's lecture in 1973 to the Investment Association of New York. In reading this discussion of how the broker should prepare himself for entering the commodities business, the speculator can get a pretty good idea of what to look for when selecting a broker.

Powers, Mark J. "Choosing a Broker." In his *Getting Started in Commodity Futures Trading*, pp. 33–40. 1973.

> Tells how to go about locating a competent commodities broker. Desirable qualities, such as mature personality and specialized training, are discussed. Initial opening of an account for speculation in commodity futures is explained.

Teweles, Richard J., and others. "The Broker in the Game; Building, Maintaining, and Servicing a Commodity Clientele." In their *The Commodity Futures Game*, pp. 315–334. 1974.

> This is very good advice for the aspiring commodity broker on such items as sales personality, knowledge of product, and how to maintain and service a commodity clientele. On pages 331 to 334 of their book, Teweles and co-authors discuss "Preparation for the Chicago Board of Trade Commodity Solicitor Examination" and give 15 questions that are typical of those on the examination (answers are also given). Traders who read this section may get some idea of just what a good broker should know.

Williams, Larry R. "How to Select the Best Broker." In his *How I Made One Million Dollars in the Commodity Market Last Year*, pp. 21–22. 1973.

> Some very frank, critical advice is given about commodity brokers. Specific firms are mentioned.

CALL OPTION. *See* Commodity Options

CAPITAL MANAGEMENT. *See* Money Management

CARRYING CHARGE SPREADS. *See* Spreads

CASH COMMODITY (*See also* Basis)
The actual, physical product. Also known as "spot commodity" or "actuals."

Gould, Bruce G. "Cash Commodity Pricing." In his *Dow Jones-Irwin Guide to Commodities Trading*, pp. 107–131. 1973.

> "Dealing with commodities on futures markets requires a good understanding of the various factors which determine prices on the cash market." Under the category of cash commodities, Gould discusses the general supply and demand factors that affect futures prices. Government regulations and government reports are emphasized, and sample pages from various reports are reproduced.

Keltner, Chester W. "The Relationship of Cash and Futures Prices." In his *How to Make Money in Commodities*, pp. 21–23. 1960.

> Explains that the cash prices and the futures price of a commodity will always come together during the delivery month of a futures contract. This is true by definition, as anyone who is short or long a futures contract when the contract matures, must deliver or take delivery of the actual cash commodity.

Kroll, Stanley, and Shishko, Irwin. "The Relationship Between the Cash and Futures Markets." In their *Commodity Futures Market Guides*, pp. 67–71. 1973.

> The differences between cash commodity contracts and futures contracts are discussed. When classified by price structure, there are three basic types of futures markets: carrying charge (premium), inverse (discount), and flat. Each of these three is explained at some length.

CATTLE
The largest single factor in American agriculture, accounting for a quarter to a third of the total value of farm products. The production of beef also accounts for the greatest use of animal feed in the United States. Tradition and various technical factors delayed the start of futures trading in live cattle until 1964 on the Chicago Mercantile Exchange.

Arthur, Henry B. "Cattle and Beef Industries." In his *Commodity Futures as a Business Management Tool*, pp. 211–260. 1971.

>General description of the live cattle futures market, with emphasis on commercial hedging. Special attention is given to breeding-herd operators, range-grown feeder cattle, feedlot operators, livestock dealers, meatpackers, processors, and retailers. Extensive information is provided about the hedging activities of Montfort Feed Lots, Inc., Wilson & Co., and Swift & Co. The live beef cattle futures market is described as having been outstandingly successful.

Chicago Board of Trade. "Beef Commodities." In *Commodity Trading Manual*, pp. 178–182. 1973.

>The following are briefly discussed: background (history), supply factors, production cycles, feedings costs, government programs, demand considerations, competitive meat products, and the import-export trade in beef. Cattle futures trading details are listed for the Chicago Mercantile Exchange (live beef cattle and feeder cattle), including delivery months, trading units, minimum price fluctuations, daily price move limits, position limits, delivery standards, and trading hours.

Oppenheimer, H. L. "How to Analyze Live Beef Futures Price Movements." In *Commodity Year Book 1965*, pp. 19–29. 1965.

>Oppenheimer is the author of the books *Cowboy Arithmetic* and *Cowboy Economics*. In this interesting article, he discusses "Life Cycle of a Steer," "Market Play and Price Patterns," "Background of Futures Trading in Cattle," "Actual Mechanics" (Chicago Mercantile Exchange procedures), and "Forecast and Survey." Specific highpoints are a consideration of industry objections to futures trading in live beef, an examination of seasonal price patterns, and a full discussion of the customs and methods of cattle marketing. Mention is made of the fact that the cattle market is free of government controls or price supports. "Violent price fluctuations are the rule rather than the exception."

Parker, George B. "New Factors in Forecasting Cattle Futures Prices." In *Commodity Year Book 1975*, pp. 35–43. 1975.

>The new factors are the changing cattle price cycle (shorter), much higher feed prices, prospective changes in grading standards, greater reliance on grass-fed animals, and actual or prospective changes in consumer preferences. Among the topics discussed are production factors, marketing practices, seasonal factors, beef quality grades, consumption patterns, and price influences. U.S. per capita consumption of beef and beef percentage of total red meat consumed is shown in tabular form for the years 1960 to 1974. October cattle futures are charted on a daily basis from 1969–1970 to 1974–1975.

Parker, George B. "Price Making Influences in the Chicago Cattle Futures Markets." In *Commodity Year Book 1969*, pp. 25-34. 1969.

> The chief items having an influence on cattle prices are said to be number of cattle, consumer population growth, level of consumer income, feed costs, weather, and production of other meats and poultry. Considerable attention is given to seasonal tendencies, but no reliable historical relationship could be established between futures and cash prices (as of 1969). Although Parker discusses beef production and consumption at some length, he states that the cattle futures trader must also take the technical side of the market into consideration. Charts show daily futures prices for April beef cattle at Chicago from 1965 to 1969.

Teweles, Richard J., and others. "Cattle." In their *The Commodity Futures Game*, pp. 443-458. 1974.

> The authors cover price factors, information sources, the cattle cycle, seasonal factors, and the marketing of live cattle. The live cattle futures market is said to be a "good trading medium" and a market that is gennerally one of relatively low volatility. Long price trends or long periods of narrow price fluctuations are characteristic.

CHARTS (See also Point-and-Figure charts; Technical Analysis; names of individual chart formations, such as Head-and-Shoulders Formation)

Representation by graphic means of commodity futures prices, volume of trading, open interest, or other data. So-called "technical" analysis of price trends makes extensive use of charts as a means of attempting to forecast price movements, but for any kind of commodity futures study, whether technical or fundamental, charts are indispensable to show price history at a glance.

Angrist, Stanley W. "Technical Trading I: Basic Chart Reading" and "Technical Trading II: Charts with Open Interest and Volume Data." In his *Sensible Speculating in Commodities*, pp. 103-134. 1972.

> Basic chart patterns and trend lines are discussed, as applied to bar charts (Angrist does not cover point-and-figure charts, stating that, in his personal opinion, they make no sense). The following formations are covered: double tops, double bottoms, head-and-shoulders, rounded tops, and rounded bottoms. Angrist recommends that fundamental crop considerations be combined with chart reading and that data on open interest and volume not be ignored. He gives the conclusions of H. S. Houthakker concerning "strong hands" versus "weak hands" (large traders versus small traders). With regard to open interest, the following situations are individually analyzed: open interest up and prices up, open interest down and prices up, open interest up and prices down, open interest down and prices down, open interest about the same and prices up, open interest about the same and prices down. Several charts are used as illustrations.

Belveal, L. Dee. *Charting Commodity Market Price Behavior.* 1969. 274 pp.

According to Belveal, commodity trading is "far less complex and a good deal safer than trading stocks for price appreciation." While the primary subject of his book is the technical or chart analysis of commodity price movements, he is of the opinion that charting must be combined with fundamental (crop) considerations for best results. Under "Major Market Indicators," the author gives ten rules, illustrated with charts, for typical situations: open interest up and price up, open interest up and price down, volume of trading up and price up, and so forth. Separate chapters are devoted to price as related to value, volume of trading as related to urgency, and open interest as related to the "Measurement of Conflicting Opinions." In his chapter "Strengths and Weaknesses of Chart Trading," Belveal reminds the speculator that a fundamental factor, such as a new crop report, can suddenly destroy even the most perfectly formed chart formation. The market goes its own way; it does not read charts. "Use technical analysis as just one more highly valuable tool in the quest for market profits." In his final chapter, Belveal explains six rules relating to price patterns, such as "head and shoulders defy definition" and "double tops and double bottoms usually hold." While one may disagree with Belveal as to commodity trading being safer than stock trading, his approach to charting is reasonable, intelligent, and certainly not fanatical.

Belveal, L. Dee. "Use of Charts in Trading Decisions." In his *Commodity Speculation with Profits in Mind*, pp. 151–190. 1967.

"A less-than-perfect tool is far better than no tool at all. Charts fall into this category." Belveal devotes a large part of his chapter on charting to an analysis of price charts covering corn for December 1966 and the May 1967 contract for soybeans. His advice is to add to winning positions at regular intervals, while keeping stop-loss orders close enough to avoid taking a large loss. The ending of a price trend will therefore be determined by the market itself and not by guesswork on the part of the trader.

Bernstein, Leonard A. "How Commodity Price Charts Disclose Supply-Demand Shifts." In *Commodity Year Book 1958*, pp. 33–42. 1958.

An article that has as its purpose the exploration of "the relationships between price charts and the operation of the law of supply and demand." Traditional supply-demand curves and the concept of market equilibrium are discussed first. Then equilibrium is considered in relation to typical charting notions, particularly trading ranges, trend channels, triangles, head-and-shoulders formations, double tops, and gaps. Volume of trading and open interest are also considered.

Chicago Board of Trade. "Charting." In *Commodity Trading Manual*, pp. 85–93. 1973.

Illustrations and discussions are provided of support areas, resistance areas, channels, trend lines, gaps, triangles, and other chart patterns. The

18 COMMODITY FUTURES TRADING

head-and-shoulders formation is said to be one of the more reliable pictures appearing on a price chart. An important caveat from the Board of Trade is that too many chartists operating in the same way will produce misleading or "false" price moves.

Cox, Houston A. "Vertical Line Chart Interpretation." In his *Concepts on Profits in Commodity Futures Trading*, pp. 116–140. 1972.

General coverage of line or bar charts, including trend lines, fan-lines, head-and-shoulders formations, triangles, rounding formations, "V" formations, diamonds, gaps, double tops, and double bottoms. Twenty-four actual commodity charts are used as illustrations. Cox believes it is necessary to include "chart-picture analysis as a major part of any overall market judgment."

"Directory of Futures Trading." Published annually in January as a special issue of *Commodities* magazine.

This special directory issue of *Commodities* lists names, addresses, and telephone numbers of about 20 commodity charting services. Descriptions, chief personnel, and subscription prices are given for about ten of the services. (The special directory edition of *Commodities* will be published as the May issue in the future, according to an announcement from the publisher.)

Feduniak, Robert. "Observations on Price Forecasting with Charts." In *Commodity Year Book 1973*, pp. 31–40. 1973.

Emphasizes the differences between stock and commodity futures price movements, so far as charting is concerned. Three important differences are discussed: (1) commodity open interest is generally unlimited, while stock supply is limited by the number of shares issued and outstanding; (2) futures contracts have relatively short lives and definite expiration dates, while stocks do not; (3) price fluctuations in futures markets are controlled as to the width of daily moves (daily price limits), while stock prices do not have formal limits. Feduniak states that charting seems to produce worthwhile results, even though "there is very little objective, explicit evidence available to support the commonly accepted rules of chart analysis...." A good explanation of the difficulty that academicians have with charting is provided. Trends, continuation patterns, support-resistance levels, and reversal formations are discussed. Well-known chart "pictures" (the triangle, the flag, head-and-shoulders, etc.) are interpreted and illustrated by means of 16 daily basis charts of actual commodity futures contracts.

Gardner, Robert L. "Chart Trading: The Automatic Way to Profits." In his *How to Make Money in the Commodity Market*, pp. 137–160. 1961.

"The chart method of trading provides safe and reliable means of predicting market swings." Gardner takes an unusually favorable view of charting, as not many would say that this method of trading is "safe and reliable." Toward the end of his discourse on charts, he backs away somewhat from his "safe and reliable" statement by saying, "Well, we're not offering the chart method as an infallible guide to easy riches.... But... the chart system is the closest thing we have to a reliable guide." Point-and-figure, line, and moving average charts are all described in detail, with the moving average chart being recommended for the novice. Support and resistance levels and trend lines are also discussed.

Gold, Gerald. "Appraisal of the Use of Price Charts." In his *Modern Commodity Futures Trading*, 6th ed., pp. 215–217. 1971.

"The tentative conclusion one comes to is that knowing the fundamentals is important.... On the other hand, keeping charts and watching them is also very important." Gold's attitude toward charts is eclectic rather than overly critical.

Gold, Gerald. "Price Chart Methods Used for Forecasting." In his *Modern Commodity Futures Trading*, 6th ed., pp. 168–184. 1971.

A general review of the charting of commodity futures prices as an aid in forecasting, including theory, bar charts, point-and-figure charts, and moving averages. Gold generally believes that chart reading should be combined with an analysis of the fundamentals for best results.

Gould, Bruce G. "Chart Construction." In his *Dow Jones-Irwin Guide to Commodities Trading*, pp. 242–247. 1973.

Line charts and their patterns are briefly explained, including channels, support-resistance levels, and "resting areas" (pennants and triangles). Gaps, islands, and reversals are also discussed. Actual commodity futures charts are used as illustrations.

Hart, John K. "The Use of Price Charts in Price Forecasting." In *Commodity Year Book 1948*, pp. 55–56. 1948.

Forecasting commodity prices by charts is said to go back as far as the sixteenth century, during which time "all sorts of methods were used to predict the course of the pepper market" in Amsterdam. However, modern chart theory probably began with Charles H. Dow (the Dow theory) during the early 1900s. Hart provides a general survey of charting, including both vertical line charts and point-and-figure methods. Construction of point-and-figure charts is covered in some detail. Hart says that, "The better informed chart traders put considerable emphasis on fundamental statistics" of a supply and demand nature.

Hayden, Jack J. "Chart Patterns and Risk-Aversion." In his *What Makes You a Winner or a Loser in the Stock and Commodity Markets?*, pp. 28–31. 1967.

States that successful chartists are that way because of their emotional control and not because of any particular technique. The best trading plan in the world will not produce profits for a commodity trader who is afraid of risk and nervous about losing money, simply because that kind of trader will not be able to follow the plan.

Jiler, William L. "Chart Analysis as an Aid to Commodity Forecasting," in *Guide to Commodity Price Forecasting*, ed. by Harry Jiler and George B. Parker, p. 23. 1965. (An earlier version of this article appears in the 1954 *Commodity Year Book*.)

> An introduction to other articles on charting. On the negative side, states that no easy road to successful price forecasting exists, that chart analysis is inexact, that formations or patterns on commodity price charts are often very indecisive, and that because of all this, considerable allowance must be made for errors. On the positive side, points out that "chart analysis can be very helpful in developing good market judgment."

Jiler, William L. "Forecasting Commodity Prices with Vertical Line Charts." In *Guide to Commodity Price Forecasting*, ed. by Harry Jiler and George B. Parker, pp. 24–32. 1965. (An earlier version of this article appears in the 1954 *Commodity Year Book*.)

> Covers trend lines, head-and-shoulders formations, triangles, rounding tops and bottoms, double tops and bottoms, flags and pennants, gaps, and key reversal days. Twenty-four small charts are used as illustrations. The problem of continuity on long-range commodity futures charts is considered (stock market charts do not have this problem, of course). The problem is usually taken care of by changing to the nearest futures contract when the contract being charted reaches expiration, but this procedure often produces a chart with an unrealistic, erratic appearance. Apparently, most commodity chartists do not object to this, but others advocate the use of some kind of averaging system to smooth out the jumps in price from one contract to another. (For example, the price charted might be the average of all delivery months for a particular commodity.) Two other distinctive aspects of commodity charting are said to be characterization and confirmation. Characterization refers to the fact that certain formations or patterns will appear with what might be regarded as unusual frequency on the price charts of a particular commodity. That is, wheat is said to be noted for flags and pennants, while soybean charts are famous for triangles, just to give two examples. Confirmation is thought by Jiler to be of great importance, and refers to trends or formations appearing at the same time on price charts of different delivery months of the same commodity.

Keltner, Chester W. "Chart Trading." In his *How to Make Money in Commodities*, pp. 101–117. 1960.

> Tells how to make vertical line charts of commodity prices, and covers the chart formations that are most common, such as head-and-shoulders, triangles, and double tops and bottoms. Keltner states that he does not include chart trading with mechanical trading rules, because the individual chart trader, "depending on the nature of the price movement and his own interpretation of it, has a considerable degree of latitude in arriving at market decisions." Nevertheless, both chartists and mechanical system

traders fall into the category of trend followers and tend to be on the same side of the market at a given time.

Kroll, Stanley, and Shishko, Irwin. "Chart Analysis." In their *Commodity Futures Market Guide,* pp. 107–157. 1973.

> An interesting survey of both line charts and point-and-figure charts. Special attention is given to trend lines and congestion areas. Top, bottom, and midformation price patterns are described, although the authors hesitate to give much weight to "individual price etchings or contours." Several pages are devoted to the use of volume and open interest data. Kroll and Shishko believe that analysis of seasonal and other fundamental factors should be combined with chart analysis. They do not believe the intelligent chart reader should worry too much about identifying chart "pictures" or patterns.

Longstreet, Roy W. "Chart Trading" and "Charts Plus Fundamentals." In his *Viewpoints of a Commodity Trader,* pp. 90–93. 1968.

> Charts are useful for timing entry and exit of trades, limiting losses, maintaining a position in a big move, and for generally staying informed about price trends. On the other hand, those who trade commodities mainly by reading charts must be psychologically prepared for many small losses. Hopefully, these losses will be offset by a few large gains. Longstreet believes that charts work best when combined on an equal basis with a thorough knowledge of crop and market fundamentals.

Reinach, Anthony M. "Recording the Action." In his *The Fastest Game in Town,* pp. 39–50. 1973

> Arithmetic charts are favored over logarithmic for commodity futures prices because commodity contracts are relatively short-lived. (Logarithmic charts are more realistic for long-term stock market prices.) Vertical line charts are "easy to make, easy to maintain, and easy to read," with daily basis charts being much more useful for trading purposes than weekly or monthly basis charts. Point-and-figure charts are also explained.

Shaw, John E. B. "How to Use Bar Charting." In his *A Professional Guide to Commodity Speculation,* pp. 87–97. 1972.

> "... the only reason for keeping charts is to find and follow a trend." While Shaw discusses the simple triangle, the upward slanting triangle, the downward slanting triangle, the flag, and the head-and-shoulders top, he does not regard price "pictures" as being as useful as simple upward or downward trend lines and channels. Several charts of actual futures prices are used as illustrations.

Shishko, Irwin. "Techniques of Forecasting Commodity Prices." In *Commodity Year Book 1965,* pp. 36–41. 1965.

> The three main purposes of price charting are to identify trends, to estimate how far prices will move, and to recognize turning (reversal) points

as soon as possible. Trend lines, channels, and gaps are discussed. A page of hypothetical charts is used to illustrate the following kinds of price bottoms (reversal patterns from down to up): fulcrum, compound fulcrum, delayed ending, inverse head-and-shoulders, V base, V extended, duplex horizontal, and saucer. Also, the following kinds of price tops are shown (reversals from up to down): inverse fulcrum, inverse compound fulcrum, delayed ending, head-and-shoulders, inverted V, inverted V extended, duplex horizontal, and inverse saucer.

Teweles, Richard J., and others. "Patterns on Price Charts." In their *The Commodity Futures Game*, pp. 167–176. 1974.

Bar charts, point-and-figure charts, and "old-time price patterns" are discussed. Chart analysis is said to have gained great popularity in 1901 when William Peter Hamilton of the *Wall Street Journal* engaged in an explanation of the price movements of U.S. Steel common stock. The advantages of charts are said to be that published charts are readily available, that successful chartists have been known to exist (very few), and that even fundamentalists can make use of charts as a source of information about market action. The disadvantages are said to be that too many people are now following charts, that analysis of chart patterns is strictly a subjective process, and that the few studies of charting that have been done revealed results that were no better than random.

Williams, Larry R. "How I Read Charts," In his *How I Made One Million Dollars in the Commodity Market Last Year*, pp. 83–91. 1973.

"Chart systems are based on whims." According to Williams, charts may be all right to help determine basic price trends or turning points, but are no good for short-term trading. He explains "buy" reversal days, "sell" reversal days, and the profitable use of gaps.

CHARTS, POINT-AND-FIGURE. See Point-and-Figure Charts

CHICAGO BOARD OF TRADE. See Commodity Exchanges

CHICAGO-KANSAS CITY WHEAT SPREAD. See Intermarket Wheat Spread

CHICAGO MERCANTILE EXCHANGE. See Commodity Exchanges

CHICAGO-MINNEAPOLIS WHEAT SPREAD. See Intermarket Wheat Spread

CHICAGO OPEN BOARD OF TRADE (now Mid-America Commodity Exchange). See Commodity Exchanges

CLEARINGHOUSE

A separate agency or corporation formed by a commodity exchange to match up (clear) buy and sell orders. The clearinghouse also assures the financial integrity of the commodity trading operation.

Arthur, Henry B. "The Clearing House Records." In his *Commodity Futures as a Business Management Tool*, pp. 32–33. 1971.

>Remarkably clear explanation of just how a commodity futures clearinghouse works. A single transaction—purchase of one wheat contract—is traced through seven clearinghouse procedures from initial obligation to delivery (in most cases, of course, the final step of delivery would not be reached).

Cox, Houston A. "The Clearing House and Your Money." In his *Concepts on Profits in Commodity Futures Trading*, p. 75. 1972.

>A brief explanation of the financial responsibilities of the commodity exchange clearinghouse and its members. As member (brokerage) firms must make their deposits to the clearinghouse without delay, individual customers are urged to make their deposits promptly to their brokers. Cox states that so far in the history of futures trading in the United States, "no clearing house of any major commodity exchange has been declared insolvent."

Gardner, Robert L. "The Role of the Clearing House." In his *How to Make Money in the Commodity Market*, pp. 43–44. 1961.

>An explanation of how the clearinghouse simplifies the whole process of futures trading. A hypothetical group of trades is used to illustrate how "a given contract changes hands many times during its life, always through the medium of the clearing house."

Gold, Gerald. "The Clearing House." In his *Modern Commodity Futures Trading*, 6th ed., pp. 41–44. 1971.

>Enphasizes that each commodity exchange's clearinghouse substitutes itself as the "other party" in all trades of futures contracts. Two topics discussed are "How Deliveries Against Contracts are Simplified by the Clearing House" and "The Financial Strength of the Clearing House."

Keltner, Chester W. "The Clearing House." In his *How to Make Money in Commodities*, pp. 19–21. 1960.

>Who is responsible for what in a futures trade? Keltner answers this question by tracing a futures trade from inception to conclusion and by clarifying the role of the clearinghouse.

COCOA (See also Cocoa—Seasonal Price Trend)

Strictly speaking, a powder made from the roasted seed (bean) of the cacao tree. However, in commodity futures terminology, the word "cocoa" means "cocoa bean," as 30,000 pounds of dried cocoa beans make up the standard futures trading contract on the New York Cocoa Exchange. The London Cocoa Terminal Market Association is also a dominant factor in cocoa futures trading.

24 COMMODITY FUTURES TRADING

Arthur, Henry B. "Cocoa." In his *Commodity Futures as a Business Management Tool*, pp. 261–289. 1971.

> General description of cocoa, cocoa bean prices, and the cocoa bean market structure. Arthur states that it would be financially dangerous to conduct commercial operations in the world cocoa market without some kind of price protection (hedging) because of the following factors: (1) early-season forecasts are not reliable, (2) intermediate-term price movements can have serious effects if one is on the wrong side of them, and (3) "an exposed position could lead to ruin . . . due to the many unpredictable short-term factors which affect cocoa and many other international commodities." The hedging operations of General Cocoa Co., A. C. Israel, General Foods Corp., Nestlé U.S.A., and Hershey Foods Corp. are described. Certainly this is a valuable discussion for those amateur speculators daring enough to trade cocoa futures, even though the emphasis is on commercial hedging.

Chicago Board of Trade. "Cocoa." In *Commodity Trading Manual*, pp. 232–235. 1973.

> After a brief history of cocoa, supply-demand factors are summarized. "World Production of Cocoa Beans in Principal Producing Countries" is given annually in metric tons for ten countries from 1962–63 to 1971–72. "World Exports of Cocoa Beans by Principal Producing Countries" in metric tons is given annually for ten countries from 1961 to 1970. "World Absorption (Consumption) of Cocoa" in long tons is given for ten countries from 1962 to 1971. Cocoa futures trading details are listed for the New York Cocoa Exchange (cocoa futures are also traded on the London Cocoa Terminal Market). The following are quoted for New York: delivery months, trading units, minimum price fluctuations, daily price move limits, position limits, delivery standards, and trading hours.

Davies, M. E. T. "Cocoa." In *Getting Started in London Commodities*, ed. by C. W. J. Granger, pp. 32–37. 1975.

> The London Cocoa Terminal Market is said to be one of the most active and talked-about futures markets in the United Kingdom. Davies provides a British view of trading in cocoa, beginning with a brief history and background of the commodity. The present London cocoa futures market is then described, including contract and trading details. The volatility of cocoa is commented upon. The rapid growth in London cocoa futures transactions is shown in the form of a table giving total trading in long tons from 1951 to 1974. A chart shows the monthly range of London spot prices from 1966 to early 1975.

Shishko, Irwin. "How to Forecast Cocoa Prices." In *Guide to Commodity Price Forecasting*, ed. by Harry Jiler and George B. Parker, pp. 98–107. 1965. (An earlier version of this article appears in the 1959 *Commodity Year Book*.)

> Cocoa has been attractive from a speculative viewpoint because of extensive and relatively consistent price moves. Shishko states that charting

is desirable or even vital in following cocoa prices, but a knowledge of fundamental crop and political factors is also essential. Influences on the price of cocoa are discussed in detail, including carryover, production outlook, consumption, grindings, seasonal aspects, and supplies available on the spot. A small chart shows a seasonal price index for cocoa from January to December, with 1947–1963 equaling 100. Cocoa straddles are briefly considered, and some "Hints on Speculation" are given. For example, be skeptical of price forecasts, go with the fundamentals, use charts as aids, and do not try to be in the market at all times. At the end of his article, Shishko presents charts of daily cocoa futures prices for the May delivery from 1956 to 1965.

Stern, William. "A Method of Forecasting Cocoa Prices." In *Commodity Year Book 1972*, pp. 13–20. 1972.

Because of high volatility and price extremes, "cocoa has not always been a happy hunting ground for the speculative community." Stern explores the "pitfalls and peculiarities" that have made cocoa profits hard to come by. He says that one of the major obstacles to accurate cocoa price forecasting is the lack of reliable statistical information—the information situation is therefore discussed in some detail. Botanical background, producer selling policies, grinding trends, warehouse stocks, international developments, seasonal patterns, and long-term supply-demand trends are also covered. A method of attempting to forecast cocoa prices according to fundamentals (supply and demand) is outlined. Cocoa stocks as of December 31 of each year and also in terms of the number of months' supply are plotted against monthly cocoa futures prices on a long-term chart covering 1935 to 1972. Charts also show daily futures prices at New York for December cocoa from 1965 to 1971.

Teweles, Richard J., and others. "Cocoa." In their *The Commodity Futures Game*, pp. 536–547. 1974.

The authors state that cocoa has been popular with speculators over the years because of "wide price moves the direction of which is relatively difficult to reverse." Factors influencing prices, sources of information, production, utilization, and seasonal tendencies are discussed. Cocoa prices are said to be difficult to forecast for the fundamentalist because of unreliable crop information and for the technician because of wide spreads between bid and asked prices, high commissions, and high margin requirements. However, price moves tend to be prolonged once they get started. Seasonal factors are of some importance.

Watling, T. F., and Morley, J. "Cocoa." In their *Successful Commodity Futures Trading*, pp. 141–150. 1974.

Several lines that should be memorized by amateur commodity speculators are quoted from G. K. Chesterton: "Tea, although an Oriental, Is a Gentleman at least; Cocoa is a cad and coward, Cocoa is a vulgar beast." General background, diseases, and factors to watch (crop fundamentals) are briefly considered. Both amateur and professional crop estimates are said to be often "hopelessly wrong." The cocoa market is said to establish long price trends, but with significant corrections that tend to wipe out chartists. Bull markets are characterized by nearby months trading at a premium over more distant months. Cocoa is a popular speculative commodity in London, so these pages by two British authors are well worth reading by those who have an interest in cocoa futures. (Complete futures trading details are given for the London Cocoa Terminal Market Association.)

Weymar, F. Helmut. "Cocoa—The Effect of Inventories on Price Forecasting." In *Commodity Year Book 1969*, pp. 15–24. 1969.

Weymar begins on an exotic note by quoting a poem by S. J. Sharpless extolling the virtues of cocoa as an aphrodisiac ("Cupid's Nightcap"). However, the topic is soon switched to the more prosaic one of the structure of the world cocoa economy. Fluctuations in the price of cocoa are characterized as long term, intermediate term, and short term. Long-term changes take years or even decades, and are caused mainly by the fact that cocoa trees require long periods to reach maximum yields. Short-term changes are measured in weeks, and are the result of "alternating speculative tides of bullishness and bearishness." Weymar is mainly concerned with intermediate price changes over periods of months. These intermediate changes "reflect basic changes in market opinion regarding cocoa production and consumption." The present article is further restricted to the price effects of cocoa inventories and inventory expectations. Inventory is among the factors included in Weymar's "Flow Diagram of the World Cocoa Economy's Structure." A great amount of fundamental cocoa data is shown by means of tables and charts, typically from 1952 or 1957 to 1968–1969. Inventory rationing and long-term equilibrium are discussed in some detail. In his conclusion, Weymar expresses the opinion that cocoa price forecasts based on supply-demand fundamentals are subject to serious errors unless "carried out on an extremely thorough basis." Charts are included that show daily futures prices for September cocoa at New York from 1958 to 1969.

COCOA—SEASONAL PRICE TREND

The marketing year for cocoa normally begins in October. Low prices for the season typically occur in May, with highs a few months later in August. However, some authorities say the seasonal high for cocoa is more likely to take place from January to March, with a double bottom in June and December. (Conflicting opinions about cocoa are commonplace.)

Teweles, Richard J., and others "Seasonal Information" and "Notes from a Trader." In their *The Commodity Futures Game*, pp. 544–547. 1974.

If November prices go above the highest prices of October, still higher prices are said to be likely. Likewise, if prices during the first half of August go above the highest prices reached during the last two weeks of July, a further increase of 100 points (1¢ per pound) or over is a good possibility. A graph shows the cocoa seasonal price index monthly from January to December, with 1947–1963 equaling 100. Two tables present "Seasonal Cocoa Prices: March Cocoa Net Price Gain from September 25 to November 30, 1953–1973 (in Cents per Pound)" and "Seasonal Cocoa Prices: September Cocoa Net Change from March 15 to May 15, 1957–1973 (in Cents per Pound)."

COCONUT OIL

A major vegetable oil produced from the dried meat or copra of the coconut. Coconut oil futures are traded on the Pacific Commodities Exchange. (Virtually all U.S. coconut oil is imported from the Philippines.)

Chicago Board of Trade. "Coconut Oil." In *Commodity Trading Manual*, pp. 165–167. 1973.

> Production and demand factors for coconut oil are explained. Coconut oil futures trading details are given for the Pacific Commodities Exchange, including delivery months, trading units, price fluctuation specifications, daily price move limits, position limits, delivery standards, and trading hours.

Teweles, Richard J., and others. "Coconut Oil." In their *The Commodity Futures Game*, pp. 603–610. 1974.

> Trading in coconut oil futures began on the Pacific Commodities Exchange in late 1972. Supply and demand factors, sources of information, factors in production, and other items influencing prices are discussed. The possibility of a coconut oil/soybean oil spread is mentioned; a line chart compares prices of the two oils from 1960 to 1972.

COFFEE

The favorite hot drink in most parts of the world that have temperate or cold climates. About three fourths of all coffee beans produced are grown in Brazil and Colombia, with Brazil alone accounting for about one half of total production. The United States is the biggest coffee user, consuming approximately one third of all coffee produced. Coffee beans of various types are represented by futures contracts on the New York Coffee and Sugar Exchange and the London Coffee Terminal Market.

Chicago Board of Trade. "Coffee." In *Commodity Trading Manual*, pp. 241–245. 1973.

> Supply-demand considerations are briefly discussed. "World Green Coffee (Exportable) Production" in thousands of bags is shown for each of ten countries annually from 1960 to 1971. "Total World Green Coffee Imports by Countries of Destination" in thousands of bags is shown for each of 12 countries annually from 1962 to 1970. "Total Coffee Imports into the U.S." in thousands of bags is given for each of 12 countries on an

28 COMMODITY FUTURES TRADING

annual basis from 1962 to 1971. Coffee futures trading details are listed for the New York Coffee and Sugar Exchange ("B," "C," and "U" contracts), including delivery months, trading units, minimum price fluctuations, daily price move limits, trading limits, position limits, delivery standards, and trading hours.

Davies, M. E. T. "Coffee." In *Getting Started in London Commodities*, ed. by C. W. J. Granger, pp. 41–43. 1975.

A British view of coffee trading, beginning with a brief history and background of the commodity. The present London coffee futures market is described, including contract and trading details for the Coffee Terminal Market Association. The 1973 International Coffee Agreement is said to have been relatively successful in stabilizing prices, resulting in relatively low activity in coffee futures markets. A table shows London coffee (Robusta) futures transactions in long tons from 1958 to 1974, while the monthly range of London spot prices is shown in chart form for the years 1966 to early 1975.

Struning, William C. "Understanding the Coffee Market." In *Commodity Year Book 1974*, pp. 22–27. 1974.

Supply, demand, inventories, methods of marketing, the coffee industry in the United States, price influences, and futures markets are discussed. In recent years, the weather in Brazil has had a dramatic effect on coffee prices. A table shows the "Major Coffee Exporting Countries of the World," with principal type of coffee, main growing regions, harvesting season, exporting season, grades traded in New York, ports of export, and number of bags of green coffee exported in 1972. All of these items are shown for each of 20 different countries.

Teweles, Richard J., and others. "Coffee." In their *The Commodity Futures Game*, pp. 523–535. 1974.

History, price factors, information sources, production, utilization, and seasonal trends (none) are discussed. Coffee is said to be a good market for those who trade by fundamental supply and demand information. However, the market is thin, and unexpected disruptions on the supply side may cause violent price moves. The coffee market "is no place for the underfinanced or the timid." Surprisingly, the authors state, the practice of buying the discounts in inverted coffee futures markets has proved to be often profitable.

Watling, T. F., and Morley, J. "Coffee." In their *Successful Commodities Futures Trading*, pp. 151–156. 1974.

Of the more than 40 varieties of coffee, only three are said to be of importance in world trade—Arabian, Robusta, and Liberian. Coffee futures markets exist in Brazil (Santos and Rio), France (Le Havre), Germany (Hamburg), the Netherlands (Amsterdam), and the United States (New York). Watling and Morley present a succinct discussion of coffee crop fundamentals. Complete futures trading details are given for the London Coffee Terminal Market Association.

COILS. See Triangles (Coils)

COMMISSIONS
Fees charged by commodity brokers for execution of orders. In an active futures trading account, commissions will be a major cost.

Hieronymus, Thomas A. "High Cost of Overhead." In his *Economics of Futures Trading*, pp. 331–333. 1971.

> While commissions charged for commodity futures trading are not high in relation to the value of the contracts, they are quite high in relation to margin requirements. As the commission must be added to a loss and subtracted from a gain, a 1¢ loss on 5,000 bushels of corn, for example, results in a total loss of $80 ($50 plus $30 commission), while a 1¢ gain results in a total gain of only $20 ($50 gain less $30 commission). Even a 2¢ gain ($100 gain less $30 commission) will not quite compensate for a trade that was previously closed out with a 1¢ loss. Hieronymus tells about the much lower commission rates that members of commodity exchanges pay. Floor traders in corn, for example, might pay a commission rate of $1.60 per contract.

Kroll, Stanley, and Shishko, Irwin. "Commissions." In their *Commodity Futures Market Guide*, pp. 222–223. 1973.

> "Selected Round-Turn (Nonmember) Minimum Commission Rates (as of December 1, 1971)" are shown in the form of a table. The regular rate, the day trade rate, and the straddle rate are given for each of 11 commodities. Commission rates are, of course, subject to frequent change. The authors provide a brief explanation of commissions on spread positions.

COMMODITY ADVISORY SERVICES. See Advisory Services

COMMODITY EXCHANGES (*See also* London Commodity Markets)
Centers where actual commodities or commodity futures contracts are bought and sold. All organized exchanges have definite rules to regulate the details of trading procedure.

Chicago Board of Trade. "Commodity Exchanges Today." In *Commodity Trading Manual*, pp. 15–26. 1973.

> Information is given about each of the following U.S. commodity exchanges: Chicago Board of Trade, Chicago Mercantile Exchange, International Monetary Market of the Chicago Mercantile Exchange, Commodity Exchange, Inc., International Commercial Exchange, Inc., Kansas City Board of Trade, Mid-America Commodity Exchange (formerly Chicago Open Board of Trade), Minneapolis Grain Exchange, New York Cocoa Exchange, New York Coffee and Sugar Exchange, New York Cotton

Exchange, Wool Associates of the New York Cotton Exchange, Inc., Citrus Associates of the New York Cotton Exchange, Inc., Tomato Products Associates of the New York Cotton Exchange, Inc., LPG Associates of the New York Cotton Exchange, Inc., New York Mercantile Exchange, and Pacific Commodities Exchange, Inc. In most cases, a brief history is given of the exchange, followed by data as to number of memberships, governing body, committees, and number of staff.

"Directory of Futures Trading." Published annually in January as a special issue of *Commodities* magazine.

This special directory issue of *Commodities* lists the names, addresses, telephone numbers, and chief personnel of the 13 major commodity exchanges of North America. A table, "Commodity Futures Trading Facts," shows contract quantities and minimum price fluctuations for all of the commodities traded on the various American exchanges. (The publisher of *Commodities* has announced that the special directory issue will be expanded and published in May in the future.)

Gould, Bruce G. "The 23 Commodity Exchanges Authorized by Law to Operate in the United States." In his *Dow Jones-Irwin Guide to Commodities Trading*, pp. 307–308. 1973.

A convenient list of 23 American commodity exchanges, although many of them are not active. Gould gives full addresses for 14 of the exchanges, dates of founding or initial trading for 11 exchanges, and names of actively traded commodities for 10 exchanges.

Granger, C. W. J. "Basic Trading Information." In his *Getting Started in London Commodities*, pp. 109–114. 1975.

The following information is given for each of 17 London commodity exchanges or market associations: lot (contract) size, deposit (margin) per lot in pounds sterling, manner of price quotation, minimum price fluctuation, maximum price fluctuation (if any), trading positions (months traded), brokerage commissions for nonmember round-turns, and trading hours.

Munn, Glenn G. *Encyclopedia of Banking and Finance*, 7th ed. 1973. 953 pp.

Major U.S. commodity exchanges are given good coverage in this standard reference work on financial matters. Over two pages are devoted to basic information about the Chicago Board of Trade, for example, and other big American exchanges are treated similarly.

Watling, T. F., and Morley, J. "Commodity Markets Overseas." In their *Successful Commodity Futures Trading*, pp. 29–36. 1974.

In this general description of futures trading around the world, trading is said to be most active in the United States, Canada, England, France, Japan, Australia, Malaya, and Singapore. "Those who are concerned to trade in commodity futures are entering a world of international trading."

Wyckoff, Peter. *International Stock and Commodity Exchange Directory.* 1974. 340 pp.

> A directory containing comprehensive information about every known domestic and foreign commodity exchange on which futures contracts are traded. Each commodity exchange description contains information about regulations, contracts, hours of business, officers, address, telephone number, Telex number, and cable address. Annual volume of trading is also indicated.

COMMODITY FUTURES (IN GENERAL) (*See also* Amateur Speculation; Commodity Futures as Inflation Hedges; History of Futures Trading; Dow-Jones Commodity Futures Index)

The books and articles described under this heading contain general overviews of commodity futures trading, usually written with the amateur speculator in mind.

Angrist, Stanley W. *Sensible Speculating in Commodities, or How to Profit in the Bellies, Bushels and Bales Markets.* 1972. 223 pp.

> A soup to nuts approach to commodity futures trading, including brief historical facts, how to open an account, fundamental analysis, technical trading methods (charts and moving averages), trading rules, and a consideration of advisory services. The author believes that fundamental analysis and technical methods should be combined for best results. A valuable "Annotated List of Advisory Services" is included in one of the appendixes to the Angrist volume, as is a glossary and a list of statistical sources. The writing is easy to understand and is intended for the beginner in commodity speculation. So far as writing style and clarity are concerned, Angrist's work is far above average.

Belveal, L. Dee. *Commodity Speculation with Profits in Mind.* 1967. 347 pp.

> For the beginner, Belveal emphatically recommends his "paper trading" system in which theoretical trades are carried out, but no actual orders are entered. (Paper trading is a good way to learn, of course, but one must be aware of the fact that changing from theory to real money results in an enormous increase in the emotional or "fear and greed" factor.) There is some coverage of charts and technical factors in this book, but the emphasis is on crop fundamentals and the development of an intelligent strategy of trading. The writing is clear, interesting, and easily understood by those who are new to futures markets. Among the topics that receive extensive treatment are leverage, short-term trading, the analysis of risk on a practical level, dealing with brokers, and pitfalls that may await the commodity trader.

Chicago Board of Trade. *Commodity Trading Manual.* 1973. 298 pp.

> The main features of this standard handbook are detailed descriptions of the 12 major U.S. commodity futures exchanges and background in-

formation on 30 individual commodities. Futures trading details are given for each of the products. Valuable information is also given about clearing operations, floor trading, exchange regulations, hedging, price forecasting, spreading, sensible speculation, and commission houses.

Cox, Houston A. *Concepts on Profits in Commodity Futures Trading*. 1972. 196 pp.

As representative of Reynolds Securities, Inc., Cox has lectured widely on the topic of successful commodity futures trading. His book is unique because of its emphasis on methodical trading capital strategy (money management), its extensive coverage of Elliott wave cycles for projecting major price trends, and its many illustrations, diagrams, and charts used to clarify the text. Cox's book is clearly written, and is obviously aimed at the "average" commodity speculator who wishes to do better than average. Fundamental analysis is covered, but the emphasis is on technical analysis, charting, and trend following.

"Directory of Futures Trading." Published annually in January as a special issue of *Commodities* magazine.

An essential item for most commodity traders. In addition to an index of articles appearing in *Commodities* magazine during the previous year, the directory contains unusually complete and informative listings of commodity advisory services, commodity books, specialized publishers in the commodity field, periodicals, charting services, computer data services, commodity educational services, discretionary account management services, commodity consultants, research services, organizations, specialized commodity brokers, and commodity exchanges. In 1975, for example, the excellent directory portion took up pages 53 to 96 of the January issue of *Commodities*. (Plans are for the special directory edition of *Commodities* to be published in May rather than January. Coverage will be expanded to include statistical data, futures contract details, and other new material. The title will be changed to "Reference Guide to Futures Markets.")

Gardner, Robert L. *How to Make Money in the Commodity Market*. 1961. 194 pp.

This volume provides broad coverage of commodity speculation, with some emphasis on the attitude and psychology of the small trader. Commodity exchanges, hedging, brokerage accounts, actively traded commodities, information sources, government support programs, charts, and trading rules are all discussed.

Gold, Gerald. *Modern Commodity Futures Trading*, 6th ed. 1971. 262 pp.

A clearly written straightforward explanation of speculative techniques in commodity futures trading. The 22 chapters of the book cover such topics as the mechanics of futures trading, the clearinghouse, sources of information, fundamental price influences, seasonal trends, hedging procedures, charting methods, stop-loss practices, spreads, and rules for successful speculating. Gold is very good at making basic futures trading operations easy to understand for the beginner.

Goss, B. A. *Theory of Futures Trading.* 1972. 116 pp.

A highly technical and mathematical work relating to the economic theory of futures trading. The ideas of John Maynard Keynes, John R. Hicks, and N. Kaldor are discussed. While Goss' book will be of interest primarily to econometricians, the chapter "The Concept of Hedging" may be helpful to commodity traders in pointing out various ways of looking at hedging.

Gould, Bruce G. *Dow Jones-Irwin Guide to Commodities Trading.* 1973. 357 pp.

Gould begins by quoting some myths about commodity futures trading and telling why the statements are untrue. Then the mechanics of commodity trading and the characteristics of futures contracts are reviewed. Part two of Gould's volume is concerned with the way in which various factors determine both cash and futures prices. One chapter is devoted to the random walk theory of market price movement. Part three goes into actual trading programs and price forecasting, with particular emphasis on figuring the odds of seasonal price trends. There is also a discussion of technical analysis and chart forecasting. Gould's book is a practical introduction to stressing the importance of using probability technique to be in the right commodity at the right time. The style of writing is clear and at the popular level.

Granger, C. W. J., ed. *Getting Started in London Commodities.* 1975. 117 pp.

The British view of such matters as risk, hedging, money management, trading technique, and the fundamentals of individual commodities. There is a glossary of commodity terms, as well as futures trading specifications, for many London commodity associations or exchanges.

Hammonds, T. M. *The Commodity Futures Market from an Agricultural Producer's Point of View.* 1972. 88 pp.

"This book was written to introduce agricultural producers to the commodity futures market. It is deliberately simplified and assumes no previous knowledge of this market." As Hammonds (Oregon State University) is writing primarily for farmers, he naturally emphasizes the use of commodity futures for hedging. In a chapter entitled "Trading Techniques for Producers," preharvest hedges, storage hedges, inventory requirement hedges, and producer speculation are discussed. As it is recognized by Hammonds that farmers sometimes speculate, a later chapter in his book considers the traditional question of supply-demand (fundamental) analysis versus price movement (technical) analysis. Hammonds recommends that producers use their own knowledge of fundamentals for basic decisions, but the advice of a commodity broker interested in the technical side of the market may be sought for help in the exact timing of trades. Other parts of the Hammonds book provide a general, elementary review of commodity futures trading. The material was originally developed for use with producers (farmers) in county extension workshops in Oregon.

Hieronymus, Thomas A. *Economics of Futures Trading for Commercial and Personal Profit.* 1971. 338 pp.

Hieronymus is professor of agricultural economics at the University of Illinois and a world authority on commodity futures trading. He states that one of the goals of his book is to place futures markets in proper perspective as an important part of commercial and economic life. Speaking of the literature of commodity futures, he remarks, "In much that has been written it is apparent that the authors failed to get out of the land of Oz." Part of Hieronymus' volume is entitled "Description" and tells about the physical or mechanical side of futures trading, including the operation of exchanges. Part two is "The Economics of Futures Trading," emphasizing that futures trading continues to be vital to the economy, despite political opposition. Part three, "Use of Futures Markets," is the practical part, but still with overtones of economics. Hieronymus talks of hedging, arbitrage activities, pricing procedures, and how to speculate (whether successfully or not). Part four, "Market Operation," considers whether or not commodity futures markets are at present functioning optimally. Regardless of what topic Hieronymus is considering, he writes with wit and style.

Jiler, Harry, and Parker, George B., eds. *Guide to Commodity Price Forecasting.* 1965. 275 pp.

A collection of 24 articles that appeared originally in various annual editions of the *Commodity Year Book*. Some of the articles have not been changed from the original, while others have been extensively revised. Many topics are covered, including chart analysis, trend-following methods, hedging, spreads, and the fundamentals of corn, wheat, soybeans, rye, cocoa, coffee, potatoes, sugar, and wool. Many pages are devoted to spread techniques, and many pages are used for detailed charts of futures prices on a daily basis, typically covering the period from 1954 to 1965. The writing style of the many different authors varies from folksy to scholarly.

Keltner, Chester W. *How to Make Money in Commodities.* 1960. 230 pp.

Most of Keltner's volume is as useful today as in 1960. He covers the functioning of commodity futures markets, mechanical trading systems, chart reading, fundamental analysis, and rules to be observed by the successful speculator. The grains are Keltner's specialty, and he includes price charts of Chicago May wheat and May soybeans from 1950 to 1960. In the introduction to his book, he makes the astounding statement that the amateur commodity trader who follows sound trading practices can realize an average annual return of 100 percent on invested capital. Keltner reveals the other side of the coin when he asserts that "commodity trading falls in a high risk field." This volume has become a standard text on futures speculation, just as the *Keltner Commodity Letter*, started in 1939, has long been regarded as one of the standard, important advisory services in the commodity field.

Kiplinger Washington Editors. "How Those Commodity Markets Work; in This Strange Game, You Bet on the Future Price of Anything from Butter and Beans to Wool and Zinc." *Changing Times*, vol. 22, May 1968, pp. 7–12.

>Futures trading is described in an elementary manner. The drawbacks of trading are listed as the necessity for learning a great deal about the mechanics of the commodity markets, the fact that no dividends or interest payments are earned on speculative capital, the necessity for constant surveillance of the markets when trading, and the fact that losses must be taken without hesitation.

Kiplinger Washington Editors. "Make a Killing in the Commodity Market? Here's How Men Make and Lose Fortunes Trading in Unplanted Soybeans, Unmined Lead, Unlaid Eggs. You'll See Why This Is No Game for an Amateur." *Changing Times*, vol. 14, November 1960, pp. 42–45.

>A general description of futures trading for the beginner. States that "The average trader won't make money in the long run . . ." because of failure to cut losses short, failure to sell short when appropriate, and a tendency to "chicken out and take small profits."

Kroll, Stanley, and Shishko, Irwin. *Commodity Futures Market Guide.* 1973. 370 pp.

>Technical (chart) analysis for speculators is emphasized by Kroll and Shishko, although good coverage of the econometric approach to commodity fundamentals is also provided. Other subjects to which a good deal of space is devoted include hedging, spreads, the technique of trading, and London commodity options. Appendixes show trading specifications for 38 different U.S. and London futures contracts (with long-term price charts), as well as seasonally adjusted open interest and volume data in chart form for 15 commodities. The authors write clearly, and are very good at putting sophisticated concepts into plain language.

Kroll, Stanley. *The Professional Commodity Trader.* 1974. 178 pp.

>In this unusually well-written volume, a successful commodity trader tells of his experiences in the market. The needed characteristics that show up most clearly are patience and courage—Kroll has the ability to stay put through some horrendous ups and downs that, in most cases, eventually work out to his great advantage. Most of the book is taken up with a description of Kroll's everyday trading activities, with good advice to the amateur thrown in where convenient. Trading only with the major price trend is the dominant theme, and specific operations in copper (the "Copper Caper"), cocoa, silver, and platinum (the "Platinum Kid") are discussed. Kroll's general advice to traders is summarized in a five-page "Epilogue" at the end of his book.

36 COMMODITY FUTURES TRADING

Merrill Lynch, Pierce, Fenner & Smith, Inc. *How to Buy and Sell Commodities.* 1972. 60 pp.

> A well-written, concise review of the fundamentals of commodity futures trading, with special emphasis on wheat. Price, supply, demand, risk, the cash market, contracts, and delivery are among the topics briefly discussed. Considerable space is devoted to "Mistakes That Speculators Make." Government price support programs and hedging are considered. There are several pages of "Questions and Answers About Wheat," with the seasonal trend of wheat prices clearly illustrated by means of a fullpage chart covering the 12-month period from July to June. The seasonal trends of farm prices, May wheat futures, and December wheat futures are shown. A similar chart shows the seasonal trend of soybean prices from September to August. A glossary of commodity trading terms is included, as well as handy tables giving basic facts about important commodity futures.

Powers, Mark J. *Getting Started in Commodity Futures Trading.* 1973. 208 pp.

> An easy-to-read, sensible, beginner's introduction to the fine art of futures trading. Powers emphasizes money management and the avoidance of overtrading, with a guest chapter on the topic by Robert Feduniak of Bache & Co. ("How to Avoid Overtrading"). Other chapters by Powers cover trading plans, brokers, orders, price forecasting (fundamental and technical), open interest, hedging, and spreads. In the chapter "What to Look For—and Where to Find It" excellent summaries in tabular form are given of supply-demand factors and sources of information for ten specific commodities or commodity groups. Much of the material in Powers' book appeared in *Commodities* magazine in 1972 and early 1973.

Prestbo, John A. "High-Flying Futures; Sharp Price Rises Make Trading in Commodities Hot Investment Field. Risks Are Great, and Pace Can be Fierce, but Many Thrive on the Excitement. Is Football Good Training?" *Wall Street Journal*, March 27, 1973, pp. 1, 18.

> General discussion of recent activity in commodity futures speculation. An estimate is given that about 500,000 people speculate in futures, with the number expected to rise to about 3 million by 1980. The author points out that anyone who had been lucky enough to buy the March 1973 soybeans contract in March 1972 and then hold it for about a year would have made a profit of approximately $18,000 on an original margin deposit of $1,000 (20¢ a bushel deposit on a contract of 5,000 bushels). The total commission cost would have been $30. On the other hand, price movements in soybean futures have been so violent recently that a speculator could have a $750 profit on one contract by lunch time and then a $750 loss by early afternoon (up the limit of 15¢ a bushel in the morning, then back to the starting point, followed by a drop of the 15¢ limit in the afternoon). Mr. Prestbo describes the experiences of some individuals who have been more or less successful in futures trading. The sharp reflexes of a trained athlete are said to be useful.

Reinach, Anthony M. *The Fastest Game in Town; Trading Commodity Futures.* 1973. 175 pp.

> Reinach's volume emphasizes charts, volume of trading as an indicator, and technical analysis in general. The key word is "action" as in commodity market action, referred to frequently by Reinach as "CMA."

Shaw, John E. B. *A Professional Guide to Commodity Speculation.* 1972. 172 pp.

> Many practical aspects of futures trading are covered in 26 concise chapters. (Eighteen of the chapter headings begin with the words "How to....") Shaw's book has a definite emphasis on automatic or mechanical, trend following systems of speculating in futures. He believes that the typical amateur trader is less likely to go astray if trend following plans are used. As Shaw indicates, several large assumptions are necessary: (1) that the speculator has sufficient, expendable capital to go through a more or less extended period of successive losses; (2) that the speculator has great nerves and will not panic while in a hopefully temporary loss position; and (3) that some definite price trends will occur in the commodities selected for trading before too much time goes by. In addition to mechanical methods, Shaw covers seasonal trades, seasonal spreads, charting (both bar and point-and-figure), computerized trading, how to deal with a broker, and margin management. Detailed results of many automatic and seasonal trading systems are given. This is a clearly written, easy-to-read book.

Shulman, Morton. "Commodity Futures—The Ideal Gamble." In his *Anyone Can Still Make A Million*, pp. 119–137. 1973.

> Speculation in futures is said to be "the quickest possible way to get rich or go bankrupt amongst all forms of market trading." Shulman says that futures trading is an exciting kind of gambling (because of low margin requirements) that can turn little money into big money—or little money into no money. The mechanism of futures trading is explained and trading methods are reviewed.

Stillman, Richard J. "Commodities." In his *Guide to Personal Finance*, pp. 249–269. 1972.

> A general review of commodity futures trading, with emphasis on the fact that amateur speculators nearly always lose money. "The commodities markets are for the venturesome who have a gambler's instinct."

Teweles, Richard J., Harlow, Charles V., and Stone, Herbert L. *The Commodity Futures Game; Who Wins? Who Loses? Why?* 1974. 638 pp.

> A completely revised and expanded version of *Commodity Futures Trading Guide* (1969), which became widely known as a standard textbook in the area of commodity markets. Section one, "Basics of the Game," explains how commodity futures markets work. Section two, "Playing the Game

(Trading)," considers the relative merits of the fundamental and the technical approaches to commodity speculation, with special attention given to risk and the problems encountered in money management. Section three, "Losers and Winners," concentrates on the behavioral skills necessary for success in commodity trading. Section four, "The Broker in the Game," presents advice for the broker who wishes to build, maintain, and service a commodity clientele. Section five, "Choosing the Game (Markets)," gives basic information about each of 30 diffrent commodities that have futures markets. Supply-demand considerations, factors generally influencing prices, sources of information, and seasonal information are featured in each case. Brief trading advice is also given for each commodity ("Notes from a Trader"). Finally, there is an excellent, classified bibliography of over 500 items. This volume by three professors of finance and management (all at California State University, Long Beach) who are also commodity consultants (Cambistics, Inc.) is not difficult to read, even though it is somewhat academic in its approach to commodity speculation. Emphasis is on actual research studies that have been done in the field of futures trading, but these studies generally point up the fact that it is very difficult for anyone to make money consistently over an extended period of time in commodity futures markets. Highly recommended as a touch of reality for those who have decided to get rich quick by speculating in futures.

Watling, T. F., and Morley, J. *Successful Commodity Futures Trading.* 1974. 227 pp.

A British view of commodity futures, with special information about London exchanges, commodity options, and market psychology. The British opinion of such international commodities as cocoa, coffee, sugar, and rubber is particularly interesting. The authors present their material in an informal, popularly written style.

Williams, Larry R. *How I Made One Million Dollars in the Commodity Market Last Year.* 1973. 130 pp.

Despite the flamboyant title, this is a very good, generally conservative book for beginners in commodity speculation. (One would want to supplement it with one of the less personal "standard" volumes, however.) While Williams does not put much faith in the usual systems of technical analysis or charting, neither does he make use of ordinary supply-demand analysis. His basic system is founded mainly on careful examination of three factors: (1) positions of large traders, (2) price relationships between near and distant months, and (3) the open interest trend. Of course, before taking an actual position in the market, other items must be taken into account, and these are explained by Williams. For example, money management is thoroughly discussed, and many market timing hints are given. The emotional problems of speculators are nicely covered in a chapter on transactional analysis. At one point in his book, Williams gives the names and addresses of nine commodity advisory services that he particularly recommends.

COMMODITY FUTURES AS INFLATION HEDGES

Along with stocks, real estate, antiques, works of art, and other items, the ownership of commodities is sometimes mentioned by financial writers as a possible hedge against inflation.

Reinach, Anthony M. "Commodity Futures as a Hedge Against Inflation." In *Commodity Year Book 1975*, pp. 6–12. 1975.

> The claim is made that "Commodity futures are the best hedge against inflation." Reinach begins his justification for this claim by providing a short history of money and inflation ("The U.S. Inflation Machine"). Then the disadvantages of diamonds, common stocks, fine art, and other inflation hedges are briefly described. Even though commodity futures are Reinach's favorite inflation hedge, he is careful to point out that sophisticated timing and money management decisions must be made by commodity investors. Prices are likely to be erratic, even while trending upward over a long period of time. Charts included show the purchasing power of the dollar from 1956 to 1975 and the Commodity Research Bureau Futures Price Index (monthly high, low, and close) from 1956 to 1975.

COMMODITY FUTURES HISTORY. See History of Futures Trading

COMMODITY FUTURES PRICE INDEX. See Dow-Jones Commodity Futures Index

COMMODITY OPTIONS

Agreements sold for a fee (premium) that give the purchaser the right to buy (call) or sell (put) a particular commodity futures contract at a specified price within a certain period of time. Options to buy are known as calls and options to sell are known as puts. A put-call combination is referred to as a double option—the holder can profit from a significant price move either down or up. Combinations other than one put to one call are also sold. In the United States commodity options are not legal in grains and other products regulated by the Commodity Exchange Act of 1936. Options are popular on the London commodity exchanges.

Biderman, Charles. "New Trading Vehicle; Commodity Options Are Growing in Popularity." *Barron's*, vol. 53, January 8, 1973, pp. 11, 19.

> A general review and explanation of commodity options. Biderman points out that options in commodity futures are not new, and were popular from about 1920 to 1934. Trading in them was stopped during the depression, because of the failure of the firms that were serving as option writers. The author points out that limited liability is the main reason for the recent

popularity of commodity options. That is, the option buyer can lose no more than he paid for his option, although there is no limit to his possible profit beyond the cost of the option. Biderman states that double options have been very popular among less sophisticated commodity speculators because of the opportunity to make money on extreme price moves in either direction. However, the recently volatile futures markets have been unusual, and double options may not work so well when "normal" market conditions prevail.

Cornish, P. J. "Options." In *Getting Started in London Commodities*, ed. by C. W. J. Granger, pp. 27–30. 1975.

States that London commodity options have been traded since before World War II, and that option trades constitute about 5 percent of the total business of London commodity exchanges. The International Commodities Clearing House, Ltd. (ICCH) guarantees the integrity of London options in cocoa, coffee, sugar, wool, and rubber. The cost of a London put or call is said to be around 5 to 15 percent of the price of the commodity contract. Cornish describes puts, calls, and double options. There have been very few occasions in recent years when double option premiums have not been covered by market price moves. Most double options have in the past furnished excellent returns, according to Cornish.

Hill, G. Christian. "Gambler's Game; Commodity Options Are the Latest Way to Get Rich—or Poor—in Hurry. SEC Frets That Potential for Fraud Is Great; How One Firm Wheels and Deals. Writing Naked Is No Disgrace." *Wall Street Journal*, February 2, 1973, pp. 1, 19.

General discussion of commodity options and dealers. According to Hill, option speculators lose money less often and lose smaller amounts than individuals who trade in commodity futures in the usual way. It is said that regular commodity speculators lose money 90 percent of the time, while the users of options lose "only" from 60 to 70 percent of the time. The author points out "serpents in this speculators' Garden of Eden." That is, there is no official regulation of dealings in commodity options because of the fact that, although the Commodity Exchange Act of 1936 forbids options in commodity futures, the act covers only "domestic" commodities and not "international" products. As a result, options are possible in sugar, cocoa, copper, platinum, plywood, and other commodities with futures markets outside the United States. Since dealers in options are unregulated, the opportunity for fraud is said to be great. Hill's article describes the activities of Goldstein, Samuelson, Inc. of Beverly Hills, California, in some detail. One gentleman, in speaking of commodity option writers (dealers) in general in early 1973, inferred that 50 to 60 percent of them were "ex-felons, individuals previously convicted of fraud and other questionable characters." One of the unsound practices engaged in is "writing naked," which means that the dealer who writes (sells) commodity options does not actually own the related futures contracts, but depends on his own speculative activities for the cash flow necessary for payoffs.

Kroll, Stanley, and Shishko, Irwin. "Commodity Put and Call Options." In their *Commodity Futures Market Guide*, pp. 258–268. 1973.

> Various uses of London commodity options are discussed, such as trading futures against options, using options to protect profitable positions, buying puts to gain a long-term tax advantage (as an alternative to selling short), and using London options to hedge in the international currency markets. Specific examples are given, with details of the use of call options for limited-risk speculation (London sugar is used as an example), to replace a long position (London silver), to protect a short position (London sugar), and to add to an existing long position at limited risk (London cocoa). Detailed examples are given of the use of put options for limited-risk speculation (London cocoa), to replace a short position (London sugar), to protect a long position (London silver), and to add to an existing short position at limited risk (London sugar). Finally, the double option is explained, with London sugar used as an example.

Loehwing, David A. "California Crackdown; Commodity Options Will Never Be the Same Again." *Barron's*, vol. 53, March 5, 1973, pp. 5, 21–22.

> Tells of the crackdown on unregulated commodity options trading in California. In early 1973, options trading was stopped by Brian Van Camp, the California Corporations Commissioner, and the leading West Coast options firm, Goldstein, Samuelson, Inc., went into receivership. Loehwing gives some historical background, indicating that puts and calls on grain futures were actively traded on the Chicago Board of Trade from 1926 to 1933, but were banned by the Board of Trade in 1933 and outlawed by the Commodity Exchange Act of 1936. That is, options on domestic, regulated commodities were outlawed—London options on international commodities, such as coffee, sugar, and cocoa, have been available for many years. Loehwing points out that, although option premiums may be almost as much as minimum margin requirements in many cases, options have the advantage of limiting risk to the amount of the premium. Another big plus for the small speculator is that margin calls are eliminated. (The largest negative factor, of course, is that losing the entire premium is very easy to do if the market moves unfavorably.) In any event, the big problem in California was the writing of "naked" options, wherein the dealers did not hedge their operations by the sale or purchase of offsetting futures contracts.

Love, J. S., and Associates. *Trading London Commodity Options.* 1974. 21 pp.

> A concise but very informative booklet on commodity puts, calls, and double options. Leverage, volatility, trading against options, advantages, risks, and the mechanics of trading are covered. Specific uses for call options, put options, and double options are outlined. London futures trading facts are summarized for sugar, cocoa, coffee, silver, and copper.

Murray, Thomas J. "The Furor Over Commodity Options." *Dun's*, vol. 101, March 1973, pp. 69–72, 119–120.

> An industry rule of thumb is mentioned, in which it is assumed that "at least 92 percent of all people who speculate directly in commodities" will be losers. Furthermore, the average commodities speculator will probably last only about six months before being wiped out. Commodity options do not appear to produce results that are much better, as it is estimated that 70 percent of options buyers are losers. Most of the *Dun's* article is devoted to a description of the rapid growth and increasing troubles of the unregulated (in 1973) commodity options business in California. The troubles were brought about by underfinancing, lack of hedging by dealers, and impending state and federal regulation. Commodity puts and calls are explained under the heading "How Options Work" on page 72 of the *Dun's* article.

Parker, George B. "Understanding the London Futures Markets." In *Commodity Year Book 1971*, pp. 36–47. 1971.

> Included in the details of futures trading for each London commodity is an indication of which commodities have call options available. Call option mechanics are discussed in some detail.

Sarnoff, Paul. *London Commodity Options Explained.* No date. 2 pp.

> Brief, but informative. The declaration date and prompt date used for London commodity options are clearly explained and contrasted with the American use of an expiration date. Sarnoff gives the straightforward warning that London options are extremely speculative, quite expensive, and not suitable for those who cannot afford to lose the cost of the premium.

Shakin, Bernard. "Commodities Options; They're Available from London Through Some N.Y. Brokers." *Barron's*, vol. 55, January 27, 1975, pp. 11–12.

> "Commodities options, a favorite of a handful of sophisticated speculators who want a crack at a fast profit, represent an off-beat way to enter the highly volatile futures markets." Shakin describes the buying and selling of London commodity options, particularly the popular "double option" or straddle (combination of a put and a call). Unfortunately, commodity options currently have a bad reputation in the United States because of the failure of certain disreputable dealers in 1973. As of early 1975, for example, large retail brokers, such as Merrill Lynch and Bache, were no longer dealing in London commodity options. However, London options were still available through certain specialty brokers in the United States who fill orders via London dealers. Shakin mentions that the lack of American interest has made the London options market thinner, resulting in premium increases to about 11 percent (in previous years, some premiums had fallen to less than 3 percent).

Shulman, Morton. "Puts and Calls." In his *Anyone Can Still Make a Million*, pp. 78–80. 1973.

> Shulman gives an example of how he made money through the purchase of a silver call option. He generally recommends commodity puts and calls, where available, for those who love to gamble with limited risk.

Watling, T. F., and Morley, J. "Option Trading." In their *Successful Commodity Futures Trading*, pp. 121–125. 1974.

> Commodity options are said to be superior to stock puts and calls in several ways: longer terms (up to 15 months), premiums that are often as little as 5 percent, and more profit potentiality resulting from commodity volatility. The uses of commodity options and double options are briefly discussed. Watling and Morley mention that the most active London options are those that are guaranteed by the London Produce Clearing House—cocoa, coffee, sugar, and rubber. "Metal options are traded between dealers and underwritten by the giver."

Zieg, Kermit C., and Zieg, Susannah H. *Commodity Options*. 1974. 158 pp.

> A detailed review of commodity options, described by the authors as "probably the most exciting investment vehicle ever made available to the general public." The authors claim that options enable the speculator to make profitable use of positive commodity leverage, while at the same time almost eliminating negative leverage. Examples of chapter headings in this clearly written volume are "Commodity Options vs. Futures," "London vs. American Commodity Options," "Call Option Trading Techniques," "Put Option Trading Techniques," and "The Chart Evaluation Method of Valuing Double Options." There are 12 chapters altogether, with 43 charts, 13 tables, and a short bibliography. Zieg and Zieg have produced an informative survey of a controversial topic.

COMMODITY PRICES AND ELECTION YEARS. See Presidential Election Years and Commodity Prices

COMMODITY PRICES AND STOCK PRICES. See Stock Prices and Commodity Prices

COMMODITY PRICES AND WAR. See War and Commodity Prices

COMMODITY STATISTICS SOURCES. See Statistics Sources

COMMODITY TERM GLOSSARIES. See Glossaries

COMMODITY TRADING HISTORY. See History of Futures Trading

COMMODITY FUTURES TRADING

COMPUTER ANALYSIS

The use of the computer in the statistical analysis of commodity supply-demand data (fundamental analysis) or as an aid in the following of price trends (technical analysis).

"Directory of Futures Trading." Published annually in January as a special issue of *Commodities* magazine.

> This special directory issue of *Commodities* lists about 20 computer data services related to commodity futures trading. Some of the services merely provide data banks of prices and other statistics, but most also furnish trading advice of a technical, trend-following nature. Names, addresses, telephone numbers, and descriptions of services are given. (It has been announced that the special directory edition of *Commodities* will henceforth be published as the May issue. Coverage will be expanded to include statistical data, futures contract details, and other material. The new title will be "Reference Guide to Futures Markets.")

Fink, Robert, and Turner, Dennis. "Computers and Commodity Price Forecasting." In *Commodity Year Book 1973*, pp. 24–30. 1973.

> Moving averages, trend lines, on-balance volume, price channels, linear regression methods, seasonal patterns, and econometric models are all discussed. While the computer cannot, of course, actually predict with any certainty what the actual price of a particular commodity futures contract will be, say, one month from now, computers are invaluable for testing speculative trading methods on historical data, compiling studies of seasonal trends, and building econometric models. Fink and Turner outline the average percentage link relative method and the ratio to moving average method of establishing a seasonal index. The authors stress the human factors of experience, intuition, and creativity in working with computers—these factors "will determine whether a given method is a success or failure."

Kroll, Stanley, and Shishko, Irwin. "The Role of the Computer in Technical Analysis." In their *Commodity Futures Market Guide*, pp. 158–166. 1973.

> A brief review is provided of the use of computers to set up automatic trading systems. The usual failings are mentioned, such as the fact that a mechanical system that works well during one time period may very well come up with losses during other periods.

Nimrod, Vance L., and Bower, Richard S. "Commodities and Computers." *Journal of Financial and Quantitative Analysis*, vol. 2, March, 1967, pp. 61–73.

> "This brief note reports successful use of an econometric model and a time-sharing computer system" for the purpose of speculation in commodity futures. The basic plan was to predict the spot price of live hogs for some future month and then "trade on the basis of any large unexplained difference between this prediction and the current price of futures for

that month." (As live hog futures were not available, pork bellies were used for speculation and mathematical adjustments were made for the substitution.) The procedure required that the following steps be taken: (1) identify variables that determine spot price; (2) determine influence of these variables on spot price; (3) estimate numerical values of variables for period being predicted. The authors include a line-by-line table showing part of the computer program used to predict the live hog spot price for August 1966, utilizing the General Electric 265 time-sharing computer system and computer language BASIC. The regression equation used in the prediction is given, as well as the equation for the econometric model fitted to August data from 1946 to 1965. When pork bellies were sold short, after analysis of data, a 70 percent profit was realized. In drawing up the basic plan, it is important to note that in addition to computer capability and econometrics, the highly personal skill of a commodity expert with knowledge of the hog market was made use of. As the authors point out, "... in spite of success, the approach reported here does not take the risk out of commodity speculation."

Pappas, Vasil. "Digital Diviners: Commodities Traders Rig More Computers to Forecast Prices. Thomte-Roper and Others Claim Success; Decisions Based on Prime Models." *Wall Street Journal*, October 8, 1975, pp. 1, 31.

Quotes a member of a leading brokerage house as saying that at least 15 firms have put together computer programs for the forecasting of commodity price trends. Although most of these programs apparently have been reasonably successful in the active futures markets of recent years, some brokers are predicting that computer trading will eventually be selfdefeating. That is, if everyone decided to buy on a particular signal, who would do the selling? The Boston trading firm of Thomte-Roper, Inc. is described at some length. Despite the firm's overall success, many of its trades are unprofitable and are terminated by "automatic" stop-loss orders. The many small losses are overcome by letting profits run.

Shaw, John E. B. "How to Use a Computer with Mechanical Methods." In his *A Professional Guide to Commodity Speculation*, pp. 119–124. 1972.

Describes an elementary, mechanical, computerized soybean trading program that Shaw devised, based on a ten-day moving average. The program worked well in actual practice over a short period of time, but has not been tested over an extended period. Approximate results are also given for a commercial, computerized, commodity forecasting service. After deducting approximate commission costs, results from eight different commodities from 1967 to 1970 were spotty, being good for commodities that happened to develop definite trends during the period studied, and poor for those that remained relatively trendless. "The computer... must not be caught too often in a trading range market." Losses from a computerized, mechanical trading scheme tend to run in streaks, meaning that the speculator must have both the patience and the capital to ride out the bad periods without abandoning ship. In any event, catching some profitable trends is absolutely essential. Tabulations show computer results in detail for wheat, oats, and copper from late 1967 to the middle of 1970.

CONGESTION AREAS. See Support and Resistance Levels; names of individual chart formations, such as Triangles (Coils) and Flags and Pennants

CONTRARY OPINION
A conclusion leading to a course of action different from what the majority is perceived to be doing. In commodity futures trading, the cue to majority opinion is often taken from what the bulk of published advisory services are saying (as reported, for example, in the weekly "Market Sentiment Index" of *Consensus* magazine).

Chicago Board of Trade. "Contrary Opinion." In *Commodity Trading Manual*, p. 99. 1973.

> Mentions a theory of contrary opinion based on published commodity advisory services. Supposedly, if more than 80 percent of these services are bullish on a particular commodity, that product is due for an important drop in price. On the other hand, if more than 80 percent of the advisors are bearish, a sharp price rally is imminent. Unfortunately, taking a "contrary position" too soon can result in financial disaster.

Teweles, Richard J., and others. "Contrary Opinion." In their *The Commodity Futures Game*, pp. 196–200. 1974.

> In this unusually complete review of the contrary opinion method, the authors point out that two basic conditions must exist before a contrary opinion position would be justified: public or trade opinion must be almost unanimous and this opinion must be supported by "weak" reasons. Furthermore, there are two characteristics of weak reasoning (one or both characteristics may be present in a potentially profitable contrary opinion situation): (1) widely publicized facts that have been well known for a good period of time; and (2) well-known "facts" that are really nothing more than suppositions. The advantages of trading according to contrary opinion are said to be that the approach is logical, that the trader is assisted in keeping his perspective, that contrary opinion often turns up overlooked facts, and that markets are sometimes "extremely vulnerable to unexpected developments not in line with current thinking." Disadvantages of the contrary opinion approach are said to be that it is difficult to get a good sample of opinions, that actual depth of opinion is hard to judge, that contrariness sometimes turns into arrogance, that points of valid crowd psychology do not come along all that often in commodities, and that there is some difficulty in knowing where to close out a position that was initiated according to a contrary opinion approach.

CONVERSION SPREAD. See Soybean Oil-Soybean Meal-Soybeans Spread

COPPER

A ductile metal noted for its ability to conduct electricity and resist corrosion, mined chiefly in the United States, Russia, Zambia, Chile, and Canada. About half of all copper mined is used to make electrical wiring. Copper in the form of standardized ingots, bars, slabs, and so forth is represented by futures trading on the Commodity Exchange, Inc. (New York) and the London Metal Exchange.

Chicago Board of Trade. "Copper." In *Commodity Trading Manual*, pp. 198–200. 1973.

> Copper supply-demand factors are discussed. Futures trading details are listed for the Commodity Exchange, Inc. (New York), including delivery months, trading units, minimum price fluctuations, daily price move limits, position limits, delivery standards, and trading hours.

Keck, Robert T. "Understanding the Copper Futures Market." In *Commodity Year Book 1971*, pp. 13–20. 1971.

> Covers the fundamentals of the copper futures market, including history, production, influence of scrap supply, characteristics and uses of copper itself, influence of refined stocks, carrying charges, general supply and demand considerations, and sources of statistical information. A short bibliography is included. Charts show daily futures prices at New York for December copper from 1959 to 1970.

Smyth, David, and Stuntz, Laurance F. "Copper—A Political Commodity." In their *The Speculator's Handbook*, pp. 92–98. 1974.

> A good, practical review of copper futures trading, including supply-demand fundamentals. Governmental influence on copper prices is emphasized.

Teweles, Richard J., and others. "Copper." In their *The Commodity Futures Game*, pp. 486–491. 1974.

> "Copper futures can be extremely volatile." This volatility is brought about by the international character of the copper market combined with a relatively small open interest. The following topics are discussed: factors influencing prices, nature of production, utilization, and seasonal trends (there is some tendency for copper prices to be low from June to August). Copper information sources are given on page 513 of the Teweles book.

Watling, T. F., and Morley, J. "Copper." In their *Successful Commodity Futures Trading*, pp. 169–172. 1974.

> Copper production and supply-demand factors are briefly discussed. Futures trading details are given for the London Metal Exchange.

Wideman, Frank L. "The Long Term Outlook for Copper." In *Commodity Year Book 1966*, pp. 6–16. 1966.

> A prediction is made of "ever increasing demand" for copper, resulting in higher prices. World supply, production sources, and utilization are dis-

cussed, and the role of the copper futures markets is briefly explained. A line chart compares the domestic producers' copper price with the London spot price on a monthly basis from 1953 to 1965. A short bibliography (five items) is included.

CORN (See also Corn—Seasonal Price Trend; Hog-Corn Ratio; Oats-Corn Spread; Wheat-Corn Spread)
The most important of the feed grains—the major source of energy for hogs, poultry, and cattle. In the United States, 90 percent of all corn grown is hard, dent corn used for animal feed and for various commercial products. Sweet corn for direct human consumption is, therefore, a relatively small part of total production. Almost one half of the world's supply of corn is grown in the Corn Belt of the United States, especially in Iowa and Illinois. Corn futures are actively traded on the Chicago Board of Trade.

Chicago Board of Trade. "Corn." In *Commodity Trading Manual*, pp. 142–147. 1973.

> Information is given as to varieties of corn (yellow, white, mixed, soft, and waxy), production factors, government corn programs, animal feed usage, industrial uses, and exports. Corn futures trading details are given for the Chicago Board of Trade and the Mid-America Commodity Exchange (formerly the Chicago Open Board of Trade). Delivery months, trading units, price fluctuation specifications, daily price limits, position limits, delivery standards, and trading hours are summarized for each exchange. The history of corn is also briefly discussed.

Clough, Malcolm. "New Guidelines for Forecasting Corn Prices." In *Commodity Year Book 1974*, pp. 6–15. 1974.

> The demand for corn has expanded greatly since 1970, with foreign needs being especially strong. Clough takes a fresh look at the factors influencing corn prices in recent years. Supply-demand balance, feed requirements, feed costs, exports, government feed grain programs, acreage, reserve stocks, and production are each discussed. The three dominant market forces affecting corn prices in the United States are said to be corn supply, livestock and poultry numbers to be fed, and the prices of livestock and poultry products. Other important influences are export demand and government programs. As a result of tight supply and big demand, corn futures prices have become much more volatile in recent years than in the past. Daily basis price charts of May corn futures at Chicago are shown from 1969 to 1974. Various corn statistics are given in tabular form, covering the past 20 years or so.

Emery, Walter L. "Understanding the Corn Futures Market." In *Commodity Year Book 1970*, pp. 15–25. 1970.

> The fundamentals of the corn market are explained, with special attention given to production factors and the carryover of corn supplies from the previous season. Seasonal price movements and variations in open interest

are emphasized, although Emery cautions against taking market positions in corn solely on the basis of seasonal considerations. Charts show daily futures prices for May corn at Chicago from 1959 to 1970. Another chart shows total "Feed Grain Production, Use, and Carryover" from 1958 to 1969.

Hieronymus, Thomas A. "Forecasting Corn Futures Prices." In *Guide to Commodity Price Forecasting*, ed. by Harry Jiler and George B. Parker, pp. 119-132. 1965.

". . . to forecast the price of corn futures, one must first forecast the price of cash corn and then relate cash corn prices to futures." As the great bulk of the corn crop is used for livestock feed, Hieronymus concentrates on the estimation of feed use as the key factor in any projection of corn prices. In a full-page table, he presents "Feed Concentrate Balance, Livestock Numbers, and Feed per Animal" from 1955 to 1964. The loan influence, the Chicago basis, and seasonal variations are discussed. Charts show "Corn Prices: Mid-Month Differences Between Chicago Cash/July Futures and National Average Farm Price" monthly from October to July for each season from 1958 through 1963, plus an average for the six years. There are also charts showing daily corn futures prices for the July delivery from 1954 to 1965.

Jones, George A. *Trading in Corn Futures.* 1972. 42 pp.

A thorough review of the fundamentals of corn trading, including economic factors, government programs, supply and demand, price analysis, and hedging.

Keltner, Chester W. "Fundamental Analysis Applied to Corn Situations." In his *How to Make Money in Commodities*, pp. 154-161. 1960.

A general discussion of how to analyze corn prices from the viewpoint of supply and demand fundamentals. Seasonal price tendencies and the price level itself are emphasized. Keltner points out that corn prices must always be scrutinized in relation to the total supply of feed from all sources and the relative number of livestock that must be fed. Tables show corn supplies, disappearance, free surplus, farm loan rate, impoundings, and seasonal price advances for each crop year from 1940-1941 to 1959-1960.

Teweles, Richard J., and others. "Corn." In their *The Commodity Futures Game*, pp. 376-390, 398-400. 1974.

Because of the big crop and the volume of hedging, corn is said to be a somewhat ponderous market, with price moves on the gradual side. At times, however, there are surprising exceptions to this. The authors discuss factors influencing prices, information sources, production, feed-concentrate utilization, government programs, spreads, carrying charges, and seasonal factors. A graph shows seasonal trends of open interest and volume for corn in the form of a ten-year average (1962-1971) plotted for each month of the year.

CORN—SEASONAL PRICE TREND (*See also* "The Voice from the Tomb")
Marketing of a new corn crop normally begins in October. Low prices for the season typically occur in November or December, with highs the following August.

Commodity Research Bureau. "Seasonal Trends in Grain Futures Prices." In *Commodity Year Book 1952*, pp. 13–15. 1952.

> A price advance in May corn occurred after the month of October in every season from 1930–1931 to 1950–1951. The advance ranged from 4¢ to 58¢ or from about 3 percent to 60 percent. A table shows "May Corn Futures Prices: 1930–31 to 1950–51, Chicago Board of Trade; Price Advance from October 31 Low to Subsequent High (Cents per Bushel)." A chart shows "Monthly Seasonal Trend in Marketing of Corn (in Percent of Total Marketings), 10 Year Monthly Average, 1941–50." The monthly percentages shown in the chart are related to corn receipts at primary markets. Other charts show daily futures prices for May corn at Chicago from 1936 to 1951.

CORN-HOG RATIO. *See* Hog-Corn Ratio

CORN-OATS SPREAD. *See* Oats-Corn Spread

CORN-WHEAT SPREAD. *See* Wheat-Corn Spread

COTTON (*See also* Cotton—Seasonal Price Trend; Cotton Spread)
A plant grown in warm or temperate climates, chiefly for the fiber attached to its seed, although the seed itself is very important for vegetable oil purposes. The leading cotton-producing countries are the United States, Russia, China, and India, with Texas being by far the leading producer in the United States. Cotton in bales is represented by a futures contract traded on the New York Cotton Exchange.

Chicago Board of Trade. "Cotton." In *Commodity Trading Manual*, pp. 219–222. 1973.

> Cotton supply factors, production, stocks, marketing procedures, demand considerations, and futures markets are discussed. Cotton futures trading details are given for the New York Cotton Exchange (cotton is also traded in Great Britain by the Liverpool Cotton Association). The following are listed for the New York Cotton Exchange: delivery months, trading units, minimum price fluctuations, daily price move limits, position limits, delivery standards, and trading hours. "World Production of Cotton" in thousands of bales is listed for each of nine countries annually from 1962–1963 to 1971–1972.

Emery, Walter L. "Understanding the Cotton Futures Market." In *Commodity Year Book 1968*, pp. 15-24. 1968.

> General coverage of the production, marketing, and use of cotton, aimed at helping the trader evaluate price making influences. Major growing areas, consumption, and exports are discussed. Details are given concerning cotton futures trading, deliveries, and hedging. Sources of information about cotton are summarized.

Teweles, Richard J., and others. "Cotton." In their The *Commodity Futures Game*, pp. 548-559, 567. 1974.

> The authors consider factors influencing prices, information sources, supply, demand, government programs, seasonal tendencies, and carrying charges. The history of cotton futures trading is somewhat erratic. The commodity was actively traded from 1947 to 1957, but declined to virtual dormancy by 1967 as government participation increased. In recent years, interest has revived.

COTTON—SEASONAL PRICE TREND

Marketing of new crop cotton normally begins in August. According to one authority, low prices for the season typically occur in January or February, with highs in August or September. Another source quotes October to December for the lows and July for the highest cotton prices.

Commodity Research Bureau. "Seasonal Influences on Commodity Futures Prices." In *Commodity Year Book 1951*, pp. 11-12. 1951.

> Cotton prices are said to have a strong tendency to rise each year from November to January. A table shows "March Cotton Futures Prices, Nov. 1, Jan. 2 and Net Changes, 1934-35 to 1950-51." Daily basis line charts show March cotton futures prices at New York from 1935 to 1951.

COTTON SPREAD

A transaction wherein a cotton futures contract for one month is bought at the same time that the contract for another month is sold, with the idea being to profit from a change in the price difference, or "spread."

Commodity Reserach Bureau. "Commodity Spreads and Straddles." In *Commodity Year Book 1948*, pp. 39-42. 1948.

> The July–October cotton spread is briefly discussed and "A Hypothetical Transaction" is presented. Daily basis price charts show July–October cotton spreads for eight years selected from the period 1916-1948.

CROP STATISTICS. See Statistics Sources

CYCLES. See Elliott Wave Principle; Moon Cycles; Seasonal Price Trend; "The Voice From the Tomb"

52 COMMODITY FUTURES TRADING

DEFINITIONS (GLOSSARIES). See Glossaries.

DELIVERY

Taking possession of the actual physical commodity. Delivery is usually pointless and expensive for commodity futures speculators. Fortunately, delivery is very easy to avoid.

Cox, Houston A. "Deliveries Not for Most of You." In his *Concepts on Profits in Commodity Futures Trading*, pp. 77–79. 1972.

> The details of a theoretical delivery of 5,000 bushels of December wheat to futures customer John Doe are presented at some length, merely to show that taking delivery of the actual commodity is expensive, time consuming, irritating, and easily avoided. Virtually all futures speculators will wish to avoid delivery.

Gold, Gerald. "Provisions Made for Deliveries" and "Advice to Traders—Liquidate Before First Notice Day." In his *Modern Commodity Futures Trading*, 6th ed., pp. 39–40. 1971.

> "Unless there are some special circumstances prevailing, a speculator would be well advised to avoid taking delivery." Fortunately, as Gold points out, delivery is very easy to avoid by simply closing out speculative positions before first notice day. (First notice day usually occurs a few days before the beginning of the delivery month, and is the first day on which a notice of intention to deliver an actual commodity can be given to the holder of a futures contract.)

Shaw, John E. B. "How to Avoid Delivery Problems." In his *A Professional Guide to Commodity Speculation*, pp. 44–46. 1972.

> Do not take delivery. Shaw emphasizes the importance to the amateur trader of finding out just when the first delivery day will occur and closing out one's position (or moving it forward) before that ominous day arrives. The difficulties caused by delivery are explained.

DEVELOPMENT OF COMMODITY TRADING. See History of Futures Trading

DISCRETIONARY ACCOUNTS

Commodity futures trading accounts in which the customer gives the broker or other party the right to initiate and execute trades without prior approval by the customer. In other words, trading is at the discretion of the broker or other party.

Angrist, Stanley W. "Discretionary Accounts." In his *Sensible Speculating in Commodities*, pp. 49–50. 1972.

> This type of account is not recommended by Angrist, as it places too much responsibility on the broker, and does not enable the customer to really learn anything about commodity trading. The author tells of his own losses by way of a discretionary account in which the broker chose not to use stop-loss orders.

DOUBLE TOPS AND BOTTOMS

Commodity futures price chart patterns in the form of an "M" at market tops and in the form of a "W" at market bottoms. These are thought to be important price-trend reversal patterns.

Angrist, Stanley W. "Double Tops and Double Bottoms." In his *Sensible Speculating in Commodities*, pp. 109–111. 1972.

> States that double top or double bottom commodity futures price formations on bar charts are easy to recognize and "seem to work sometimes."

Gold, Gerald. "The Double Top or Bottom." In his *Modern Commodity Futures Trading*, 6th ed., pp. 201–204. 1971.

> Double bottom and double top chart formations are discussed in some detail, with specific buy and sell points illustrated on two hypothetical charts. However, these buy and sell points will vary from one situation to the next, depending upon the strategy being employed by the individual trader. For example, some traders will wait until a complete, double bottom, "W" shaped formation is complete, while others will try to anticipate the market by establishing positions early.

DOW-JONES COMMODITY FUTURES INDEX

An index of the combined prices of a group of active commodity futures contracts, published daily in the *Wall Street Journal*, and having the years 1924 through 1926 as a base (1924–1926 equals 100). There is also the Commodity Research Bureau Futures Index, which is published daily in the *Journal of Commerce* (1967 equals 100).

Keltner, Chester W. "The General Price Level." In his *How to Make Money in Commodities*, pp. 183–187. 1960.

> A consideration of the relationship between the general trend of commodity prices, as measured by the Dow-Jones Commodity Futures Index, and the prices of individual commodity futures contracts. An interesting chart shows the monthly average of Chicago May wheat prices superimposed on the Dow-Jones Commodity Futures Index. The period covered is 1949 to 1960.

Shaw, John E. B. "How to Trade on the Futures Index." In his *A Professional Guide to Commodity Speculation*, pp. 141–151. 1972.

> Presents an interesting and logical mechanical trading system that coordinates transactions in individual commodity futures with the direction of a ten-week moving average of the Dow-Jones Commodity Futures Index. Extensive tabulations show how the method worked with soybeans, wheat, pork bellies, and cocoa during the three-year period from the beginning of 1968 to the end of 1970. Results were very good during those particular years. Shaw lists seven rules that he recommends following if one is going to speculate according to the moves of the futures index.

ECONOMETRIC ANALYSIS. See Computer Analysis; Fundamental Analysis

EGGS

In this case, chicken eggs—an important foodstuff and source of protein. The United States produces many more eggs than any other country, with California being the leading egg-producing state. Fresh shell egg futures contracts are traded principally on the Chicago Mercantile Exchange.

Chicago Board of Trade. "Eggs." In *Commodity Trading Manual*, pp. 185–187. 1973.

> History and supply-demand factors are briefly discussed. Egg futures trading details are listed for the Chicago Mercantile Exchange and the Pacific Commodities Exchange, including delivery months, trading units, minimum price fluctuations, daily price move limits, position limits, delivery standards, and trading hours.

Inkeles, David M. "How to Forecast Egg Futures Prices." In *Commodity Year Book 1966*, pp. 28–37. 1966.

> Because of the perishability of eggs, the number of fundamentals influencing shell egg prices is high. Inkeles discusses egg supply, production factors, weather factors, effects of price change, demand considerations, seasonal variations, U.S. government purchases, exports during short supplies abroad, imports when domestic supplies are short, and demand from egg "breakers" (commercial egg users). Several pages are devoted to an analysis of both the shell egg and the frozen egg futures markets. Charts show daily futures versus cash prices for September shell eggs at Chicago from 1960 to 1965 and January shell eggs from 1961 to 1966. Daily futures prices are charted for October frozen eggs at Chicago from 1960 to 1965.

Inkeles, David M. "Understanding the Egg Futures Market." In *Commodity Year Book 1971*, pp. 6–12. 1971.

> Covers the fundamentals of the egg futures market, including supply and demand, hatching, molting, culling, imports, weather, holiday demand, commercial breaker demand, cash markets, and delivery considerations. Few commodities are said to have such consistently wide price fluctuations as eggs. Charts show daily futures prices at Chicago for the September shell egg contract from 1965 to 1970.

Shaw, John E. B. "Profiting from Cyclical Markets." In his *A Professional Guide to Commodity Speculation*, pp. 66–69. 1972.

> A specific method of taking advantage of the six-month egg cycle is discussed in some detail. The cycle is based on "the time from a chick to a layer of medium sized eggs." Shaw's egg trading method was profitable in six of the eight years from 1964 to 1971.

Teweles, Richard J., and others. "Fresh Eggs." In their *The Commodity Futures Game*, pp. 459–470, 476. 1974.

> History of egg marketing, factors influencing prices, five major sources of information, nature of production, consumption, and seasonal information are discussed. In 1969, 85 percent of all variation in Chicago egg prices was explained by three variables (number of layers, egg-feed ratio, and retail beef price). These three variables are shown in a regression analysis formula taken from a Chicago Mercantile Exchange research report. A chart shows "Fresh eggs: monthly open interest and volume as a percentage of average monthly open interest and volume for the years 1962–1971 at the Chicago Mercantile Exchange." The complexity of egg pricing factor interaction leads Teweles and co-authors to recommend that heavy commitments in the egg futures market be left to commercial traders. As demand is relatively inelastic, the trader should concentrate on impending changes in supply.

ELECTION YEARS AND COMMODITY PRICES. See Presidential Election Years and Commodity Prices

ELLIOTT WAVE PRINCIPLE (*See also* Time Cycles)
A theory formulated by the late R. N. Elliott, which states that stock and commodity prices exhibit periodicity and therefore move in regular patterns or waves. Some of the waves are tidal, while others are quite small. Elliott introduced his theory in an article relating primarily to the stock market, appearing in *Financial World*, April 5, 1939. R. N. Elliott died in 1947.

Cox, Houston A. "Elliott Wave Cycles for Major Trend Projection." In his *Concepts on Profits in Commodity Futures Trading*, pp. 89–106. 1972.

> For those interested in Elliott wave or cycle forecasting, Cox presents an unusually complete explanation. As the emphasis is on long-range forecasting, most of the dozen or so commodity charts used as examples are on a monthly basis and cover periods of over 30 years. In addition, many theoretical charts are used to illustrate principles and show common errors in Elliott wave interpretation. Several pages are devoted to wave extensions, corrections, and failures. Cox regards the Elliott principle as often useful in following long-term commodity price trends.

Kroll, Stanley, and Shishko, Irwin. "Wave Theory of Trend Analysis." In their *Commodity Futures Market Guide*, pp. 110–114. 1973.

> A full-page chart of prices for December 1968 orange juice is used to illustrate "Possible I, II, III, IV, V Elliott wave upcount." Kroll and Shishko take a neutral attitude toward wave theory, but mention the difficulty of determining the number of price swings or waves that have actually taken place within a certain period.

56 COMMODITY FUTURES TRADING

Teweles, Richard J., and others. "The Elliott Wave Theory." In their *The Commodity Futures Game*, pp. 208–214. 1974.

> Two pages of charts are used to illustrate "basic Elliott wave sequences" and "corrective patterns and triangles." A full-page chart of monthly rye futures prices from 1935 to 1970 is used to illustrate "major Elliott wave sequences." Advantages of the Elliott wave method are said to be that Elliott himself, as well as some of his followers, has been able to make surprisingly accurate forecasts of stock prices, that the Elliott system is based on the all-pervasive Fibonacci summation, and that therefore the method really does seem to have some viability. Disadvantages of the Elliott wave theory are said to be that the method was not designed for commodity prices, that highly subjective judgment must be used in counting Elliott waves, that leading Elliott interpreters are in constant disagreement, that wave moves can be extended in number without warning, that it is often impossible on individual commodity charts to get any kind of wave count, and that the originator, R. N. Elliott, was a mystic who believed, for example, that mathematical relationships in an Egyptian pyramid predicted future world events and corroborated his own wave theory.

EMOTIONS OF TRADERS. See Psychology

ENGLISH COMMODITY MARKETS. See London Commodity Markets

EVOLUTION OF COMMODITY TRADING. See History of Futures Trading

EXCHANGES. See Commodity Exchanges

FOLKLORE (ADAGES). See Trading Rules

FORECASTING OF PRICES. See Fundamental Analysis; Random Walk Theory; Technical Analysis

FOREST PRODUCTS. See Lumber and Plywood

FROZEN ORANGE JUICE CONCENTRATE. See Orange Juice

FROZEN PORK BELLIES. See Pork Bellies, Frozen

FUNDAMENTAL ANALYSIS (*See also* names of individual commodities)
The study and forecasting of commodity price trends according to basic supply-demand considerations.

Angrist, Stanley W. "Fundamental Analysis." In his *Sensible Speculating in Commodities*, pp. 72–102. 1972.

A discussion of how to use basic supply-demand factors in attempting to predict the future price of a commodity. The new crop, the old crop carryover, and imports are arrayed on the supply side against domestic utilization and exports on the demand side of the fundamental commodity price balance. Angrist describes the government agricultural programs having to do with loans and acreage control and considers the effects of government programs. He describes various seasonal price tendencies, and mentions that buying May soybean futures on October 1 and selling on January 31, as one example, has been profitable "66 percent of the time in a twelve-year period." Charts of daily prices of May soybeans are shown for the years 1961 to 1971. Finally, scare situations and inflation and deflation in general are considered.

Belveal, L. Dee. "Introduction to Market Analysis," "Analyzing the Long-Term Market Situation," and "Analyzing the Medium-Range Market Situation." In his *Commodity Speculation with Profits in Mind*, pp. 55–89. 1967.

These three chapters cover the general principles involved in making an analysis of fundamental or crop or supply and demand factors that are likely to have an influence on the future price of a commodity. Some of these factors are world prices, crop forecasts, governmental crop controls, farmer holding, politics, and the weather.

Chicago Board of Trade. "The Fundamental Approach." In *Commodity Trading Manual*, pp. 79–84. 1973.

Topics covered are supply, demand, econometric models, and the practical use of fundamental analysis. Five steps are given for the development of a model to forecast the price of a storable commodity. Fourteen questions are listed, the answers to which are important when making a supply-demand analysis of an individual commodity.

Cox, Houston A. "The Know-How's of Commodity Trading." In his *Concepts on Profits in Commodity Futures Trading*, pp. 45–54. 1972.

Emphasizes the commodity "balance sheet," or balance between supply and demand. Basis is discussed as a factor in fundamental analysis, after which Cox gives a short, general summary of this kind of commodity study.

Gold, Gerald. "Price Making Influences—How to Analyze Them Profitably." In his *Modern Commodity Futures Trading*, 6th ed., pp. 54–59. 1971.

Lists and briefly discusses the factors in addition to basic supply and demand considerations that have a major influence on the prices of commodity futures: government agricultural policy, international events, the weather, devaluation of money, business conditions in general, prices in general, and seasonal trends in prices. On pages 58 and 59 of his book, Gold outlines "A General Method of Price Analysis." An 11-point checklist is given to assist the commodity trader in making a methodical analysis of fundamentals.

Hieronymus, Thomas A. "Technical Versus Fundamental." In his *Economics of Futures Trading*, pp. 269–271. 1971.

". . . the position taken here is on the side of the fundamentalist." Nevertheless, Hieronymus regards conflict between technicians and fundamentalists as unfortunate. He states that chart followers are usually well aware of fundamentals when trading, and fundamentalists are generally conscious of price patterns.

Keltner, Chester W. "The Fundamental Analysis Approach." In his *How to Make Money in Commodities*, pp. 46–48. 1960.

In this general introduction to fundamental analysis of commodity price movements, Keltner asserts that the fundamental approach relies heavily upon the study of seasonal price tendencies. He believes that the fundamentalist can make good use of technical or chart methods to improve timing. The main attractions of the fundamental approach are said to be that a longer term view can be taken, with less attention paid to day-to-day fluctuations, and that the fundamentalist has a better understanding of *why* price changes take place.

Keltner, Chester W. "Fundamental Market Analysis." In his *How to Make Money in Commodities*, pp. 119–196. 1960.

The commodity speculator who buys or sells on the basis of fundamentals must know what statistics are used to arrive at supply and demand balances. He or she must also be knowledgeable about the seasonal price tendencies and the relative price levels of whatever commodities are contemplated for trading. Fundamentals are Keltner's specialty, and he covers the various market factors very well. Common situations, such as supply scarcity, supply surplus, and crop scares, are briefly considered in a general way that would apply to any commodity. Then Keltner tells how to apply fundamental analysis for practical commodity trading, emphasizing the great importance of keeping the analysis simple. "Too often traders . . . clutter their minds up with so much unessential information that they completely lose sight of the impotant background factors. . . ." To demonstrate, there are detailed discussions of fundamental factors as applied to wheat, corn, oats, rye, and soybeans. These basic factors are then summarized in a step-by-step, five-part guide to the application of fundamental market analysis. The strong points of the fundamental analysis approach are said to be that the trader can take a relatively long-term viewpoint without worrying about temporary price fluctuations and that there is a certain satisfaction in knowing *why* prices are likely to behave in a certain way. The chief weakness is that a trader who sticks to a fundamental position that proves to be wrong may have to absorb a large loss. Keltner recommends, therefore, that fundamental traders use technical or chart methods to place stop-loss orders when positions are taken. Stop-loss orders do not always work well, but they are important for psychological reasons.

Kroll, Stanley, and Shishko, Irwin. "Fundamental Analysis—An Econometric Approach." In their *Commodity Futures Market Guide*, pp. 167-198. 1973.

> Kroll and Shishko believe that the trend of commodity analysis on Wall Street is toward "objective econometric analysis," as opposed to more informal, subjective approaches. A clear presentation is made of basic econometric concepts, intended for readers who are not mathematicians or statisticians. The authors wisely state that "reliance on high-powered techniques is no guarantee of forecasting accuracy." Cocoa in 1967 is used to illustrate in detail and step by step just how a practical econometric analysis is put together. Good data and a thorough understanding of the commodity are emphasized. To show how more advanced analysis works, econometric model building is explained, using copper and wheat as examples. A concise, universal model is shown, with side-by-side mathematical statements and explanatory verbal statements. The authors provide a useful, realistic, and even readable introduction to a formidable topic.

Longstreet, Roy W. "Trading the Fundamentals." In his *Viewpoints of a Commodity Trader*, pp. 88-89. 1968.

> Advises that a thorough knowledge of commodity fundamentals is the key to big profits in futures trading. However, Longstreet does not believe in being a pure fundamentalist because of the danger of pitting one's personal opinion against the trend of the market and staying in a losing position. "The commodity market is no place for heroes." Specialization is advised; the trader who is interested in fundamentals should learn more and more about less and less.

Powers, Mark J. "Forecasting Prices" and "More About Forecasting Prices." In his *Getting Started in Commodity Futures Trading*, pp. 47-66. 1973.

> Supply-demand factors, data sources, seasonal movements, secular trends, ratios, index numbers, and correlation are discussed. As a final word, Powers warns against falling into "the common trap of arriving at erroneous conclusions drawn from purely statistical manipulations." Deductive reasoning is said to be very important.

Powers, Mark J. "What to Look for—And Where to Find It." In his *Getting Started in Commodity Futures Trading*, pp. 147-158. 1973.

> Individual tables list the following for each commodity or group of commodities: short-term (less than three months) supply factors, long-term supply factors, short-term demand factors, long-term demand factors, and sources of information (reports and publications). The commodities covered are the grains, potatoes, the metals, eggs, hogs, beef cattle,

pork bellies, soybeans, lumber, and feeder cattle. These tables provide very handy summaries of fundamental considerations.

Reinach, Anthony M. "Approaching the Action." In his *The Fastest Game in Town*, pp. 31–38. 1973.

Reinach says of a purely fundamental (product supply and demand) approach to commodity futures speculation: "To so trade profitably requires a knowledge and prevision that is virtually impossible to sustain." Technical or chart trading is greatly preferred by Reinach.

Shishko, Irwin. "Techniques of Forecasting Commodity Prices." In *Commodity Year Book 1965*, pp. 30–36. 1965.

Using 1964–1965 cocoa as an example, Shishko shows how to do informal fundamental analysis ("interpretive forecasting") as well as more systematic, econometric price forecasting. The "ABC's of Econometrics" are discussed, and various mathematical equations are examined.

Teweles, Richard J., and others. "The Fundamental Approach." In their *The Commodity Futures Game*, pp. 137–164. 1974.

A very good elementary introduction to economic analysis and price forecasting as applied to commodity markets. Such items as model building, demand curves, elasticity of demand, and disequilibrium (cobweb theorem) are clearly explained. While stating that careful fundamental analysis is a powerful tool for the commodity trader, the authors also admit that "there are several rocky detours along the way." Fundamental analysis can go wrong because of errors in basic data, errors in judgment when constructing the analytical framework, and poor timing of trades.

Williams, Larry R. "My Million Dollar Fundamental System." In his *How I Made One Million Dollars in the Commodity Market Last Year*, pp. 25–38. 1973.

"Traders who . . . attempt to disregard fundamentals will certainly find themselves in trouble." Nevertheless, Williams says, commodities should not be regarded as having intrinsic value levels—each product is worth only what someone is willing to pay for it (supply and demand). The Williams method of applying what he regards as fundamental analysis is based on observing the actions of commercial interests and large traders. He explains in detail just how to use his three "smart money tools" for determining the market sentiment of the professionals. The three tools are the government report *Commitments of Traders in Commodity Futures*, the price relationship of near and distant futures contracts (carrying charge market or premium market), and open interest data interpreted in a special way. Eight charts are used to illustrate the profitable use of open interest figures.

FUTURES (IN GENERAL). *See* Commodity Futures (In General)

FUTURES PRICE INDEX. *See* Dow-Jones Commodity Futures Index

FUTURES TRADING HISTORY. See History of Futures Trading

GAPS

On price charts, a gap is a blank space representing prices at which a commodity did not trade, as when a particular commodity contract opens at a price higher than the previous day's high and does not fall back for at least a day.

Gold, Gerald. "Gaps." In his *Modern Commodity Futures Trading*, 6th ed., pp. 211–215. 1971.

> Describes the common gap, the breakaway gap, the runaway gap, and the exhaustion gap. A chart is used to illustrate specific trading action that should be taken when these price gaps occur.

Kroll, Stanley, and Shishko, Irwin. "Market Gaps." In their *Commodity Futures Market Guide*, pp. 135–137. 1973.

> Gaps are often caused by heavy buying or selling by the public at a commodity market's opening. The common gap, the breakaway gap, the runaway gap, and the exhaustion or key reversal gap are all described. According to market technicians, a runaway gap often occurs halfway along a major price move. Heavy volume of trading is usually associated with key reversal gaps.

GLOSSARIES

Definitions of terms relating to commodity futures trading are provided in many of the books on the subject.

Angrist, Stanley W. "A Brief Glossary of Terms Used in Commodity Trading." In his *Sensible Speculating in Commodities*, pp. 198–206. 1972.

> These are concise definitions of about 130 terms that are important to commodity traders. The definitions range in length from one line to about a dozen lines.

Arthur, Henry B. "Glossary." In his *Commodity Futures as a Business Management Tool*, pp. 371–378. 1971.

> Arthur says that his definitions were drawn from a variety of sources and in some cases represent his own interpretations. About 60 terms are clearly defined. This glossary is especially good for terms relating to commercial hedging by means of commodity futures.

Belveal, L. Dee. "Glossary." In his *Charting Commodity Market Price Behavior*, pp. 235–266. 1969.

> Short, clear definitions of about 350 words and phrases relating to commodity futures are provided.

Belveal, L. Dee. "Glossary." In his *Commodity Speculation with Profits in Mind*, pp. 291–321. 1967.

> Over 300 terms relating to commodities and speculation are succinctly defined.

62 COMMODITY FUTURES TRADING

Chicago Board of Trade. "Glossary." In *Commodity Trading Manual*, pp. 273–280. 1973.

    About 130 commodity terms are briefly defined.

Clifton, Frederick T. "Defining Types of Spreads and Concepts." In *Commodity Year Book 1973*, pp. 41–42. 1973.

    A total of 40 terms relating to spreads and spread concepts are defined. About half of the terms are placed in a special colloquial category, examples include dead leg, butterfly, lift leg, and straddle-up.

Commodity Research Bureau. "Glossary of Commodity Terms." In *Commodity Year Book 1939*, pp. 85–86. 1939.

    The first edition (1939) of the *Commodity Year Book* gives clear definitions of 44 terms "which have definite meanings, but of which the public has little understanding." Virtually all of the definitions are still valid 35 years later.

Cox, Houston A. "Glossary of Terms." In his *Concepts on Profits in Commodity Futures Trading*, pp. 187–194. 1972.

    Approximately 150 commodity words and phrases are briefly defined. Cox states that this is a "practical, common sense glossary."

Gardner, Robert L. "Glossary." In his *How to Make Money in the Commodity Market*, pp. 181–185. 1961.

    Sixty commodity terms are briefly defined.

Gold, Gerald. "Glossary." In his *Modern Commodity Futures Trading*, 6th ed., pp. 246–253. 1971.

    ". . . a selected list of terms used in commodity futures trading and their usual meaning." Short definitions of 118 terms are presented.

Gould, Bruce G. "Glossary." In his *Dow Jones-Irwin Guide to Commodities Trading*, pp. 341–353. 1973.

    Clear definitions are given for 185 terms.

Granger, C. W. J., ed. "Glossary." In his *Getting Started in London Commodities*, pp. 104–108. 1975.

    Fifty commodity trading terms are defined from a British point of view.

Hammonds, T. M. "Glossary." In his *The Commodity Futures Market from an Agricultural Producer's Point of View*, pp. 78–85. 1972.

    About 80 commodity futures trading terms are defined in an easy-to-understand manner.

Jiler, Milton W. "Commodity Market Terms." In *Guide to Commodity Price Forecasting*, ed. by Harry Jiler and George B. Parker, pp. 18–21. 1965.

    Brief definitions of about 90 terms. About 20 of the terms are preceded by an asterisk to indicate definitions relating to the cash market rather than futures.

Kallard, Thomas. "Glossary of Terms." In his *Make Money in Commodity Spreads!*, pp. 179–190. 1974.

> About 250 commodity trading terms are briefly defined. Many terms relating to spread positions are included.

Keltner, Chester W. "Trade Terms and Their Meaning." In his *How to Make Money in Commodities*, pp. 219–227. 1960.

> About 120 commodity terms are defined. The definitions vary greatly in length. "Free supply scarcity" and "government support program," for example, are fully explained by means of examples.

Merrill Lynch, Pierce, Fenner & Smith, Inc. "Commodity Trading Terms." In *How to Buy and Sell Commodities*, pp. 40–54. 1972.

> Concise definitions of about 130 trading terms are given "to help the uninitiated to understand the jargon of the Exchanges."

Munn, Glenn G. *Encyclopedia of Banking and Finance*, 7th ed. 1973. 953 pp.

> There are a surprising number of terms relating to commodities and commodity futures trading in this standard reference book of banking. Most of the definitions are considerably longer than those appearing in the typical glossary found in a book on futures trading. Background information is given on individual commodities, as well as on the larger U.S. commodity exchanges.

Powers, Mark J. "Glossary of Commodity Futures Terms." In his *Getting Started in Commodity Futures Trading*, pp. 185–202. 1973.

> A glossary of about 180 commodity terms, compiled with the aid of the Research and Education Department of the Chicago Mercantile Exchange.

Shaw, John E. B. "Glossary of Terms." In his *A Professional Guide to Commodity Speculation*, pp. 163–164. 1972.

> Shaw states, "I have listed only those terms which you may encounter in the normal course of your trading activities." Forty terms are briefly defined.

Stillman, Richard J. "Commodity Trading Terms." In his *Guide to Personal Finance*, pp. 343–349. 1972.

> "Definitions in this section are adapted from Merrill Lynch, Pierce, Fenner & Smith, Inc., *How to Buy and Sell Commodities*. . . ." About 150 terms are included.

Watling, T. F., and Morley, J. "Glossary: Terms Used in Commodity Trading." In their *Successful Commodity Futures Trading*, pp. 205–214. 1974.

> These British definitions of about 60 commodity terms are, with very few exceptions, the same as American definitions.

Wyckoff, Peter. *The Language of Wall Street*. 1973. 247 pp.

> While stock market terms make up the bulk of Wyckoff's book, many commodity definitions are also included.

GOLD

A precious metal, widely used for monetary and commercial purposes. The purity of gold is measured in carats—24 carat gold is pure gold. Although there are important gold mines in Russia, Canada, and the United States, two thirds of the world's newly mined gold comes from South Africa. Gold ownership was made legal for U.S. citizens on January 1, 1975, and gold futures contracts of varying sizes are now available on the Chicago Board of Trade, the New York Mercantile Exchange, the Commodity Exchange, Inc. (New York), the International Monetary Market (Chicago), and the Mid-America Commodity Exchange (Chicago), not to mention the Winnipeg Commodity Exchange.

Carabini, Louis E. ed. *Everything You Need to Know Now About Gold and Silver.* 1974. 176 pp.

> A collection of question-and-answer interviews that were published originally in Carabini's *Gold and Silver Newsletter* (Carabini is also president of the Pacific Coast Coin Exchange). The interviews are mainly on the subject of how gold and silver prices will be affected by inflation, depression, devaluation, and other monetary matters. The persons who are interviewed include Franz Pick, Thomas J. Holt, Murray N. Rothbard, Harry Browne, and others with favorable attitudes toward investing in precious metals. A good bibliography is included.

Conway, Vincent J. "Understanding Gold and the World Gold Markets." In *Commodity Year Book 1974*, pp. 28-34. 1974.

> Sources of supply, gold mining in the United States, techniques of mining, scrap recovery, private hoards, central bank holdings, and industrial uses are among the gold topics discussed. Also covered are Winnipeg gold futures, the London gold market, the influence of hoarding gold, and the gold standard. Line charts show daily spot prices for gold at London in dollars per troy ounce from January 1971 to May 1974. A bar chart shows "Gold: Winnipeg (Weekly High, Low & Close of Nearest Futures)" from November 1972 to May 1974, with prices in dollars per ounce. This article provides an excellent review of the world gold situation in 1974, including basic supply and demand factors.

Green, Timothy. "Gold Futures Markets." In his *How to Buy Gold*, pp. 81-85. 1975.

> Size of trading unit, fineness of gold, trading hours, minimum price fluctuation, and daily price-move limit are given for the Commodity Exchange, Inc., New York Mercantile Exchange, Chicago Board of Trade, and International Monetary Market of the Chicago Mercantile Exchange. Green states that, "Action in a gold futures market is not quite like a casino, but it can be risky." In addition to gold futures, *How to Buy Gold* gives a great deal of information about investing in gold coins and gold bars. A directory, "The Gold Buyer's Address Book," is included to provide the exact addresses and telephone numbers of wholesale bullion and coin dealers, futures markets, banks and other retail outlets, brokerage firms,

and North American coin dealers. In addition to U.S. listings, addresses are given for wholesale gold dealers in Canada, Britain, and Switzerland.

International Monetary Market of the Chicago Mercantile Exchange, Inc. *Understanding Gold Futures Trading.* 1974. 32 pp.

A concise, practical discussion of gold futures trading, including monetary perspective, supply factors, demand factors, and hedging by producers and users. Emphasis, of course, is on futures trading in gold at Chicago's International Monetary Market. Tables show gold flows and gold fabrication by end use from 1968 to 1973. A line chart shows weekly London gold prices in dollars per ounce from January 1972 to October 1974 (high, low, close). Weekly London gold prices (London P. M. gold fix) are also shown in tabular form for all Mondays from June 1972 to September 1974.

Rosen, Lawrence R. "How to Buy and Sell Gold Futures." In his *When and How to Profit from Buying and Selling Gold,* pp. 227–252. 1975.

A general explanation of gold futures trading, with specific details for the Winnipeg Commodity Exchange, the International Monetary Market of the Chicago Mercantile Exchange, the Commodity Exchange, Inc. (New York), the New York Mercantile Exchange, the Chicago Board of Trade, and the Mid-America Commodity Exchange (Chicago). Rosen recommends gold futures only for speculative purposes. (The Rosen volume also covers the gold standard, gold mining stocks, exchange rates, the International Monetary Fund, and other gold-related topics.) A small chart shows weekly high-low-close prices for Winnipeg gold futures from November 1972 to the end of 1974.

Smyth, David, and Stuntz, Laurance F. "Gold—The Ultimate Security." In their *The Speculator's Handbook,* pp. 66–77. 1974.

A general discussion of the advantages of owning gold, including gold coins, gold mining stocks, gold futures, and gold bullion.

GOVERNMENT STATISTICS. *See* Statistics Sources

GRAINS. *See* Corn; Oats; Rye; Wheat

GROSS PROCESSING MARGIN. *See* Soybean Oil-Soybean Meal-Soybeans Spread

HEAD-AND-SHOULDERS FORMATION
A commodity price pattern that makes a formation on a chart similar in appearance to the outline of a head and shoulders. This best known of the many chart-price patterns is thought by chart analysts to be a reasonably reliable indicator of a price-trend reversal. A regular head-and-shoulders is supposed to signal a change from an uptrend to a downtrend, while an upside-down head-and-shoulders is supposed to signal a reversal from down to up.

Angrist, Stanley W. "Head-and-Shoulders Formations." In his *Sensible Speculating in Commodities*, pp. 111–114. 1972.

> Angrist believes that "probably a majority" of commodity bull markets end with a head-and-shoulders top. This formation in inverted form is seen less frequently at the end of bear markets (head-and-shoulders bottom).

Gold, Gerald. "The Head and Shoulders Formation." In his *Modern Commodity Futures Trading*, 6th ed., pp. 204–207. 1971.

> Both the head-and-shoulders top and the head-and-shoulders bottom are pictured and discussed. Price objectives and logical places for stop-loss orders are described for those who wish to trade according to the development of this chart formation.

Keltner, Chester W. "Head and Shoulder Formations." In his *How to Make Money in Commodities*, pp. 105–106. 1960.

> States that a good majority of major bull markets in commodities have ended with head-and-shoulders top formations. The head-and-shoulders formation in both its top and bottom configurations is briefly described and illustrated.

Kroll, Stanley, and Shishko, Irwin. "Top and Bottom Formations." In their *Commodity Futures Market Guide*, pp. 128–132. 1973.

> Although Kroll and Shishko do not believe in spending much time or energy in attempting to recognize individual chart formations ("pictures"), they do state that the head-and-shoulders formation displays "a surprising degree of uniformity" and reliability. The development of this pattern is thoroughly described.

HEDGING (*See also* Basis)

The use of futures contracts by commercial interests, such as farmers or food companies, to assure that the current price of a commodity will be received or paid in the future. By hedging, commercial interests transfer part of their price risk to speculators. Commodity futures markets exist primarily to make hedging possible.

Arthur, Henry B. *Commodity Futures as a Business Management Tool*. 1971. 392 pp.

> Commodity futures speculation as such is hardly touched upon in this volume by the first George M. Moffett Professor of Agriculture and Business at the Harvard Business School. The subject matter here is entirely commodity hedging by business firms. A theory of commercial hedging operations is presented in which hedging is said to consist of an analogous part and a residuals part. The analogous part consists of the price risk that is offset by commodity futures contracts; the residuals part

is made up of unhedged costs or premiums. These residual risks are "quality, time and service factors, from which the skilled hedger expects to gain a trading or merchandising profit." A major portion of Arthur's book is devoted to "Policies and Programs in the Use of Futures" by the following industries: wheat (flour milling), soybean, cattle (beef), cocoa, and frozen orange juice. This is useful and well-written information for speculators who wish to increase their knowledge of the commercial side of commodity futures activity.

Belveal, L. Dee. "How Hedgers Use the Market." In his *Commodity Speculation with Profits in Mind*, pp. 103–118. 1967.

A detailed but clearly written explanation of commodity hedging operations. Charts are used to illustrate premiums, normal markets, inverted markets, and "basis."

Berlin, Bruce S. *Corporate Use of Commodity Futures*. 1972. 33 pp.

After a general introduction to commodity futures markets, this pamphlet concerns itself with "the use of commodity futures contracts by business enterprises as a means of reducing risks...." Results of a survey are given in which 124 companies of considerable size responded to questions from the Conference Board. Forty-nine of the companies were actively engaged in futures trading at the time of the survey, and, as might be expected, most of these large corporations were interested in commodity futures markets as a means of hedging against the risks of price changes. "Policies of Companies That Trade in Commodity Futures" and "Performance Measurement" are briefly summarized.

Beveridge, E. A. "Hedging and Speculative Procedures in Carrying Charge and Discount Markets." In *Guide to Commodity Price Forecasting*, ed. by Harry Jiler and George B. Parker, pp. 82–87. 1965. (An earlier version of this article appears in the 1955 *Commodity Year Book*.)

A detailed discussion of various hedging techniques and considerations, providing background information for commodity futures speculators.

Beveridge, E. A. "How to Hedge Commodities." In *Commodity Year Book 1949*, pp. 14–36. 1949.

A practical, intelligently written review of hedging that should still be useful to hedgers, even though some of the details are, of course, out of date. Beveridge points out that commodity hedging in the usually accepted sense can take place only where a futures market exists. He states that hedging is far from being an automatic process; it requires specialized knowledge to avoid mistakes and considerable skill to achieve results that are above average. Sample topics are "How the Hedger Makes His Profit or Loss in the Basis," "Successful Hedging Is a Highly Skilful Business," and "What to Watch for in Hedging."

68 COMMODITY FUTURES TRADING

Business Week. "Hedging Against Disaster; Wild Price Swings Force More Companies to Cover Their Commodities Bets." *Business Week*, February 10, 1975, p. 62.

> Volatile price movements in commodities have caused more business firms than ever before to take a look at futures as a means of hedging; for example, "Plenty of feedlot operators saved their necks in 1974 by hedging in live cattle futures." The general principles of commodity hedging are briefly explained.

Chicago Board of Trade. "Hedging in Commodity Markets." In *Commodity Trading Manual*, pp. 65–77. 1973.

> Covers the basis, basis trading, carrying charges, selling hedges, and buying hedges. Examples are given of selling hedges in corn and cattle and buying hedges in plywood and cocoa. These are unusually clear and well-presented examples. In conclusion, it is stated that, while hedging does not eliminate all price fluctuation risk for producers and dealers, this method of operation does limit risk to the generally small and predictable changes in the basis.

Clifton, Frederick T. "How to Adjust Trading and Hedging Methods to the Volatile Markets of the Seventies." In *Commodity Year Book 1974*, pp. 48–50. 1974.

> Bakers, bottlers, edible oil manufacturers, and others have been too casual about hedging in the past, and thus in many cases did not take advantage of the futures markets to fix costs ahead during recent phenomenal price increases. Under such headings as "The Hedger Must Study Recent Factors in the Same Manner as the Speculator," Clifton tells how hedging must be done in modern, inflationary times.

Clifton, Frederick T. "New Hedging Concepts in Commodity Futures." In *Commodity Year Book 1970*, pp. 33–39. 1970.

> A clearly written, perceptive account of hedging. Under the subheading "The Pitfalls of Oversimplification," Clifton states that it is absurd to refer to hedging as "insurance," and that hedging should remain flexible—taking price probabilities into account may rule out hedging altogether. Much space in this article is devoted to a painstaking explanation of "the basis" (the difference between a cash or spot commodity price and a futures contract price for the same commodity). Nine concepts of the basis are summarized. Schematics of basis models show buy and sell hedges with a baseline visualized as cash and buy and sell hedges with a baseline visualized as futures. After listing various things that hedging will *not* do, Clifton cites the edible oil processing industry as an example of a very successful user of the futures markets for hedging. Hedgers are urged to keep simple business precepts in mind, and to realize that success may well require both talent and hard work.

Gardner, Robert L. "The Part Hedging Plays." In his *How to Make Money in the Commodity Market*, pp. 49–62. 1961.

". . . hedging affects the speculator only indirectly, but it is important to understand its impact." To demonstrate how hedging works, Gardner gives the example of "Mr. Johnson," a cotton planter who anticipates a harvest four months in the future. Mr. Johnson sells short in the futures market because he likes the prevailing price of cotton, and the price may drop by harvest time. Any loss caused by selling the cash crop at a low price will be offset by a profit from the short sale in the futures market.

Gold, Gerald. "Advanced Hedging Procedures." In his *Modern Commodity Futures Trading*, 6th ed., pp. 159–167. 1971.

Buying and selling by use of the basis, on-call trading, and ex-pit transactions are discussed. Quoting cash commodity prices only in their relationship to futures prices ("quoting the basis") makes automatic hedging easier.

Gold, Gerald. "Hedging in Practice." In his *Modern Commodity Futures Trading*, 6th ed., pp. 144–158. 1971.

Four examples are given of hedges as they might actually occur: (1) "A Selling Hedge in a Normal Market Followed by a Price Decline for the Spot Commodity," (2) "A Selling Hedge in a Normal Market Followed by a Price Increase for the Spot Commodity," (3) "A Buying Hedge in a Premium Market Followed by a Price Advance for the Actual Commodity," and (4) "A Buying Hedge in a Premium Market Followed by a Price Decline." Gold emphasizes that hedging must be done carefully or it can, at worst, lead to losses greater than if no hedge were used. The following relationships are clearly explained: (1) futures prices will generally be stronger than cash prices over the long term; (2) distant months will normally be less volatile than near months; (2) a buying hedge will be effective over a period of time in a discount market; and (4) a selling hedge in a discount market may be only partially effective or even ineffective. Gold concludes by saying that automatic hedging is not necessarily desirable for those dealing with cash commodities—unhedged or partially hedged positions may be called for, depending upon basis changes and other factors.

Gold, Gerald. "The Theory of Hedging." In his *Modern Commodity Futures Trading*, 6th ed., pp. 130–143. 1971.

Hedging is said to be the basic reason for the existence of futures markets. A specific example is given of the "selling hedge," in which commodity futures contracts are sold by the operator of a grain elevator to protect against a drop in the price of an actual commodity that has been bought and is being held in storage. An example is also given of the "buying hedge," in which commodity futures contracts are bought by a commodity exporter to protect against a rise in the price of an actual commodity that has been sold for future delivery at a fixed price (the exporter does not have the commodity in storage). Gold mentions that hedging in actual practice does not give complete protection against adverse price movements, for these reasons: (1) the cash price of a particular commodity and its price for various futures delivery months do not necessarily go up or down at the same time by exactly the same amount; (2) the prices of different grades of a cash commodity change at different rates; (3) fixed-size futures contracts may not exactly match the physical amount of the actual commodity involved in a hedge; and (4) a processed commodity such as flour may be involved in a hedge against adverse price changes in a primary commodity such as wheat, even though special marketing factors may make flour prices move independently of wheat.

Goss, B. A. "The Concept of Hedging." In his *Theory of Futures Trading*, pp. 29–36. 1972.

The "old" concept of hedging, in which hedging neatly eliminates price risk for the producer, is contrasted with the "modern" concept, in which the producer-hedger assumes the risk of loss from an unfavorable change in the basis.

Gould, Bruce G. "The Hedger." In his *Dow Jones-Irwin Guide to Commodities Trading*, pp. 35–39. 1973.

General review of hedging, provided as background information for the commodity speculator. Points out that producers and others who generally hedge will gladly remain unhedged if a windfall profit appears imminent.

Hammonds, T. M. "Trading Techniques for Producers." In his *The Commodity Futures Market from an Agricultural Producer's Point of View*, pp. 49–58. 1972.

While Hammonds' entire book may be considered an elementary introduction to hedging for the producer (farmer), this chapter deals specifically with a preharvest hedge for a grain producer, a storage hedge, and an inventory requirement hedge. Seven detailed reasons are given for hedges not turning out in real life the way they do in textbooks. The reasons have to do with such items as contract expiration dates, commodity grades, volume multiples, price patterns, and deviations in the basis from the normal pattern.

Hieronymus, Thomas A. "Hedging." In his *Economics of Futures Trading*, pp. 147–150. 1971.

An iconoclastic view of hedging. Hieronymus states that hedgers should not see hedging as insurance, but rather as "an intricate activity, requiring substantial knowledge and operational skill." Hedging is not so much an academic shifting of risk as it is the business of trying to make a profit out of variation in the basis (the difference between cash price and future price). Of course, hedging does enable the dealer in the actual (cash) commodity to avoid catastrophic losses from large, unforseen price changes. Hieronymus points this out, but adds that business people hedge with profits in mind, not risk avoidance. Hedgers are speculators of a special kind.

Hieronymus, Thomas A. "Warehousemen and Merchants." In his *Economics of Futures Trading*, pp. 173-198. 1971.

A detailed, sophisticated, and clearly written account of commercial grain hedging. Includes "Hedging in Detail," plus discussions of specific hedging operations by rural storage elevator operators, interior grain merchants, feed ingredient merchants, cash grain commission merchants (a discussion of practices prior to World War II), independent terminal storage elevator operators ("a dying breed"), and exporters. Hieronymus mentions that the favorable image of hedging as opposed to speculation "leads to all sorts of things being called hedging."

Keltner, Chester W. "Hedging in Futures." In his *How to Make Money in Commodities*, pp. 23-24. 1960.

Two examples are used to explain hedging. In the first, a wheat storage firm sells wheat futures at a price that will protect storage and merchandising profits. In the second example, a flour mill sells flour for delivery at a future date and, at the same time, buys futures contracts for a sufficient amount of wheat to make the flour. This enables the mill to establish its profit margin on the manufacture of flour without worrying about a rise in the price of wheat. Keltner points out that hedging transfers the risk of price fluctuation from business firms to speculators.

Kroll, Stanley, and Shishko, Irwin. "Case Histories of Trade Hedging." In their *Commodity Futures Market Guide*, pp. 297-305. 1973.

In these case histories, commodity futures markets are used for hedging purposes in the chocolate industry ("The ABC Chocolate Company"), the copper industry ("The Amalgamated Copper Corporation"), the potato chip business ("The Crispy Potato Chip Company"), the textile industry ("General Cotton Corporation" and "Muffy Puffy Mills"), and corn producing ("General Farm Corporation"). Both selling and buying hedges are used in these cases.

Kroll, Stanley, and Shishko, Irwin. "Hedging for Insurance and Profit." In their *Commodity Futures Market Guide*, pp. 278-296. 1973.

The selling hedge (short futures and long actuals) and the buying hedge (long futures and short actuals) are said to be the two fundamental kinds of hedging operations. After a discussion of "The Need for Hedging," detailed examples are given of these two types of transactions. Then price differences that occur between cash markets and futures markets (the basis) are explained at some length. The authors point out that, while hedging does not eliminate the risk of loss from unfavorable changes in the basis, commercial interests usually find basis risks much more acceptable than speculative price risks. Various pitfalls of hedging, such as the temptation to speculate, are covered in a few "words of caution." Charts of spot and futures prices for frozen pork bellies and cattle are used as illustrations. In a hedging recapitulation, seven general observations and seven specific observations are given (the seven specific observations amount to practical suggestions for actual hedging). The writing of Kroll and Shishko is clear; they make hedging as easy to understand as possible.

Powers, Mark J. "Hedging . . ." In his *Getting Started in Commodity Futures Trading*, pp. 107–114. 1973.

The following kinds of hedges are described in a popular, readable manner: carrying charge, operational, anticipatory (forward pricing), selective, and risk avoidance ("insurance").

Seim, Dick. "It Cost Me $70,000 to Learn About Futures—A Look at the Other Side of Commodity Trading, by a Farmer Who Came as Close as You Can to Going Broke and Still Survive." *Farm Journal*, vol. 98, February, 1974, pp. H-6, H-8, H-9, H-16.

The sad story of Reno Stoebner, a South Dakota hog farmer who decided to "lock in" his market price by hedging (he sold futures) and wound up becoming a heavily losing speculator. Stoebner advises farmers to think the matter over carefully before deciding to hedge. Four rules are suggested for those producers who do decide to hedge: (1) limit hedge positions to amounts covered by actual crops; (2) remember that a hedge locks in a market price, not a specific profit (costs will continue to fluctuate); (3) no hedge is perfect. Expect to pay a few hundred dollars as a price protection premium; (4) do not leave decisions to commodity brokers. Stoebner succumbed to the temptation to lift his hedge and begin outright speculation against the market trend.

Shaw, John E. B. "How to Take Advantage of Hedging." In his *A Professional Guide to Commodity Speculation*, pp. 30–32. 1972.

States that "Hedging is the only reason for having a commodity futures market." As the amateur speculator should at least have an idea of how hedging is used by producers to reduce risk, Shaw provides an easy-to-read summary, complete with examples.

Snider, Thomas E. "Using the Futures Market to Hedge; Some Basic Concepts." *Federal Reserve Bank of Richmond Monthly Review*, vol. 59, August 1973, pp. 2–7.

"This article is designed to acquaint businessmen who might use futures markets in their production, warehousing, and processing activities, and the lenders who finance them, with the basic principles underlying the operation of the futures market." An elementary, well-written review is presented of hedging, hedging arithmetic, the storage hedge, establishing a price in advance, forward contracting, and bank financing of hedged inventories. Successful hedging is said to require detailed study and broad knowledge.

Teweles, Richard J., and others. "Nature of Cash and Futures Price Relations." In their *The Commodity Futures Game*, pp. 32–44. 1974.

> Various kinds of hedging operations are described: "hedging carried out to eliminate the risks associated with price fluctuations," "hedging carried out to profit from movements in the basis," and "hedging carried out to maximize expected returns for a given risk (variability of return) or minimize risk for a given expected return." Teweles and co-authors describe the philosophy or theory behind all of these hedges. They state that they dwell on hedging in their book so that the speculator will realize that futures trading itself depends on hedging. Also, most literature on hedging is oversimplified or even wrong. However, the speculator should realize that even a good understanding of hedging is not likely in itself to improve his trading record.

HISTORY OF FUTURES TRADING (See also War and Commodity Prices)

The concept of using contracts to set prices for goods to be delivered in the future is an ancient one.

Angrist, Stanley W. "How Futures Markets Evolved." In his *Sensible Speculating in Commodities*, pp. 17–20. 1972.

> Points out that "As early as 1840 grains began to trade on a deferred basis in Chicago" simply because farmers arrived in Chicago and sold grain while it was still in transit (sales were on a "to arrive" basis). To prevent defaulting, cash deposits to a disinterested third party were made by both buyer and seller. These cash deposits to assure performance are still made today, but modern futures traders refer to them as "margin." (As Angrist states, commodity futures margin is really a deposit as a performance bond. Unlike margin on stocks and bonds, there is no loan and no interest involved.) As commodity trading increased in volume, informal arrangements had to be formalized, and the Chicago Board of Trade was organized in 1848, followed by the New York Produce Exchange in 1862, the New York Cotton Exchange in 1870, and the New York Coffee Exchange in 1885.

Belveal, L. Dee. "Evolution of Trade." In his *Commodity Speculation with Profits in Mind*, pp. 11–22. 1967.

> Begins with the Stone Age and proceeds through Roman times, the Renaissance (trade fairs), the evolution of credit and cash-forward contracts up to the development of the Chicago grain market and modern futures trading. Professional speculation is said to be a somewhat recent innovation, having probably originated only a few hundred years ago in Japan.

Chicago Board of Trade. "The Making of a Market." In *Commodity Trading Manual*, pp. 1–5, 1973.

> Modern commodity markets are said to have evolved from the medieval fairs of the thirteenth century. Interestingly enough, there was an early

form of rice futures trading in Japan, beginning around 1730 on the Osaka Rice Exchange. U.S. futures trading (contracts for forward delivery) in grains developed slowly in Chicago, starting shortly after the incorporation of the town of Chicago in 1833. The Chicago Board of Trade was formed in 1848, with futures trading becoming standardized in the late nineteenth century.

Cowing, Cedric B. "Agrarians and Commodity Speculators." In his *Populists, Plungers, and Progressives: A Social History of Stock and Commodity Speculation, 1890-1936*, pp. 3-24. 1965.

States that speculation during the Civil War years "led to the formal organization of futures trading in provisions and commodities." Although the Chicago Board of Trade was the main attraction, commodity exchanges were also developed in St. Louis, New York, New Orleans, Minneapolis, Kansas City, and several other cities during the first ten years after the end of the Civil War. The futures contract itself was an outgrowth of earlier "to sail," "to arrive," and "forward delivery" forms of agreement. Cowing gives the history of agrarian (Populist) attempts to outlaw futures trading in the latter part of the nineteenth century. The Hatch Bill is discussed in some detail.

Cox, Houston A. "Theory of Commodity Futures as the Historical Ultimate in Marketing." In his *Concepts on Profits in Commodity Futures Trading*, pp. 67-70. 1972.

Cox takes his brief history of the development of commodity futures markets all the way back to the exchange of gifts between primitives. However, he states that, except for some early experiments in Japan (1697-1730) and England (1826), true futures trading did not emerge until 1865 (Chicago Board of Trade).

Gardner, Robert L. "The Development of Commodity Trading." In his *How to Make Money in the Commodity Market*, pp. 5-11, 1961.

Brief, informal history of the commodity futures market. Chaotic conditions in nineteenth-century commodity trading and the great cocoa bean crash of 1921 are mentioned.

Gold, Gerald. "Origin and Development of Commodity Exchanges." In his *Modern Commodity Futures Trading*, 6th ed., pp. 6-11. 1971.

States that the first commodity futures exchange was the Chicago Board of Trade, founded in 1848, with trading beginning in 1859. In a footnote, Gold points out that the Japanese Grain Dealers Association claims that futures trading began in Japan a century earlier than the Chicago Board of Trade.

Hieronymus, Thomas A. "Historical Development." In his *Economics of Futures Trading*, pp. 69-92. 1971.

In addition to the history of futures trading in general, specific histories are given for corn and wheat, cotton, eggs, soybeans, and soybean products.

Speculative activity at the Chicago Board of Trade in the nineteenth century is discussed at some length. In those days, there were frequent efforts to "corner the market" in one commodity or another (in the corner were short sellers, who could not buy their way out except at exorbitant prices demanded by speculators who created the corner initially by heavy purchases). "Clearly, the interest and emphasis was on speculative trade," Hieronymus states in regard to the Board of Trade in the late nineteenth and early twentieth centuries. He devotes a few pages to "bucket shops," which existed from about 1876 to 1915 without creating actual contracts for delivery. According to Hieronymus, bucket shop customers did not appear to know the difference between bucket shops and legitimate commission houses.

Kroll, Stanley, and Shishko, Irwin. "The History of Futures Markets." In their *Commodity Futures Market Guide*, pp. 3–8. 1973.

Emphasizes the development of trading in "to-arrive" and futures contracts in the United States from about 1820 to 1870, although active commodity markets are mentioned as having existed in Asia around 1200 B.C. An interesting summary is given of the chaotic grain marketing conditions that were characteristic of Chicago in the early 1850s. These conditions led to the development of the Chicago Board of Trade and the modern commodity futures contract. The standardized contract was needed to encourage trading by speculators (speculators were needed to assume the price risks that producers wished to avoid).

Labys, Walter C., and Granger, C. W. J. "Commodity Market Development." In their *Speculation, Hedging and Commodity Price Forecasts*, pp. 2–7. 1970.

Discusses "Europe: Early Development" (tenth to fourteenth centuries), "England: The Forward Contract" (1570 to 1881), and "United States: The Futures Contract" (1848 to date).

Powers, Mark J. "Historical Development of Commodity Futures Trading." In his *Getting Started in Commodity Futures Trading*, pp. 159–169. 1973.

The development of commodity markets through cash markets to forward markets to futures markets is discussed. Japan is said to have had a form of futures trading in 1697, about 150 years before forward contracts became common in the United States. Powers describes the early activation of rice futures trading in Osaka, Japan. The evolution of the Midwest grain markets in the United States is considered, leading to the organization of the Chicago Board of Trade in 1848. A short history of the Chicago Mercantile Exchange is given. "Commodity Futures Trading and the Law" (pp. 167–169) tells about commodity market legislation in the United States from 1884 to recent times, including the banning of onion futures trading in 1958.

76 COMMODITY FUTURES TRADING

Teweles, Richard J., and others. "The Evolution of Futures Trading," "Development of the Futures Contract," and "Attacks Against Futures Trading." In their *The Commodity Futures Game*, pp. 5-14. 1974.

> States that two great trading centers had begun to flourish in Europe by the twelfth century, one in northern Italy and the other in the Flanders region. Year-round meeting places known as exchanges were established in London in the sixteenth century (the Royal Exchange, for example, later became the London Commodity Exchange). Forward trading was engaged in to a certain extent at these exchanges, but true futures contracts had not yet been developed. "The first recorded case of organized futures trading occurred in Japan during the 1600s." This trading in "rice tickets" or rice futures is described in some detail. In the United States, the Chicago Board of Trade was established in 1848, although futures trading did not begin until 1851. Considerable opposition to futures trading developed in the 1890s.

HOG-CORN RATIO

The price per hundredweight (100 pounds) of live hogs divided by the price per bushel of corn. When corn prices rise sufficiently relative to the price of hogs, lowering the hog-corn ratio to a figure below the breakeven point for hog sales, farmers can make more money by selling their corn than they can by feeding it to hogs. This causes a drop in hog production.

Angrist, Stanley W. "Hog-Corn Ratio." In his *Sensible Speculating in Commodities*, pp. 78-79. 1972.

> States that one may think of the hog-corn ratio as the number of bushels of number three yellow corn that would be required to buy 100 pounds of live hog. Charts show the annual average of the hog-corn ratio from 1958 to 1970 and the percent change in sows farrowing for the same years. Angrist points out that 90 percent of all corn produced in the United States is used as livestock feed and discusses briefly the significance of the hog-corn ratio in the fundamental analysis of futures prices.

HOGS (LIVE)

The source of about 40 percent of the meat supply in the United States. As hogs are great consumers of corn, hog raising tends to be concentrated in the major corn-producing states, such as Iowa and Illinois. Live hog commodity futures are traded on the Chicago Mercantile Exchange.

Chicago Board of Trade. "Pork Commodities." In *Commodity Trading Manual*, pp. 173-176. 1973.

> Among the items discussed are feeding costs, production scheduling, supply considerations, and demand factors. Live hog futures trading details are given for the Chicago Mercantile Exchange, including delivery months, trading units, minimum fluctuations, daily price limits, position limits, delivery standards, and trading hours.

Elberty, Mary. "Analyzing Hogs and Pork Bellies Price Trends." In *Commodity Year Book 1975*, pp. 13–23. 1975.

> The four-year cycle in hog prices (two years up and two years down) is clearly explained, and is said to be one of the more reliable economic cycles. To illustrate, a theoretical four-year cycle is printed at the bottom of a line chart of cash hog prices in the United States from 1912 to 1975. Other charts show "Hypothetical Relationships Between Measures of the Hog Cycle" (price, pig crop, and slaughter). The cobweb theory is also used to explain the hog price cycle. The importance of corn in hog production is discussed, particularly with reference to the complicating factors of inflation and increasing export demand for corn. Both medium-term and short-term forecasting of hog supplies are briefly considered, along with seasonal patterns and demand factors. A chart and a table show meat consumption per person for beef, pork, and lamb from 1950 to 1974. The demand for pork bellies is said to be relatively inelastic (people must have bacon for breakfast), resulting in price volatility. Finally, a list of important government reports relating to hogs is provided, and futures prices are shown in chart form on a daily basis for both July hogs and July pork bellies from 1969–1970 to 1974–1975.

Lessiter, Frank. "Forecasting Hog Futures Prices." In *Commodity Year Book 1972*, pp. 6–12. 1972.

> An understanding of the hog production cycle is said to be essential for anyone attempting to forecast live hog prices. The hog-corn ratio is also important, although the ratio is more useful as an indicator of production direction than amount of production change. Seasonal factors in the hog business are decreasing in importance because producers are turning toward complete confinement of the hogs. Lessiter explains hog supply and demand factors, and tells how to use U.S. Department of Agriculture statistical reports. Charts show daily hog futures prices at Chicago from 1966 to 1971. In addition, daily volume and open interest are shown in chart form from 1968 to 1971.

Shaw, John E. B. "Profiting from Cyclical Markets." In his *A Professional Guide to Commodity Speculation*, pp. 63–66. 1972.

> A specific method of taking advantage of the two-year price cycle in hog futures is discussed in some detail. A line chart shows hog slaughter in millions, 1951 through 1968, while a bar chart shows the yearly average price for hogs for the same period.

Teweles, Richard J., and others. "Live Hogs." In their *The Commodity Futures Game*, pp. 437–442. 1974.

> Supply and demand factors are discussed, including the hog-corn price ratio.

ICED BROILERS

Ready-to-cook, broiler-fryer chickens packed in ice. In 28,000 pound lots, they are represented by futures contracts traded on the Chicago Board of Trade.

Bailey, Fred. "Understanding the Iced Broiler Futures Market." In *Commodity Year Book 1969*, pp. 35–42. 1969.

> Famous poultry fanciers of the past are mentioned, such as Napoleon, Sir Francis Bacon, Henry IV of France, and Herbert Hoover ("a chicken in every pot..."). To show the remarkable growth of the broiler industry, it is pointed out that annual production was only about 30 million birds in Hoover's day, 310 million in 1947, and an astounding 2.5 billion in 1969. Average consumption of broiler meat per person in the United States grew from about 5 pounds at the end of World War II to almost 33 pounds in 1969. Bailey discusses production, marketing, supply-demand factors, and price determination. A chart shows "Relationship Between Per Capita Consumption and Broiler Prices, 1953–1968." Various U.S. Department of Agriculture publications are listed as sources of statistical information on poultry, hatcheries, and feed. The futures market is vital to the broiler industry, simply because this is a very large industry with small profit margins—"even nominal price variations can spell economic catastrophe" to an unhedged producer. By using the futures market to hedge, processed poultry producers can establish prices in advance of marketing or even in advance of production. Bailey explains the mechanics of the iced broiler futures market at Chicago.

Chicago Board of Trade. "Iced Broilers." In *Commodity Trading Manual*, pp. 188–191. 1973.

> Broiler supply and demand considerations are discussed. Iced broiler futures trading details are listed for the Chicago Board of Trade, including delivery months, trading units, minimum price fluctuations, daily price move limits, position limits, delivery standards, and trading hours.

Liuzza, Vincent J. *Trading in Iced Broiler Futures*. 1972. 24 pp.

> Iced broiler market fundamentals are reviewed, including price volatility, processing, production factors, price negotiations, and major determinants of supply and demand. Hedging is well covered. A three-page bibliography is included.

INCOME TAX CONSIDERATIONS. See Tax Considerations

INDEX OF COMMODITY FUTURES PRICES. See Dow-Jones Commodity Futures Index

INFLATION HEDGES. See Commodity Futures as Inflation Hedges

INFORMATION SOURCES. See Advisory Services; Bibliographies; Statistics Sources

INSTITUTIONAL INVESTING

The investment activities of those who manage endowment funds, pension funds, and other large accumulations of capital. Trading in the commodity futures markets is an unusual activity for institutional investors.

Young, Clarke D. "Commodity Futures for Institutional Investors? Commodities Offer the Money Manager Many Ways to Adjust His Risk-to-Reward Ratios in Light of His Portfolio Objectives and Overall Market Appraisal." *Bankers Monthly*, vol. 91, October 15, 1974, pp. 36–38.

> The advantages of commodity futures trading for institutional investors are said to include rational pricing, ease of specialization (a few commodities as opposed to hundreds of stocks), margin flexibility (risk can be varied from very high to quite low), liquidity, and ease of selling short.

INTERMARKET WHEAT SPREAD (*See also* Wheat Spread)

Typically, the buying of July Kansas City wheat while simultaneously selling short July Chicago wheat. Kansas City futures contracts are for hard red winter wheat, while Chicago wheat is soft red winter. However, Kansas City wheat may be delivered against Chicago contracts, and will be if the price of Chicago wheat rises too much relative to Kansas City. The Kansas City-Chicago spread is generally one with limited risk, in that Kansas City wheat can sell at as high a premium "as it wants to" over Chicago wheat, while hedgers will usually prevent Chicago prices from rising more than 13¢ or so over Kansas City. Naturally, if one believes that Chicago wheat will gain on Kansas City during a particular time period, Chicago may be bought while Kansas City is sold. Wheat spreads are also possible between Chicago and Minneapolis or Kansas City and Minneapolis.

Angrist, Stanley W. "Intermarket Spreads." In his *Sensible Speculating in Commodities*, pp. 169–170. 1972.

> Concise description of why the Kansas City versus Chicago wheat spread usually works, including the transportation factors (Gulf Coast ports for Kansas City and Great Lakes ports for Chicago). A chart shows that the intermarket wheat spread worked quite well from 1955 to 1969, but not so well in 1970 and 1971.

Clifton, Frederick T. "Wheat Spreads Between Chicago, Kansas City and Minneapolis." In *Guide to Commodity Price Forecasting*, ed. by Harry Jiler and George B. Parker, pp. 250–262. 1965. (An earlier version of this article appears in the 1962 *Commodity Year Book*.)

> Clifton begins his discussion with a consideration of money management and the extremely high leverage factor (margins as low as 2 or 3 percent) involved in commodity spreading operations. Even a very small adverse price move can seriously impair a minimum margin capital position. The fundamentals of the various U.S. wheat markets are presented, including "The Basic Elements Accounting for Market Differences." Then charting or "technical" methods of analysis are explained as they relate to intermarket spreads. Separate, detailed discussions are given for the Kansas

City-Chicago spread, the Minneapolis-Chicago spread, and the Minneapolis-Kansas City spread. Charts show all three spreads on a daily basis from 1955 to 1963.

Lowell, Fred R. "Intermarket Spreads—Chicago vs. Kansas City." In his *The Wheat Market*, pp. 257–293. 1968.

> Makes the observation that if a trader believes he knows which way the price of wheat is going to move, he may as well take a simple buy or sell position. The profit potential in a straight trade is normally greater than in a spread, and, for the average speculator, the straight position has no greater risk than a spread would have. Lowell devotes pages 269–279 of his book to a reproduction of charts showing the spread of daily prices of Chicago May wheat over Kansas City May wheat from the 1956–1957 season to 1966–1967. Then pages 283–293 show the spread of Chicago July wheat over Kansas City July from 1956–1957 to 1966–1967.

INVERTED MARKET (*See also* Basis; Spreads)

A situation in which the distant months of a commodity are selling at lower prices than the near month. Normally, because of carrying (storage) charges, the highest prices are quoted for distant months.

Gardner, Robert L. "Normal Markets and Inverted Markets." In his *How to Make Money in the Commodity Market*, pp. 23–28. 1961.

> Discusses the normal market situation and then explains why and how inverted markets develop.

JOURNALS. See Periodicals

KANSAS CITY-CHICAGO WHEAT SPREAD. See Intermarket Wheat Spread

LEVERAGE (*See also* Margin; Pyramiding)

Generally, the magnification of both risk and possibility for profit that results from having a little bit of money represent a lot of money. In the case of commodity futures trading, margin deposits often represent only from 5 to 10 percent of the actual value of the commodity specified in a futures contract. Therefore, disregarding such practical matters as commissions and margin calls, a mere 5 percent rise in the price of a commodity would double a 5 percent margin deposit, while a 5 percent drop in price would reduce margin capital to zero. A commodity speculator can reduce leverage, of course, merely by making a larger margin deposit. One hundred percent margin, for example, would equal zero leverage and would make futures trading very dull.

Belveal, L. Dee. "Leverage Theory in Speculation." In his *Commodity Speculation with Profits in Mind*, pp. 47–54. 1967.

> General discussion of how low margin requirements (generally 5 to 7 percent, for commodity trading result in futures speculators having much

greater leverage at their disposal than stock speculators. The margin requirement for stocks is typically about ten times greater than for commodities. Price risk and daily price fluctuation limits are viewed.

LINE CHARTS See Charts

LITERATURE. See Advisory Services; Bibliographies

LIVE BEEF. See Cattle

LIVE HOGS. See Hogs (Live)

LONDON COMMODITY MARKETS (See also Commodity Exchanges; Commodity Options)

There are important British futures markets in cocoa, coffee, copper, silver, wool, and other commodities. In addition, current activity in commodity options (puts and calls) is centered in London.

Granger, C. W. J., ed. *Getting Started in London Commodities*, 1975. 117 pp.

> Nine chapters by various British authors provide a general survey of the London futures markets. The English view of risk, hedging, money management, and trading technique is presented. Individual commodities discussed include cocoa, sugar, coffee, soybean meal, wool, tea, rubber, gold, and silver. In addition to a glossary of about 50 commodity trading terms, the following information is provided for each of 17 London commodity futures associations or exchanges: lot size, deposit per lot, method of quotation, minimum and maximum fluctuations, months traded, commissions, and trading hours.

Parker, George B. "Understanding the London Futures Markets." In *Commodity Year Book 1971*, pp. 36–47. 1971.

> Contract quantity, length (time) of contract, what quotations mean, minimum price fluctuation, daily price limit, market hours, commission, arbitrage equivalents, price conversion data, call option availability, notice days, last trading day for spot commodity, and standard deliverable grade are given where applicable for the following London commodity futures: cocoa, coffee, copper, lead, rubber, silver, soybean oil, sugar, sunflower seed oil, tin, wool, and zinc. Some data are given also for barley, coconut oil, maize (corn), and shellac, but futures in these four commodities have limited trading. Call option mechanics for London futures are discussed in some detail.

Watling, T. F., and Morley, J. "Commodity Markets in Britain." In their *Successful Commodity Futures Trading*, pp. 19–27. 1974.

> The statement is made that "The London Commodity Exchange is possibly the most powerful international commodity exchange in the world, being

larger than its New York and European rivals." In addition to the London Commodity Exchange (sugar, cocoa, coffee, rubber, vegetable oils), the following commodity exchanges in London are described: the London Metal Exchange (copper, lead, tin, zinc, silver), the Baltic Mercantile Exchange (including the London Grain Futures Market, with trading in barley and wheat), and the London Silver Market. The London Produce Clearing House is also described.

LONDON COMMODITY OPTIONS. See Commodity Options

LOSSES (See also Amateur Speculation; Money Management; Psychology; Stop-Loss Orders; Trading Rules)
That which commodity speculators seek either to avoid or to accept with aplomb. Learning to "cut losses short" would appear to be a major goal of most traders.

Dunbar, Ernest A. "Commodity Trading? I've Had a Pork Bellyful! Some People Make Fortunes Trading in Commodities. Want to Try It? First Read This Wry Confession by a Doctor Who Gave It a Whirl." *Medical Economics*, vol. 50, February 19, 1973, pp. 143, 147–148.

> The touching tale of a physician who went into commodity futures trading with $10,000 and came out with 60¢! He traded in copper, frozen orange juice, pork bellies, sugar, cotton, hogs, eggs, soybean oil, and live cattle, with his greatest losses being in bellies, orange juice, and eggs. The good doctor started out rather well, and ran his $10,000 up to $13,264 in about three months. Then came a string of small losses followed by some larger ones, and by continuing to trade on the buy side in a falling market, the doctor was eventually done in. The total time that passed from $10,000 to 60¢ was about six months.

Kroll, Stanley. "The Most Important Chapter in the Book." In his *The Professional Commodity Trader*, pp. 25–33. 1974.

> In which Kroll tells about how everyone talks about cutting losses short, but hardly anyone does, and therefore many speculators get taken to the cleaners when speculating in commodity futures. Specific instructions are given for closing out a position.

Longstreet, Roy W. "Your First Loss." In his *Viewpoints of a Commodity Trader*, pp. 15–16. 1968.

> An admonition to *expect* losses in commodity speculation and to *accept* them when they occur.

Seim, Dick. "It Cost Me $70,000 to Learn About Futures—A Look at the Other Side of Commodity Trading, by a Farmer Who Came as Close as You Can to Going Broke and Still Survive." *Farm Journal*, vol. 98, February, 1974, pp. H-6, H-8, H-9, H-16.

> Seim tells the sad story of a hog farmer who changed from a hedger to a speculator. The farmer sold futures short in increasing amounts as the

market price rose, and was forced to take on a heavy debt load (mortgages) to cover his losses. Suggestions for proper hedging are given.

LUMBER AND PLYWOOD
Wood products used extensively by the construction industry. The principal lumber-producing countries are Russia and the United States; the leading lumber-producing states are Oregon and California. Stud lumber (two by fours) futures contracts are traded on the Chicago Board of Trade, as are futures in exterior grade plywood. The Chicago Mercantile Exchange also has a contract in construction grade lumber.

Chicago Board of Trade. "Forest Product Commodities." In *Commodity Trading Manual*, pp. 211–215. 1973.

> Forest product development, production, and consumption are briefly considered. Stud lumber and plywood futures trading details are listed for the Chicago Board of Trade (lumber, plywood), the Chicago Mercantile Exchange (lumber), and the New York Mercantile Exchange (plywood). The following are given for each exchange: delivery months, trading units, minimum price fluctuations, daily price move limits, position limits, delivery standards, and trading hours.

Gray, Roger W. *Trading in Plywood Futures.* 1972. 26 pp.

> The fundamentals of the plywood market are reviewed, including the development of futures trading, price relationships, and hedging.

Olmedo, James P. "How to Trade and Hedge in the Lumber and Plywood Futures Markets." In *Commodity Year Book 1975*, pp. 24–34. 1975.

> A brief history of the lumber and plywood futures market is given (trading began in late 1969). After discussing the long-term and short-term fundamentals of lumber and plywood price movements, Olmedo thoroughly explains the ramifications of hedging with futures. Charts show November plywood futures and March lumber futures relative to cash prices from 1970 to 1975 (cash prices are represented by a zero baseline). Other charts show actual futures prices on a daily basis for July lumber and July plywood from 1969–1970 to 1974–1975. While the emphasis of this article is on commercial hedging, there is also a consideration of trading strategy, including market appraisal, technical analysis, and seasonal analysis.

Olmedo, James P. "Understanding the Lumber and Plywood Futures Markets." In *Commodity Year Book 1973*, pp. 6–15. 1973.

> Plywood and lumber futures contracts in use in 1973 are described, and their trading history since 1969 is summarized. Supply-demand factors are explained, with emphasis on production costs and housing demand. Fundamental analysis of the forest industry market is said to require both long-term and short-term approaches, in that long-term trends are subject to the short-term aberrations of seasonal influences, changes in govern-

ment policy, strikes, consumer attitudes, and so forth. A table presents "Average Monthly Seasonal Indices of Major Supply, Consumption, and Economic Factors Related to Lumber and Plywood Markets," January–December, based on averages for the periods 1961–1971 and 1964–1971. Olmedo tells how to analyze trends in forest product futures prices, based on supply-demand fundamentals. Cash-futures relationships are described. Two pages of charts show daily futures prices for March lumber and March plywood at Chicago from 1970 to 1973. Monthly totals of volume and open interest are charted for the same period. A short bibliography is included, giving 14 sources of forest products data on an annual basis and four sources of weekly data.

Sayers, W. B. "The Long-Term Outlook for Lumber and Plywood." In *Commodity Year Book 1970*, pp. 6–14. 1970.

Major attention is given to softwood products, as softwood is specified in lumber and plywood futures contracts. Domestic and international supply and demand factors are considered in some detail. The conclusion is reached that "The decade of the 70's will probably witness an unprecedented demand for lumber and plywood." Twelve publications and nine associations are listed under "References."

Teweles, Richard J., and others. "Plywood and Lumber." In their *The Commodity Futures Game*, pp. 401–422. 1974.

Factors influencing prices, information sources, production, distribution, and utilization are discussed separately for lumber and plywood (softwood in both cases). The authors state that it is doubtful "that a price seasonal would occur that could be profitably utilized by the futures trader." Both plywood and lumber are said to be affected by the stock market more than other commodities generally are. The outlook for housing also has an important effect on the price of forest products.

LUNAR TRADING. See Moon Cycles

MAGAZINES. See Periodicals

MAINE POTATOES. See Potatoes

MARGIN (*See also* Leverage; Money Management; Pyramiding)
A deposit made by a buyer or seller of a commodity futures contract to assure good faith and fulfillment of the contract. A futures trading deposit, unlike stock market margin, is not considered to be a partial payment against the value of the contract, so no balance due has to be borrowed by the trader from his or her broker and no interest has to be paid. Initial margin is the amount per contract that must be deposited when a trade is opened. Maintenance margin is the amount of customer's equity per contract that must be maintained until the

trade is closed out. Most brokers also have overall minimums regarding the amount of capital that must be deposited to open a commodity account in the first place.

Angrist, Stanley W. "Margin Requirements." In his *Sensible Speculation in Commodities,* pp. 45–48. 1972.

>States that nearly all brokers require a deposit of at least $1,000 to open an account to trade in commodity futures. Angrist says, "In my opinion you would be wise not to consider trading until you can put down a deposit of at least $3,000." This permits some diversification and reduction of risk. It is pointed out that commodity futures rarely require more than 10 percent of the value of the contract as initial margin. Margins vary from broker to broker, but may not be less than the minimums set by the various commodity exchanges. Brokers commonly ask for more margin if the amount on deposit has absorbed a loss of 25 percent (for example, if $1,000 initial margin drops to $750 because of a loss of $250, most commodity houses will issue a margin call for an additional deposit of $250). To provide at least a small cushion, Angrist strongly recommends that speculators with $3,000 on deposit use no more than $2,200 as initial margin. He also is of the opinion that "trader with borrowed money as capital will be trader with sweaty palms."

Belveal, L. Dee. "Commodity Margin." In his *Commodity Speculation with Profits in Mind,* pp. 42–46. 1967.

>Tells how the practice of requiring margin deposits evolved and states that margin amounts typically represent something like 5 to 7 percent of the value of commodity contracts. Belveal points out that, while futures trading margin requirements are relatively thin, the institution of the clearing house has so far eliminated default. No one has suffered financial loss because of the default of another party when dealing in Chicago Board of Trade commodities.

Cox, Houston A. "The Sensitive Subject of Margin." In his *Concepts on Profits in Commodity Futures Trading,* pp. 76–77. 1972.

>States that commodity futures margins are typically 5 to 10 percent of contract value. "The tremendous leverage occasioned by traditional commodity futures margins is at the same time an outstanding opportunity and a danger to the uninitiated." High margins would cause the vital hedging function to become uneconomic. Cox states that if a trader's margin deposit drops considerably in value (generally 25 percent) because of an unfortunate price move, the trader will receive a call from his broker for additional funds to replace the loss. If prices are moving widely and rapidly, the customer may have less than 24 hours to meet his margin call. Minimum margin requirements are typically set higher for public speculators than for commercial hedgers.

Gould, Bruce G. "Margin." In his *Dow Jones-Irwin Guide to Commodities Trading*, pp. 57–64. 1973.

> The difference is explained between margin as money borrowed to buy stocks and margin as a surety deposit for commodity futures trading. Initial margin, maintenance margin, margin for spreads, and brokerage house rules are discussed. Some brokers require a margin deposit of $10,000 to open a commodity trading account, but most firms will accept an amount in the neighborhood of $1,000. A table shows initial, maintenance, and spread margin amounts that were recently required by a leading commodity broker for all products traded on active exchanges.

Hieronymus, Thomas A. "Margin Requirements." In his *Economics of Futures Trading*, pp. 62–65. 1971.

> States that initial margins for commodity futures tend to be established at a level of from 5 to 10 percent of the value of the contract, with maintenance margins at from 60 to 85 percent of initial margins. The urgency of brokers' requests to customers for additional margin varies greatly, according to size of account, volatility of the market, and past record of customer. Hieronymus makes some witty comments on the situation.

Hieronymus, Thomas A. "Margin Requirements." In his *Economics of Futures Trading*, pp. 318–322. 1971.

> An argument for retaining the present system of low margin requirements and no government regulation of margin. High margin requirements would greatly reduce the economic usefulness of commodity futures markets—the markets would be much less attractive to farmers and processors as a means of hedging.

Keltner, Chester W. "Margin Requirements." In his *How to Make Money in Commodities*, pp. 27–30. 1960.

> A discussion of initial margin deposits and margin calls. According to Keltner, most brokers will call for additional margin if a trader's losses bring his margin deposit down to an amount that equals from 70 to 75 percent of the initial minimum requirement. For example, if a speculator loses $150 on a trade for which the minimum margin deposit is $500, his broker will probably issue a margin call for $150. This assumes, of course, that the speculator initially deposited only the minimum of $500.

Kroll, Stanley, and Shishko, Irwin. "Commodity Margins." In their *Commodity Futures Market Guide*, pp. 217–222. 1973.

> A general review of commodity futures margins or deposits, with actual minimum initial requirements quoted for both net and straddle positions for 11 different commodities as of December 1, 1971. Naturally, requirements change rapidly as price levels and volatility change, but requirements are said to be typically 8 to 15 percent of market value for net positions and perhaps 4 percent for spread positions. Margin calls and how to avoid them is one of the topics discussed.

Shaw, John E. B. "Why Commodity Margins Are Needed." In his *A Professional Guide to Commodity Speculation*, pp. 33-36. 1972.

> The minimum margin requirements for trading commodity futures are said to be "much too low" in most cases. That is, the speculator should always begin trading with a margin deposit of at least 25 percent to allow room for price fluctuation. The technique of pyramiding (using paper profits to margin additional contracts) is not recommended, because pyramiding magnifies the importance of small price changes to the point that most traders become unnerved.

Teweles, Richard J., and others. "Commodity Futures Versus Securities and Other Speculations." In their *The Commodity Futures Game*, pp. 17-18. 1974.

> Makes the wise observation that low margin requirements make commodity prices seem much more volatile than they really are, and that the individual speculator can easily reduce the apparent volatility (and the very real risk) merely by voluntarily putting up more margin than the minimum. For example, 20 percent margin can be deposited with the broker in cases where only 10 percent is required. On the other hand, using all available capital to trade commodities at minimum margin can be hazardous to one's financial health. The authors observe that margins for speculating in commodity futures typically run between 5 and 10 percent, or even less for "low risk" spread positions.

MARKET SCARES. See News Events

MAXIMS. See Trading Rules

MECHANICAL TRADING SYSTEMS (See *also* Computer Analysis; Moving Average; Random Walk; Trend Following)

Speculative procedures in which decisions to buy or sell are made automatically according to price moves or trends, and not according to the speculator's analysis or intuition. Judgment does come into play, of course, in the initial selection of the plan. Even the best mechanical trading systems do not work well all of the time.

Keltner, Chester W. "Mechanical Trading Systems." In his *How to Make Money in Commodities*, pp. 49-99. 1960.

> The automatic trading system that never fails is a will-o'-the-wisp pursued by many commodity speculators. Keltner points out that the idea of a perfect mechanical trading rule is so intriguing that literally hundreds of automatic systems have been devised over the years. Unfortunately, the great majority of them are worthless, either because they fit price patterns that may easily be nonrecurring or because they are so vaguely worded as to make practical application impossible. At the same time, Keltner says, there are a few mechanical plans that have real value. Any plan should be judged by how well it has performed over a period of at last ten years and by

the extent to which it is based on sound, trend-following principles. Nearly all plans can be expected to make money in markets with lengthy, well-defined price trends and to lose in erratic or narrowly fluctuating markets. The bulk of this chapter is devoted to a consideration of the minor trend rule (see Trend Following), "Trading Rule No. 19" (see Trend Following), and the ten-day moving average rule (see Moving Average).

Keltner, Chester W. "The Principal Weakness of Mechanical Rules." In his *How to Make Money in Commodities*, pp. 90–94. 1960.

The big weakness of mechanical or automatic trading systems is their inability to cope with markets that are erratic and that do not show a definite trend. Markets of this kind, and they are common enough, will produce many small losses for the commodity speculator using a typical mechanical trend-following system. For example, Keltner's minor trend rule, when followed faithfully in Chicago December wheat from April 30 to July 21, 1952, produced 13 consecutive losses. The wheat market during this period did show a slight downward trend, but the day-to-day fluctuations were just enough to "whipsaw" the minor trend trader back and forth, in and out of losing transactions. The psychological stumbling block to automatic plans is the difficulty in following them after they have done badly. The trader is sorely tempted to abandon his plan after a long losing streak, but formula plans have a perverse way of performing brilliantly immediately after being dropped!

Kroll, Stanley, and Shishko, Irwin. "A Simple Automatic Trading System." In their *Commodity Futures Market Guide*, pp. 159–161. 1973.

Using spot mercury prices on a weekly basis, as published in *Metals Week*, Kroll and Shishko demonstrate how a simple mechanical trading system is set up. In this case, mercury was bought and previously established short positions closed out if the price went up $10 per flask. Mercury was sold short and previously established long positions liquidated if the price dropped $10. Results were "astonishingly good" during the period 1965–1967. Unfortunately, and as always seems to be the case with such plans, the system produced losses during other time periods.

Shaw, John E. B. "How to Use Mechanical Methods of Trading." In his *A Professional Guide to Commodity Speculation*, pp. 107–118. 1972.

States that there is nothing new about using mechanical or automatic trading systems in commodity speculation, as some of the mechanical methods go back to the time of World War I. Shaw says, "I have used mechanical methods for a long time and I have yet to find one that is invariably successful year after year." He also says, however, that the best mechanical methods should work well three years out of four. Needless to say, the speculator will not be happy at all if the bad year coincides with the beginning year. In any event, Shaw presents his favorite mechanical method, which is a fairly complicated system based on a ten-day moving average of pork belly prices. The plan has worked well in recent years (1967–1971), but is not, of course, guaranteed for the future. Shaw gives the seven rules necessary to use his method, and includes nine pages of tabulation for the year 1967.

Teweles, Richard J., and others. "Trade Selection and Evaluation." In their *The Commodity Futures Game*, pp. 234–238. 1974.

Few advertised trading systems are said to be worthy of serious study and "some can produce dangerous errors in thinking." Any trading system must be validated by the speculator himself before actual use, regardless of whether the plan is homemade or comes from an outside source. The following qualities are said to be essential for any worthwhile trade-selection method: (1) The system must be logical and make sense. (2) The system must not be tested solely after the fact. Tests must be done in "real time" that extends over a sufficient period and covers varying market conditions. (3) Entry and exit prices must be realistic. For example, too many systems assume that the opening price on the "day of action" will be the same as the previous day's closing. (4) The system must not be too erratic; 50 small losses followed by one sensational gain would hardly be practical. (5) Realistic stop-loss points must be provided.

MID-AMERICA COMMODITY EXCHANGE. See Commodity Exchanges

MINNEAPOLIS-CHICAGO WHEAT SPREAD. See Intermarket Wheat Spread

MONEY MANAGEMENT (*See also* Overtrading; Trading Rules)
The control or apportionment of available, speculative capital. Because of the high risk involved, money used in commodity futures trading must be carefully administered.

Bache & Co., Inc. *Money Management Concepts for Commodity Traders.* No date. 10 pp.

Successful commodity speculation is said to require self-discipline, planning, correct diagnosis of market conditions, and a knowledge of how to make the best use of available capital. Six rules are discussed: (1) set aside a specific amount of capital for futures trading; (2) never enter a trade before choosing both a stop-loss point and an initial profit objective; (3) be sure that your net potential profit/potential loss ratio is at least 2 to 1; (4) risk no more than 10 percent of your trading capital on any single position and no more than 30 percent on all positions combined; (5) do not take a position unless your profit objective is at least eight to ten times your commission; and (6) remember that margin requirements are irrelevant to profit and loss objectives. According to how he employs his capital, each speculator sets his own level of conservatism or recklessness.

Clifton, Frederick T. "General Trading Plan" and "Risk of Capital." In *Commodity Year Book 1972*, pp. 39–40. 1972.

    As a proper minimum, Clifton recommends that a speculator in spread positions have from $8,000 to $10,000 available. $5,000 would be used for eight or so different spread situations, thus achieving adequate diversification, while $3,000 to $5,000 would be held in reserve. If capital is increased by 50 to 100 percent through profits, this newly won cash should be removed from the commodity speculation fund and placed elsewhere.

Cox, Houston A. "Budgeting Your Money" and "Money Management Expanded." In his *Concepts on Profits in Commodity Futures Trading*, pp. 15–34. 1972.

    To be practical, Cox says, the beginning commodity trader should have a minimum of $5,000 as speculative money. Furthermore, this speculative money should represent no more than 10 percent of the inexperienced trader's net quick assets. In other words, beginning commodity speculators should be worth at least $50,000 in liquid assets, only 10 percent of which should be used for trading. (Experienced traders, Cox states, could reasonably use 25 percent of quick assets for speculation.) As a further safeguard, 20 percent of the speculative money should be maintained as a reserve. This means that, in the case of a $5,000 account, $4,000 should actually be put to use as margin for trading. Cox gives two principal rules and five subsidiary rules to help the commodity trader achieve "monetary consistency." The basic idea behind monetary consistency is that the speculator should think in terms of money units when diversifying, not in terms of numbers of contracts. The rules prevent overtrading in commodities with low margin requirements. Conservative pyramiding and the logical placement of stop-loss orders are also among the topics covered by the rules. For larger accounts, Cox shows how trading units should be developed. For example, a $25,000 account should be thought of in terms of four $5,000 trading units and one $5,000 reserve unit (as each of the $5,000 trading units would have its own $1,000 reserve, the total reserve fund would be $9,000).

Gould, Bruce G. "Position Management." In his *Dow Jones-Irwin Guide to Commodities Trading*, pp. 281–282. 1973.

    "Margin equity is not money." That is, margin should not be looked upon as money invested, but rather as so many game tokens that enable the player (speculator) to take part in the game. Margin should be viewed dispassionately. As the speculator's primary objective is to stay in the game, a position should never be taken that has the obvious potential to knock the player out of the game. Even the best players of the commodity futures game do not expect to be right more than 40 percent of the time, so it is essential to stay in the game and catch profitable trends as they occur.

Hieronymus, Thomas A. "Capital Management." In his *Economics of Futures Trading*, pp. 261-263. 1971.

(1) Commodity trading may be an avocation. In this case, risk capital should be no larger than that which is necessary to provide some diversification and allow the player of the game to absorb a few losses without having to quit "early." (2) Commodity trading may be part of a diversified investment program. This would be a limited risk operation designed to produce a steady rate of return higher than that available from other investment media. (3) Commodity trading may be used in an attempt to turn a small amount of money into an important amount of money. However, if the amount risked is *too* small, the trader may not take commodities seriously enough to have much chance of success.

Kroll, Stanley, and Shishko, Irwin. "Budget Concepts." In their *Commodity Futures Market Guide*, pp. 224-227. 1973.

Sensible management of money for futures speculation is nicely explained in seven rules or elements: (1) capital for futures speculation is high-risk capital; (2) capital should be divided into speculative units; (3) possible gain relative to possible loss should be calculated; (4) loss limits and profit targets should be established for all trades; (5) trade only in markets that seem to promise some "action"; (6) taking short-term profits is sometimes prudent; (7) impulses to buy scale-down or sell short scale-up must be carefully controlled to avoid financial disaster. Kroll and Shishko elaborate on each of these seven rules.

Lynch-Garbett, P. "Capital Management." In *Getting Started in London Commodities*, ed. C. W. J. Granger, pp. 68-77. 1975.

Capital that is designated for futures trading should be limited to an amount that can be lost "without endangering your peace of mind." Stop-loss orders should be used, and profit objectives should be set. The potential of profit over loss for each trade should be at least 2 to 1. Lynch-Garbett believes that no more than 30 percent of available trading capital should be in use at any one time, and that 10 percent should be the limit for each position. Profit objectives should be at least eight to ten times commission costs.

Teweles, Richard J., and others. "The Management of Risk." In *Commodity Year Book 1975*, pp. 50-55. 1975.

This discussion by Teweles and co-authors of the relationship between risk and reward is more or less a condensation of material appearing originally in their book *The Commodity Futures Game* (1974). After giving the mathematical formula for determining the average payoff for a series of trades (assuming that the probability of outcomes is known), the authors outline the four steps that must be taken to develop and validate a trading system: (1) plan a system that would appear to be profitable based on what has happened in the past, (2) test the system unchanged through a large number of trades in various kinds of markets in past time, (3) test the system unchanged through a large number of simulated trades in real time, but only if past time results were favorable, and (4) take the ultimate step of testing the system with real dollars, if this seems warranted. The authors present a rather full discussion of the "Probability of Ruin," including mathematical formulas for traders to use in determining their chances of going broke. "When all is said and done, a trader must work out his own probabilities given his personal opinions, attitudes, and beliefs." Multiple positions, stop-loss orders, strategies following great success or failure, trading fallacies, and size of commitments are all considered in this article by Teweles, Harlow, and Stone.

Teweles, Richard J., and others. "Money Management." In their *The Commodity Futures Game*, pp. 251-273. 1974.

It is very difficult for a commodity trader to use logic and discipline in handling his trading capital. Under the heading "Expectation of the Game Played," Teweles and co-authors discuss the probability of winning, how to figure the "payoff," fair bets, good bets, bad bets, strategy for a favorable game, and real-time validation. This is mathematical probability theory applied to commodity futures trading, and three tables are presented showing percentage probabilities for unsuccessful trades assuming, respectively, a 0.55 probability of winning (10 percent advantage), a 0.60 probability of winning (20 percent advantage) and a 0.65 probability of winning (30 percent advantage). Under "Probability of Ruin," mathematical formulas are given for determining the probability of losing all of one's trading capital. A table shows "Trader's Chance of Ruin When He Has a .10, .20, or .30 Advantage Attempting Either to Double His Initial Capital or Trade Indefinitely." In general, trading on a small scale is recommended, simply because the chance of being ruined goes down rapidly as the number of available trading units increases (assuming that the trader is engaged in a favorable game). Periods of bad luck ("severe adversity") are said to be inevitable, even in a favorable game, so these periods must be planned for.

Teweles, Richard J., and others. "Risk, Reward, and You." In their *The Commodity Futures Game*, pp. 109-136. 1974.

The four elements of money management are discussed: (1) attitude toward money, (2) risk capital, (3) expectations, (4) probability of ruin. A somewhat involved mathematical method is presented, enabling the commodity trader to use computation of utilities (measures of preference) as a means of constructing a personal "trading curve." After being plotted on graph paper, the trading curve's shape will reveal the risk attitudes of the speculator. Curves with various meanings are illustrated.

Williams, Larry R. "My Key Ingredient to Market Success." In his *How I Made One Million Dollars in the Commodity Market Last Year*, pp. 9–16. 1973.

> Williams states that it is possible to forecast the commodity market brilliantly, but still go bankrupt because of poor money management. He describes his system in detail, based on strictly limiting the amount of speculative capital in use (20 to 30 percent) at any one time, limiting losses to 5 percent of capital, not trying to follow too many positions at one time, and completely eliminating pyramiding or plunging (overtrading). Williams emphasizes the importance of setting up a plan and sticking with it.

MOON CYCLES

Short-term changes in commodity prices that coincide with changes back and forth from new moon to full moon, or long-term price changes that coincide with orbital movements of the moon over a period of years.

Williams, Larry R. "The Great Silver Secret." In his *How I Made One Million Dollars in the Commodity Market Last Year*, pp. 92–99. 1973.

> While most people make fun of the moon theory of trading, Williams claims that there is actually something to it, in the sense that new moons are often bearish (negative influence) and full moons often bullish (positive influence). Several price charts are used as illustrations of how new moons tend to occur at price peaks and full moons at price valleys.

MOVING AVERAGE (*See also* Mechanical Trading Systems; Oscillator Method; Trend Following)

An arithmetic mean that changes or moves according to a specified period of time. Ten-day moving averages, for example, are often used to measure commodity futures price trends. In this case, assuming that an ordinary moving average is being used, the figure calculated each day would be the average or mean of closing prices for the most recent ten-day period. Commodity traders and advisers have come up with ingenious ways to construct and use moving averages.

Angrist, Stanley W. "Technical Trading III: Moving Averages." In his *Sensible Speculating in Commodities*, pp. 135–154. 1972.

> The standard moving average, the linearly weighted moving average, and the exponentially weighted moving average are considered in relation to commodity futures price forecasting. Also discussed are the two-moving-averages method, the seven-week-moving-average method of D. D. Dunn and E. F. Hargitt, and the price-difference method. Two detailed tables summarize the work of Seymour Smidt, with moving averages varying in length from one to ten days, using decision rules based on movements of the averages of from 0.5¢ on any one day to 4¢ on any one day. The results of using each of 20 different "action signals" are shown annually from

1951–1952 to 1960–1961. Total profits or losses after commissions from trading soybeans with these signals over a ten-year period varied from a loss of 476¢ per bushel (1¢ movement of a one-day average) to a gain of 197¢ (1¢ movement of a ten-day average). However, one year (1953–1954) accounted for half of the 197¢ profit. Angrist's conclusion is that, while moving average methods will most assuredly not result in a profit for every trade, if these methods are used consistently they will enable the careful trader "to catch his share of the big moves."

Cox, Houston A. "Modern Computed Trends as Adjunct to Standard Technical Analysis." In his *Concepts on Profits in Commodity Futures Trading*, pp. 149–161. 1972.

Cox states that an ordinary, "unsophisticated" moving average superimposed on a standard line chart is helpful in forecasting commodity prices, "but usually produces certain inaccuracies which throw doubt on its consistent forecasting value." He therefore describes a rather complicated "computed market trend" utilizing a weighted composite of 10-, 20-, and 40-day moving averages of daily closing prices. Action points are determined by a combination of price difference, rate of price change (velocity), and volatility. Various charts are used to explain the method.

Fink, Robert, and Turner, Dennis. "Moving Averages." In *Commodity Year Book 1973*, pp. 25–26. 1973.

Moving average trading methods are based on the belief that prices will continue for some time in a trend, once the trend is established. Academicians call this "serial correlation in the price movement." Moving average trading methods are not much good in stable markets; wide price moves of some duration are necessary to produce worthwhile profits. Computers can be used to advantage to test moving average schemes against historical price data and also to help determine if fundamental supply-demand factors are favorable.

Gold, Gerald. "The Moving Average Method." In his *Modern Commodity Futures Trading*, 6th ed., pp. 179–184. 1971.

The moving average is considered as a price forecaster by itself and also in combination with bar charts of commodity futures prices. The technique of using two moving averages of different time periods (five-day and ten-day, for example) is discussed. Gold states that commodity futures speculation based on moving averages can work well when there are definite price trends, but prices that fluctuate within a narrow range will likely produce a string of small losses.

Keltner, Chester W. "The Ten-Day Moving Average Rule." In his *How to Make Money in Commodities*, pp. 58–61, 65–67, 81–84. 1960.

Keltner feels that ten days is just about the right length of time for a moving average used in commodity futures trading. To determine buy and sell points, he recommends that a moving average of daily price *ranges* be compiled, in addition to the usual moving average of the prices themselves. A buy signal is given when the price of a commodity rises above its moving average by an amount equal to the price range moving average. A sell signal results when the price falls below its moving average by an amount equal to the price range moving average. Keltner does not discuss the results that were obtained from the ten-day moving average rule, although he does give results from other trend-following rules.

Kroll, Stanley, and Shishko, Irwin. "Computer Use in Designing a Moving Average System." In their *Commodity Futures Market Guide*, pp. 161–163. 1973.

A brief discussion is given of the use of computers to generate moving averages for mechanical trading systems. "It is possible to construct systems of impressive complexity." However, Kroll and Shishko recommend simplicity (such systems are, after all, based merely on trend following).

Kroll, Stanley, and Shishko, Irwin. "Moving Averages." In their *Commodity Futures Market Guide*, pp. 154–157. 1973.

Moving average decision rules that work very well during one time period may fail miserably during another. The advisory firm of Dunn and Hargitt, Inc. has arrived at the conclusion that the price movements of some commodities are simply too random to permit the profitable use of moving averages. However, a 40-day weighted moving average chart line works well with most grains, cattle, and sugar. Pork bellies and silver apparently do best with a 20-day line, while a 60-day line is preferred for soybean oil and copper. Another firm, Commodity Research Bureau, Inc., is represented by a reprint of a page from their weekly "Computer Trend Analyzer."

Maxwell, Joseph R. *Commodity Futures Trading with Moving Averages.* 1975. 76 pp.

A unique, in-depth study of moving averages as applied to commodity futures speculation. In the first part of his book, Maxwell shows what happens when moving averages of various kinds and lengths are plotted against four typical theoretical price chart movements. The theoretical chart patterns are the trend reversal, the retracement, the breakout, and the sideways movement. In some 30 pages of charts and tables, each of these four basic price patterns is shown with conventional, average-modified, and weighted moving averages. Three-day, five-day, and ten-day averages are illustrated. In the last half of the book, results are given from applying some 600 different moving average trading systems to an actual commodity futures contract: the May 1972 pork belly contract from January 3, 1972 to March 13, 1972. Even though this 50-day time period is not very long, the data presented by Maxwell will be of great interest to commodity futures traders using or contemplating the use of moving average systems. While some of the trading methods tested by Maxwell were quite profitable from January to March 1972, he warns that a different time period could produce entirely different results.

96 COMMODITY FUTURES TRADING

Shaw, John E. B. "How to Use Other Mechanical Methods." In his *A Professional Guide to Commodity Speculation*, pp. 125–136. 1972.

> Shaw's general attitude is that the average speculator may as well take his or her chances with a mechanical or technical system of trading rather than dabble in the fundamentals of one commodity or another. This would not hold true, of course, for someone with access to specialized information. Shaw discusses various moving average methods, and presents a system for trading sugar based on totals for three successive ten-day moving averages. Nine pages are devoted to a "Triple Average Sugar Method Tabulation," covering the calendar year 1968.

Teweles, Richard J., and others. "Moving Averages." In their *The Commodity Futures Game*, pp. 176–179. 1974.

> While there are many moving average systems for trading stocks or commodities, they are all based on variations of only two factors: (1) *Time*. Short-term moving averages get the trader in at the beginning of a price move but greatly increase the possibility of whipsaws. Long-term moving averages reduce the number of whipsaws but often result in missing an important part of a price move. (2) *Penetration*. Small or large penetration requirements (trading indicators) have the same advantages or disadvantages as small or large time factors. A table shows "Computation of a 10-day moving average for a typical May soybeans contract" and a chart shows "Weekly May and November soybeans, weekly closing price versus 10-week moving average. . . ." The period covered by the chart is late 1951 through 1956.

Williams, Larry R. "How Technical Data Can Identify the Fundamentals." In his *How I Made One Million Dollars in the Commodity Market Last Year*, pp. 77–81. 1973.

> A ten-week moving average of Friday closing prices is described. The function of this moving average is merely to point out the basic price trend; the timing of actual trades must be based on other considerations.

NATURE'S LAW. *See* Elliott Wave Principle

NEW YORK MERCANTILE EXCHANGE. *See* Commodity Exchanges

NEWS EVENTS

Happenings or developments that affect commodity prices.

Williams, Larry R. "How to Evaluate All Fundamental News." In his *How I Made One Million Dollars in the Commodity Market Last Year*, p. 38. 1973.

> Did the market react as expected to a particular news event, or did it react differently than expected? That is the key point in the Williams method of evaluating the constant flow of news stories about commodities.

NORM TRADING. See Fundamental Analysis

OATS (See also Oats—Seasonal Price Trend; Oats-Corn Spread)
An important cereal grain used chiefly as food for livestock, especially horses. Oats are generally planted in the spring and harvested in the summer. The main oats-growing countries are the United States, Canada, and Russia, while the leading oats-growing states are Minnesota and Iowa. Oats futures are traded on the Chicago Board of Trade and the Winnipeg Commodity Exchange.

Chicago Board of Trade. "Oats." In *Commodity Trading Manual*, pp. 150–153. 1973.

> Concise information is given regarding the early history of oats, production factors, and usage. Oats futures trading details are given for the Chicago Board of Trade and the Mid-America Commodity Exchange (formerly the Chicago Open Board of Trade). Delivery months, trading units, price fluctuation specifications, daily price limits, position limits, delivery standards, and trading hours are summarized for each exchange.

Inkeles, David M. "Understanding the Oats Futures Market." In *Commodity Year Book 1972*, pp. 29–35. 1972.

> "A gentleman never trades oats." Inkeles states that this old adage refers to the stodgy reputation of the oats market as a place to speculate. Wheat, for example, is supposed to be more sporting. Be that as it may, Inkeles presents a detailed discussion of oats fundamentals. Oats is a desirable, healthy food for laying hens, milk cows, horses, and other valuable animals, even though corn is a better energy source. Also, about 6 percent of oats production is used as human food, mainly in the form of breakfast cereal. Supply-demand factors and the long-range outlook are considered by Inkeles, with the prediction that the use of oats as animal feed will become more specialized in the future. Charts show daily futures prices for May oats at Chicago 1961 to 1972. A short bibliography (nine items) is included.

Keltner, Chester W. "Fundamental Analysis Applied to Oats Situations." In his *How to Make Money in Commodities*, pp. 161–167. 1960.

> Points out that oats prices are greatly influenced by the supply of corn, as corn is the primary feed grain and oats is also used chiefly as feed. Supply and demand considerations for oats and seasonal price tendencies are discussed. Tables show oats supplies, disappearance, free surplus, impoundings, farm loan rate, and seasonal price advances for each crop year from 1945–1946 to 1959–1960.

Teweles, Richard J., and others. "Oats." In their *The Commodity Futures Game*, pp. 390–400. 1974.

> These subjects are commented upon: factors that influence prices, sources of information, production, utilization, and seasonal tendencies. A graph shows seasonal trends of open interest and volume for oats in the form of a

98 COMMODITY FUTURES TRADING

ten-year average plotted for each month of the year. The authors point out that the oats market is not as big as it seems because of the simple fact that it takes 43 percent less oats than corn by weight to fill a bushel container and the feed value of the two grains is considered to be about the same per pound. This, plus dominance of the oats market by a few large commercial traders, makes the market more volatile at times than might be expected.

OATS—SEASONAL PRICE TREND

Marketing of the new oats crop normally begins in July. Low prices for the season typically occur in August, with highs the following May.

Commodity Research Bureau. "Seasonal Influences on Commodity Futures Prices." In *Commodity Year Book 1951*, pp. 14–16. 1951.

> Oats prices are said to have a definite tendency to rise each season after the first of November. A table shows "May Oats Futures Prices—1935-36 to 1949-50; Price Advances from November 1 Low to November-May High." Among data given for each season are net advance in cents per bushel, percent advance, and date of highest price. Daily basis price charts show the May oats futures delivery at Chicago from 1936 to 1951. Price advances after the first of November ranged from about 1¢ to 35¢.

Commodity Research Bureau. "Seasonal Trends in Grain Futures Prices." In *Commodity Year Book 1952*, pp. 15–17. 1952.

> A price advance in May oats occurred after the month of August in every season from 1936–1937 to 1950–1951. The advance ranged from about 3¢ to 30¢ or from about 6 to 49 percent. A table shows "May Oats Futures Prices: 1936-37 to 1950-51; Price Advance from August 31 Low to September-May High (Cents per Bushel)." A chart shows "Monthly Seasonal Trend in Marketing of Oats (in Percent of Total Marketings), 10 Year Monthly Average, 1941–50." The monthly percentages shown in the chart are related to oats receipts at primary markets. Other charts show daily futures prices for May oats at Chicago from 1936 to 1951.

Keltner, Chester W. "Chicago December Oats—Seasonal Price Advances Following the July-August Low in Past Years." In his *How to Make Money in Commodities*, p. 164, 1960.

> This is a table showing loan rate, July-August low price, September high price, October high, November high, December high, and extreme price advance for each year fom 1940 to 1959.

OATS-CORN SPREAD

Usually the buying of two contracts of December oats while simultaneously selling short one contract of December corn, or the selling short of two contracts of December oats while simultaneously buying one contract of December corn. April is the popular time to go into this spread; what is sold and what is bought depend upon the relative value of oats and corn at the time the spread is initiated.

Oats and corn are both feed grains, and the success of the oats-corn spread is brought about by fluctuations that occur in the "normal" price relationship of the two grains.

Angrist, Stanley W. "Intercommodity Spreads." In his *Sensible Speculating in Commodities*, pp. 166-169. 1972.

> The margin requirement for the proportion generally used in this spread (two contracts for oats and one for corn) is said to be about the same as the margin for trading one contract of corn. Angrist views the oats-corn spread as "One of the most consistently reliable intercommodity spreads. . . ." He says that, as a rule of thumb, two December oats contracts are bought and one December corn contract is sold short if the price of two bushels of oats is less than 15¢ more than one bushel of corn, around the first of April. If, on the other hand, the oats premium is over 15¢ the oats contracts are sold short and the corn contract is bought. A table shows "Spread Between December Oats and December Corn" annually from 1952 to 1971, with profit or loss that would have resulted each year from April to November.

Greenberg, Stephen. "Oats-Corn Price Spread." In *Guide to Commodity Price Forecasting*, ed. by Harry Jiler and George B. Parker, pp. 222-223. 1965.

> Oats and corn are both feed grains and interchangeable to a large extent. As a bushel of corn (56 pounds) is much heavier than a bushel of oats (32 pounds), the usual spreading operation uses one unit of corn to equal roughly two units of oats. Greenberg points out that from 1948 to 1959 buying oats while selling corn was nearly always a profitable spread. Unfortunately, seasonal trends reversed themselves enough to make the opposite spread (buy corn, sell oats) more profitable from 1960 to 1964. A table shows "Net Change in Premium of Price of Two Bushels of Oats Over One Bushel of Corn from April 1 to November 1 (1948-1964 inclusive)." Charts show the daily spread of December corn over December oats at Chicago from 1949 to 1964.

Teweles, Richard J., and others. "Seasonal Information and Spreads." In their *The Commodity Futures Game*, pp. 397-398. 1974.

> States that the rationale behind buying December oats and selling December corn on April 1, with the spread to be closed out on November 1, is that oats prices should be relatively firm after the summer harvest has passed, while corn prices should be relatively weak during fall harvest. A table shows "December Oats-December Corn: Net Change in Premium of Price of 2 Bushels of Oats Over 1 Bushel of Corn, April 1 to November 1 (1948-1973 inclusive)." The authors state that the success of this spread depends upon proper appraisal of the total supply of corn and oats, the rate of usage, and stocks at Chciago. Because of increasing speculator sophistication, the traditional spread of buying two bushels of oats per one bushel of corn sold short has not worked well during most recent years.

ON BALANCE VOLUME. See Volume of Trading

OPEN BOARD OF TRADE, CHICAGO (now Mid-America Commodity Exchange). See Commodity Exchanges

OPEN INTEREST (See also Volume of Trading)
The number of unfilled contracts for future delivery of a commodity that exists at a particular time. Long open interest and short open interest are always equal in a particular delivery month for a particular commodity, in that each contract that is bought must also be sold. Open interest in commodity futures differs radically from shares outstanding in stocks because open interest is not a "set" figure. The open interest in futures fluctuates continuously and sometimes violently as contracts are created and cancelled (offset). As a result, speculators in soybean futures, for example, may buy and sell more future soybeans than will actually exist (open interest may easily be larger than expected physical supply). As the delivery date for a particular futures contract approaches, the open interest drops sharply, reflecting the fact that relatively few contracts result in actual delivery of a physical supply of a commodity. (Physical supplies are taken care of in the spot or cash markets.) Incidentally, the beginning commodity speculator should keep in mind that open interest figures as quoted in newspapers and elsewhere represent one side only—either all contracts long or all contracts short (take your pick, as the two sides are equal). That is, if trader A enters the market for the first time and sells one contract to trader B, who also has no prior position, the resulting new open interest equals one. This is true even though two sides are involved, with A having sold short and B having bought. The combined actions of A and B have created one open contract. (However, open interest in grains is usually quoted in thousands of bushels rather than in number of contracts.)

Angrist, Stanley W. "Open Interest and Price Correlations." In his *Sensible Speculating in Commodities*, pp. 125–134. 1972.

> Open interest is discussed at some length and is illustrated on various charts. The rules for open interest are summarized as follows: (1) open interest and prices moving in the same direction equals price strength; and (2) prices are technically weak when prices and open interest move in opposite directions. Angrist is a firm believer in the helpfulness of open interest data when attempting to forecast futures prices from charts.

Belveal, L. Dee. "Understanding Open Interest as a Measurement of Conflicting Opinions." In his *Charting Commodity Market Price Behavior*, pp. 125–136. 1969.

> Emphasizes the fact that open interest measures the quantitative aspects of a futures market situation. That is, open interest indicates the size of the two equal groups that are opposing each other on the opposite sides (bought and sold short) of a futures contract. The significance of changes in open interest is analyzed by Belveal.

Beveridge, E. A. "The Significance of Open Interest in Commodity Futures Markets." In *Commodity Year Book 1954*, pp. 13–20. 1954.

> Synonyms for open interest that are mentioned are "open commitments," "open position," and "open contracts." All refer to unliquidated com-

modity futures contracts. After discussing the function of commodity clearinghouses, Beveridge lists transactions affecting open interest in July 1953 cotton futures to illustrate just how open interest figures are compiled. He starts from the beginning of the first day of trading in the contract, at which point the open interest was zero, of course. At the end of the first day, volume of trading was already greater than open interest, and Beveridge shows in detail how this could happen. Next the effects of the following on open interest are considered: a contract that is close to expiration, seasonal factors, and government agricultural support programs. The author closes his article with a discussion of the use of open interest to predict price trends. He states that open interest data are undoubtedly of some value some of the time, but not always. Interpretation is often difficult.

Cox, Houston A. "Use of Volume and Open Interest in Commodity Analysis." In his *Concepts on Profits in Commodity Futures Trading*, pp. 140–149. 1972.

Cox's first rule is that an uptrend is valid if prices, volume, and open interest are all up. Likewise, a downtrend is valid if volume and open interest are up, but the price is down. His second rule is that an uptrend is doubtful if the price is up, but volume and open interest are down. Likewise, a downtrend is doubtful if volume and open interest are down, even though the price is also down. In other words, volume and open interest must rise if a price trend in either direction is to be confirmed. Furthermore, according to Cox, one must adjust changes in open interest according to seasonal variations to determine if the change is truly significant or merely a reflection of a seasonal pattern. To assist the trader in this adjustment, Cox reprints the Commodity Research Bureau's charts showing seasonal trends of open interest and volume (ten-year average, 1955–1964). Cocoa, coffee, copper, corn, cotton, cottonseed oil, shell eggs, grease wool, hides, oats, potatoes, wheat, rye, soybean meal, soybean oil, soybeans, domestic sugar, and world sugar are shown in individual charts.

Gardner, Robert L. "The Open Interest." In his *How to Make Money in the Commodity Market*, pp. 166–168. 1961.

States four conclusions that experienced commodity traders generally draw from changes in open interest and prices: (1) rising open interest and rising prices equal a strong market; (2) falling open interest and rising prices equal a weak market; (3) rising open interest and falling prices equal a weak market; and (4) falling open interest and falling prices equal a strong market. Gardner briefly discusses each of these four situations. He states that only strong and rapid changes in open interest are useful clues to speculators (minor fluctuations are not important). Hedging and seasonal influences must also be taken into consideration when looking at open interest. Gardner cautions his readers to pay attention only to *total* open interest for a particular commodity, not to individual delivery months.

Gold, Gerald. "Significance of Open Interest Changes." In his *Modern Commodity Futures Trading*, 6th ed., pp. 218–221. 1971.

> Price improvement is indicated when prices and open interest both move in the same direction (both up or both down). However, prices are likely to be weak when prices and open interest move in opposite directions (one increasing and the other decreasing). Unfortunately, open interest movements are "complicated" by seasonal patterns, and only reasonably sharp or rapid changes in open interest are likely to be significant. Gold states that because of difficulties in timing, analysis of open interest "has rarely been successfully used *alone* as a means of price forecasting." He mentions that open interest analysis is likely to be helpful in the interpretation of price charts.

Jiler, William L. "Volume and Open Interest Analysis as an Aid to Price Forecasting." In *Guide to Commodity Price Forecasting*, ed. by Harry Jiler and George B. Parker, pp. 61–73. 1965. (An earlier version of this article appears in the 1958 *Commodity Year Book*.)

> Although analysis of price movement is said to be by far the most important procedure in any technical study of commodity trends, "the proper interpretation of volume and open interest changes is an extremely valuable supplementary technique." Jiler tells how to read volume and open interest statistics as they appear in newspapers. The important statistics are said to be total open interest and total volume for any particular commodity (various futures contract months combined). Instructions are given for the essential step of making seasonal adjustments in open interest data according to charts showing open interest monthly as a percentage of the ten-year average (1955–1964, in this case). Jiler includes 19 separate charts in his article, giving seasonal trends of open interest and volume for the following commodities: cocoa, coffee, copper, corn, cotton, cottonseed oil, eggs, hides, oats, potatoes, rubber, rye, soybean meal, soybean oil, soybeans, domestic sugar, world sugar, wheat, and wool. Under "How Volume and Open Interest Changes Can Reveal Forthcoming Price Trends," eight specific tendencies are described. To illustrate his various points, Jiler analyzes the September 1957 futures contracts for Chicago wheat, corn, and soybeans. Charts are shown for these three contracts, giving daily prices, daily total open interest (all delivery months combined), and daily total volume (combined). In his conclusion to this article, Jiler states that any analysis of price trend can be completely disrupted by weather, government, foreign affairs, or strikes. He says that analysis of volume and open interest should be regarded as a minor analytical technique.

Keltner, Chester W. "Open Interest and Volume of Trading." In his *How to Make Money in Commodities*, pp. 187–193. 1960.

> While open interest is usually mentioned in connection with the technical analysis of commodity price trends, it can also be useful in fundamental

analysis. That is, the trader who uses fundamentals primarily should check open interest for technical weakness or technical strength and should re-examine his strategy if the open interest appears to be out of tune (technically strong when the trader is short, for example). Keltner gives a set of rules for analyzing open interest. He illustrates his points by making detailed commentary on a chart of prices, open interest, and trading volume for Chicago November soybeans, May–August 1960. "Changes in open interest and in volume of trading have forecasting value only when considered in connection with price change."

Kroll, Stanley, and Shishko, Irwin. "Seasonally Adjusted Open Interest and Volume Charts." In their *Commodity Futures Market Guide*, pp. 348–352. 1973.

Charts show seasonal trends of open interest and volume for 15 different commodities. Open interest is plotted as of the middle and end of the month, January through December, based on a ten-year, 1955–1964, average. The data plotted represent percentages of the ten-year average.

Kroll, Stanley, and Shishko, Irwin. "What Do Volume and Open Interest Show?" In their *Commodity Futures Market Guide*, pp. 137–148. 1973.

When open interest is unusually high, the breaking of an established price trend should be looked upon as a "potent warning." This is especially true in delivery months that are close to expiration. The four possibilities for price and open interest are stated as follows: (1) A rise in both price and open interest is caused mainly by new buying. (2) A rise in price while open interest declines is caused mainly by short covering. (3) A decline in both prices and open interest is caused mainly by liquidation of long positions. (4) A decline in price while open interest rises is caused mainly by new selling. The conclusions traditionally arrived at by market technicians are that (1) price and open interest moving in the same direction is a technically strong factor of bullish potential, but (2) a divergence in price and open interest is probably bearish. Unfortunately, the relationships are both subtle and complex. Kroll and Shishko suggest the refinement that rising price and open interest (with high volume) is a factor of greatest significance at the beginning of a price move. A price, open interest, and volume chart of July 1971 corn is used to illustrate the point. The importance of using seasonally adjusted open interest is stressed. The authors' discussion of open interest is a rational one that should be helpful to commodity speculators.

Powers, Mark J. "Volume and Open Interest." In his *Getting Started in Commodity Futures Trading*, pp. 79–83. 1973.

Open interest figures for all delivery months of one crop year of a particular commodity should be added together for purposes of analysis. Changes in open interest are helpful in forecasting only when considered together with price changes. Mention is made of the fact that many pitfalls await those who casually apply rules of thumb to changes in open interest and volume.

Shaw, John E. B. "How to Use Open Interest as a Trading Guide." In his *A Professional Guide to Commodity Speculation*, pp. 52–55. 1972.

> States that if open interest for a particular commodity grows to an amount that is three times the average or "normal" amount, there is a probability of unwise public participation, and selling short should be considered. However, to be successful in this short selling, one needs patience and adequate capital. A full-page chart of May 1968 sugar at New York from December 1966 to October 1967 is given as an example of the excessive buildup and subsequent collapse of open interest.

Teweles, Richard J., and others. "Analysis of Open Interest to Determine Activities of Large and Small Traders." In their *The Commodity Futures Game*, pp. 193–196. 1974.

> A discussion of the use of government reports on the long and short positions of bona fide hedgers, large traders, and small traders. The basis for analysis of such reports would be the assumption that big traders are usually right and the small trader is usually a loser. The advantages of such analysis are said to be that similar analysis has met with some success in the stock market, that it is important to know what large traders are doing, and that little work has been done so far in this area as far as commodities are concerned. Disadvantages are that "smart money" data are published too late and too infrequently, that small speculators are more likely to trade haphazardly than be consistently wrong, and that large trader-small trader study may be an arid field.

Teweles, Richard J., and others. "Traditional Volume and Open Interest Methods." In their *The Commodity Futures Game*, pp. 185–188. 1974.

> (1) Buying of an aggressive nature may be indicated when seasonally adjusted open interest rises along with prices. (2) Short covering instead of aggressive buying is suggested when prices rise but seasonally adjusted open interest drops. (3) The market may be stronger after seasonally adjusted open interest drops along with prices. The advantages of open interest analysis are said to be logic, a three-dimensional outlook (assuming that volume analysis is added), and, at least, the provision of additional information for the trader to base decisions on. Some disadvantages of open interest analysis are ill-defined terms (for example, what quantity or percentage constitutes a valid "increase in open interest"?), overpublicizing of the standard rules of open interest analysis, and lack of proof of usefulness.

Williams, Larry R. "The Second Indication of a Million Dollar Trade." In his *How I Made One Million Dollars in the Commodity Market Last Year*, pp. 52–59. 1973.

> As a general rule, according to Williams, an increase in open interest means an increase in short selling by commercial interests, simply because commercial interests dominate the market and are more often on the short side than public speculators. Likewise, a decline in open interest means that the professionals are buying to close out their short positions. Williams tells

how to make profitable use of these changes in open interest, with eight charts used to illustrate his points.

OPTIONS, COMMODITY. See Commodity Options

ORANGE JUICE
In this case, frozen concentrated orange juice (FCOJ) as traded in futures contracts by the Citrus Associates of the New York Cotton Exchange. Florida is by far the largest producer of oranges for frozen orange juice.

Arthur, Henry B. "Frozen Concentrated Orange Juice." In his *Commodity Futures as a Business Management Tool*, pp. 290–314. 1971.

> General discussion of the frozen orange juice market, with emphasis on commercial hedging. The viewpoints of growers, processors, dealers, and retailers are considered. Arthur describes the use of orange juice futures by Lykes-Pasco Packing Co., H. P. Hood & Sons, Citrus World, Coca-Cola Co. (Minute Maid), Kraftco Corp., Kroger Co., and First National Stores. Kroger and First National are said to be atypical, in that most retailers make little or no use of commodity futures. Arthur says that the typical orange grower making use of the orange juice futures market can probably best be described as an "informed speculator."

Chicago Board of Trade. "Orange Juice." In *Commodity Trading Manual*, pp. 239–241. 1973.

> Supply and demand factors are briefly discussed. Frozen concentrated orange juice futures trading details are shown for the Citrus Associates of the New York Cotton Exchange, including delivery months, trading units, minimum price fluctuations, daily price move limits, trading limits, position limits, delivery standards, and trading hours.

Goldberg, Ray A. "Florida Oranges." In his *Agribusiness Coordination*, pp. 149–178. 1968.

> A scholarly look at the fundamentals of the Florida orange industry in two parts: "The Florida Orange Industry: Its Dynamics and Structure" (production, consumption, processors, marketing) and "Behavioral and Performance Patterns of the Florida Orange Economy" (storage, pricing, competition). Goldberg uses a systems approach.

Green, Leslie. "Understanding the Frozen Orange Juice Market." In *Commodity Year Book 1968*, pp. 25–32. 1968.

> General coverage of the frozen concentrated orange juice market, including orange crop hazards, processing, trends in juice consumption, and futures contract details. Two tables give statistics on 17 different supply-demand factors from the 1957–1958 season to 1966–1967. Charts show daily futures prices for frozen orange juice at New York from October 1966 to March 1968. Charts also show weekly futures (high, low, close) from

October 1966 to April 1968 and total open interest-volume figures on a daily basis for the same period.

Hershman, Arlene. "The OJ Play: Tough and Tangy; in the Fast-Moving World of Commodities, Frozen Orange Juice Is a Weird Concoction of Timing and Intangibles." *Dun's,* vol. 97, April, 1971, pp. 55–57.

>The unique characteristics of the frozen orange juice market are said to be regional concentration (90 percent of the oranges for frozen juice are grown in central Florida), unusually high weather risk (the crop is vunerable to sudden freezes), lack of timely information (government crop reports appear only once a month), severe short-term price swings that wipe out speculators who may have been right for the long-term price move, and overreaction of the market to rumors of freezes. Therefore, the orange juice futures market is jittery and dangerous. Weather scares become more important than fundamental supply-demand factors.

Rosenbaum, Clarence H. "How to Analyze the Orange Juice Futures Market." In *Commodity Year Book 1972,* pp. 21–28. 1972.

>The fundamentals of the frozen concentrated orange juice market are presented, including supply-demand factors, aspects of juice production, import-export significance, the relationship of futures prices to spot prices, the function of growers' cooperatives, hedging, and long-term production trends. The "crop scare season" for oranges is said to run from September to March, with hurricanes a danger in September and October and disastrous freezing possible from late November to March. In fact, freeze scares produce a kind of seasonal pattern in orange juice futures, with prices often peaking toward the end of January. Charts in this article show daily futures prices for March frozen orange juice at New York from 1967 to 1972. A bibliography of 18 items is included.

Teweles, Richard J., and others. "Orange Juice." In their *The Commodity Futures Game,* pp. 569–576. 1974.

>"Fluctuations in orange juice prices in recent years have been violent." The authors suggest that those speculators whose nerves are not steady should stay away from the orange juice market. The dominant factor is said to be the weather in Florida. Price influences, information sources, production, and utilization are discussed.

ORDERS TO BROKERS (See also Brokers; Stop-Loss Orders)

"Buy," "sell," and other instructions given by commodity traders to their brokers, nearly always by telephone. To avoid confusion, these instructions must be explicit.

Angrist, Stanley W. "Orders—Instructing Your Broker." In his *Sensible Speculating in Commodities,* pp. 56–59. 1972.

>The following kinds of orders are described and proper procedure given: day orders, open orders (good till canceled or GTC), market orders, price-

limit orders, stop-loss orders, buy-stop orders, sell-stop orders, stop-limit orders, on-close stop orders, and one-cancels-the-other orders (OCO). The trader must be able to give instructions to his broker in a clear and proper manner or great difficulties will arise. Further on in his book, under "Placing Spread Orders" (pp. 163-164), Angrist gives specific, clear instructions about dealing in spreads.

Belveal, L. Dee. "Order Placement and Execution." In his *Commodity Speculation with Profits in Mind*, pp. 237-247. 1967.

". . . a broker cannot read a customer's mind." Order execution in the commodity futures markets is generally very efficient, but requires a certain knowledge on the part of the customer. Belveal emphasizes the importance of knowing the customs of various markets. For example, "five March wheat" means one contract of 5,000 bushels, but "five March soybean oil" means five contracts of 60,000 pounds each. Belveal discusses many different types of orders, including those involved in intermarket spreads and intercommodity spreads.

Chicago Board of Trade. "Orders." In *Commodity Trading Manual*, pp. 130-133. 1973.

Orders described are fill or kill, stop, stop-loss, stop-limit, board (MIT—market if touched), day, open (GTC—good till canceled), time limit, straight cancel, cancel former order (CFO), and OCO (one cancels the other). Orders establishing spreads are briefly discussed.

Cox, Houston A. "The Commodity Order as Your Command Decision." In his *Concepts on Profits in Commodity Futures Trading*, pp. 171-186. 1972.

An unusually complete presentation of the kinds of buy or sell orders that can be given to commodity futures brokers. Among the types of orders included and described in some detail are market orders ("at the market"), buy-stop, sell-stop, stop-limit, OB (limit price "or better"), MIT (market if touched), OCO (one cancels the other), CFO (cancel first order), EOS (enter open stop if executed), market scale, limit scale, MIT-scale, stop-scale, market basis, limit basis, stop basis, market-switch, over-switch, under-switch, straddle (spread), FOK (fill or kill), GTC (good till canceled), open (same as GTC), GTM (good through current month), GTW (good through current week), WRI (without responsibility), discretionary, and "all-or-nothing." Needless to say, the average amateur commodity speculator will not need to use all these orders, and, in any event, not all commodity brokers will execute all of these. Nevertheless, Cox has provided a useful catalog of detailed order forms designed to fill specific purposes without ambiguity.

Gould, Bruce, G. "Order Variations." In his *Dow Jones-Irwin Guide to Commodities Trading*, pp. 83-85. 1973.

Fifteen kinds of commodity trading orders are briefly described, and 21 order abbreviations are listed.

108 COMMODITY FUTURES TRADING

Gould, Bruce G. "Sample Commodity Orders as Written by Commodity Brokers and Wired Directly to the Floor of Commodity Exchanges to Be Filled on Behalf of the Customer by a Floor Trader." In his *Dow Jones-Irwin Guide to Commodities Trading*, pp. 309–340. 1973.

> Thirty-one reproductions of actual order forms are shown, with informative explanations. The teletype input that matches each order is also reproduced. An excellent, comprehensive presentation is provided in which a different point is illustrated by each of the 31 examples.

Hieronymus, Thomas A. "Kinds of Orders." In his *Economics of Futures Trading*, pp. 59–62. 1971.

> The following kinds of orders are described: market, limit, stop, stop-limit, trailing stop, scale, contingent, spread, time, and discretionary. Hieronymus states that "the broker can usually be given any instructions that can be understood and kept track of." He points out, however, that brokerage houses vary in their willingness to accept complex or difficult orders.

Keltner, Chester W. "Placing Buying and Selling Orders." In his *How to Make Money in Commodities*, pp. 40–41. 1960.

> Market orders, limit orders, and open orders are defined. As types of limited orders, Keltner also explains stop orders, day orders, quick orders, market-if-touched (MIT) orders, and limit-stop orders.

Powers, Mark J. "The Order." In his *Getting Started in Commodity Futures Trading*, pp. 41–46. 1973.

> Orders are discussed under the categories of "time element" (day, open, good till canceled, good through a specific date, time-of-day, off-at-specific time, fill-or-kill, quick, on-the-opening, and on-the-close), "price" (at the market, limit, and market-if-touched), "stop orders" (stop-loss, stop-limit, and scale), and "combination orders" (alternate, contingent, and spread). Exact instructions about how to place an order are given.

Shaw, John E. B. "How to Specify Orders." In his *A Professional Guide to Commodity Speculation*, pp. 41–43. 1972.

> Various situations and solutions are given to show the beginning speculator just how different types of commodity orders should be given to brokers. The solution to each situation explains a particular kind of order.

Teweles, Richard J., and others. "Types of Orders." In their *Commodity Futures Games*, pp. 61–66. 1974.

> Briefly explains buy-stop, buy-limit, sell-stop, sell-limit, trailing stop, stop-limit, market-if-touched (MIT), scale, take your time (TYT), not held, contingent, and spread orders.

ORIGIN OF FUTURES TRADING See History of Futures Trading

OSCILLATOR METHOD (See also Moving Average)
A system of technical analysis of commodity futures that involves the adding up of changes in a moving average of prices, as when, for example, daily changes in a three-day moving average are added for seven days. Trading rules then revolve around changes in direction of the seven-day totals (plus to minus or minus to plus). The amount of the seven-day total at a point of change is also usually considered to be an important factor in oscillator trading schemes. Another name for the oscillator method is "price-difference method."

Angrist, Stanley W. "Price-Difference Method." In his *Sensible Speculating in Commodities*, pp. 148–153. 1972.

> Chiefly, this is a discussion, chart, and table of the "7-Day Oscillator Method Applied to the December, 1971 Soybean Oil Contract," although there is some comment on oscillator or price-difference methods of trading in general. Angrist says that these systems appear to work well in trading markets but not in markets where sustained, long-term price trends develop, the problem being that when the long-term trend pauses to catch its breath, the oscillator throws the poor trader out of the trend and into an opposite position, with disastrous results. In other words, the oscillator method is good for minor but not major, trends, leaving the speculator with the nice problem of figuring out what kind of trend he is involved with.

Teweles, Richard J., and others. "Oscillators." In their *The Commodity Futures Game*, pp. 182–185. 1974.

> A chart shows "November 1970 shell eggs daily close versus 20-day net change oscillator for May-October 1970," with overbought and oversold points indicated. The advantages of oscillators are said to be that they work well in trading (trendless) markets, that overbought or oversold signals can act as controls on the emotions, and that indications of loss of market momentum are often given well in advance of the actual change in price trend. Disadvantages of oscillators are uselessness during long price trends (the very trends that one would normally want to take advantage of), uncertainty as to the actual overbought or oversold zones (volatility changes make old zones obsolete), and uncertainty as to interpretation of oscillator trend lines.

OVERTRADING (See also Money Management; Trading Rules)
Overuse of available speculative capital. That is, if a speculator has trading capital of, say, $10,000 and uses this entire amount as margin to enter as many orders as possible for futures contracts of a particular commodity, an adverse price move may result in complete loss of capital within an amazingly short period of time (a "wipeout"). Overtrading is avoided by being an astute money manager.

Belveal, L. Dee. "Over-Trading." In his *Commodity Speculation with Profits in Mind*, pp. 264–265. 1967.

> States that overtrading is like playing Russian roulette—one mistake can put the speculator out of the game forever. Traders must always leave themselves latitude for loss. The following principles are set forth as rules of thumb: (1) Never put more than one half of available speculative capital into an *initial* position. (2) When adding to initial positions (presumably under favorable conditions), never use more than 90 percent of speculative capital.

Cox, Houston A. "Consistency, Money Management, and Profits." In his *Concepts on Profits in Commodity Futures Trading*, pp. 169–171. 1972.

> "The Five Success Rules of Money Management" are quoted. Cox's rules for money management in futures trading are quite specific regarding the amounts of capital that should be utilized in individual situations.

Feduniak, Robert. "How to Avoid Overtrading." In *Getting Started in Commodity Futures Trading*, by Mark J. Powers, pp. 89–95. 1973.

> "... one of the most striking differences between winners and losers in the futures game is the failure on the part of consistent losers to manage their money intelligently." Feduniak provides a sobering account of those who open commodity accounts with $5,000 and risk $1,000 on each trade. While this proportion may seem relatively conservative, the mathematical chances (probability theory) of going broke within a year are about three out of four, if one assumes there will be 50 trades within one year at a 50-50 chance of profitability. That is, the chances of having five consecutive losses are relatively high within 50 trades, and if one risks 20 percent of one's speculative capital on each trade, one must not be a genius to determine that five times 20 percent equals 100 percent! In any event, Feduniak wisely states that the prudent thing to do is to limit one's risk to no more than 10 to 12 percent of available speculative capital on any one trade. Feduniak describes his plan to avoid overtrading, in which losses are limited to 10 percent of trading capital and gains are allowed to accumulate to the point of being ten times commission cost.

Longstreet, Roy W. "Overtrading." In his *Viewpoints of a Commodity Trader*, pp. 84–85. 1968.

> In addition to the traditional meaning of overextension of market position because of limited capital, Longstreet asserts that overtrading can mean overextension of nerves with an accompanying paralysis of action. "If you find it hard to sleep," he states, "reduce your position some or all."

PALLADIUM. See Platinum and Palladium

PERIODICALS (See also Advisory Services; Bibliographies; Statistics Sources)
In this case, magazines that have commodities and futures trading as major subjects.

Carabini, Louis, E., ed. "Publications." In his *Everything You Need to Know Now About Gold and Silver*, pp. 174–176. 1974.

> A listing of 28 periodicals and services that are related in one way or another to gold and silver.

Commodities: The Magazine of Futures Trading. Published monthly by Investor Publications, Inc. (1000 Century Plaza, Columbia, Md. 21044).

> The fundamentals of individual commodities as well as general speculative techniques are featured in *Commodities*. Nearly all of the articles are popularly written and easy to understand. An important regular feature of each issue of the magazine is "Commodity Alert," a day-by-day listing of government crop reports and other statistical commodity reports that are scheduled for publication during the current month. Each January issue features the invaluable "Directory of Futures Trading," with unusually complete lists of commodity books, services, publishers, consultants, brokers, computer data services, charting services, and periodicals. (It has been announced that the special directory edition of *Commodities* will henceforth be published as the May issue. Coverage will be expanded to include statistical data, futures contract details, and other new material. The title will be changed to "Reference Guide to Futures Markets.")

Commodity Journal. Published bimonthly by the American Association of Commodity Traders (286 Fifth Ave., New York, N.Y. 10001).

> Each issue usually contains four or five articles of some length dealing with a wide variety of topics. The articles range from theoretical treatises on econometrics to practical explanations of charting systems and moving averages. Each issue contains a complete, annotated listing of articles that have appeared in *Commodity Journal* since volume one in 1965. A few back issues are out of print, but most are still available to subscribers at one dollar per copy.

Consensus: National Commodity Futures Weekly. Published weekly by Consensus, Inc. (30 W. Pershing Rd., Kansas City, Mo. 64108).

> Published each Saturday, *Consensus* is similar to the *Wall Street Transcript*, except that the world of commodity futures is covered. Each issue presents summaries of brokers' reports and recommendations for 24 different commodities or commodity groups. Various crop or production statistics are given, and recent prices are quoted for a wide variety of domestic and Canadian commodity futures. Among the regular departments are daily price charts (about seven pages), commodity commentary, commodity calendar, commodity spreads, USDA reports, technical comments, and

112 COMMODITY FUTURES TRADING

a unique "Market Sentiment Index" showing the percentage of brokers that appear to be bullish on each of 18 leading commodities. Each weekly issue of *Consensus* contains a wide variety of useful information for the commodity trader.

"Directory of Futures Trading." Published annually in January as a special issue of *Commodities* magazine.

This special directory issue of *Commodities* lists and describes some 70 magazines and newspapers that may contain information of importance to commodity traders. Complete address information is given in each case. (Plans are for the directory issue of *Commodities* to be published in May rather than January.)

PERSONAL CHARACTERISTICS OF TRADERS. See Psychology

PHASES OF THE MOON. See Moon Cycles

PHILOSOPHY OF TRADING. See Money Management; Psychology; Trading Rules

PLATINUM AND PALLADIUM
Malleable white metals useful for their corrosion-resistant and catalytic properties and often used in alloys. Palladium is harder, lighter, and less costly than platinum. The platinum-group metals are produced mainly by Russia, South Africa, and Canada, while U.S. production is relatively small. Platinum and palladium each have futures contracts traded on the New York Mercantile Exchange.

Chicago Board of Trade. "Platinum and Palladium." In *Commodity Trading Manual*, pp. 200–203. 1973.

Supply, production, U.S. supplies, and demand are discussed. Platinum and palladium futures trading details are listed for the New York Mercantile Exchange, including delivery months, trading units, minimum price fluctuations, daily price move limits, position limits, delivery standards, and trading hours.

Lynde, Harold W. "The Long Term Outlook for Platinum and Palladium." In *Commodity Year Book 1968*, pp. 33–42. 1968.

A brief history of the platinum group of metals is given covering the period from 1557 to the modern era. In recent years, industrial usage of these metals has become much more important than jewelry and decorative applications. Lynde summarizes the many industrial uses and consumption outlets of the platinum group, and discusses production sources. The futures markets are briefly considered. A considerable amount of supply-demand statistical information is given in tabular form, covering 1900–1920 to 1967. A table gives platinum prices (spot and futures) monthly from January 1963 to March 1968. Finally, the prediction is made that both consumption and production of platinum will have major increases in the future.

Teweles, Richard J., and others. "Platinum Group." In their *The Commodity Futures Game*, pp. 498–507. 1974.

> Factors influencing prices, production, utilization, and lack of seasonal trends are discussed. Platinum information sources are given on page 513 of the Teweles book.

PLATITUDES. *See* Trading Rules

PLYWOOD. *See* Lumber and Plywood

POINT-AND-FIGURE CHARTS
Commodity price graphs that consider price movement only; time periods and volume of trading are ignored. Therefore, an inactive commodity with small, infrequent price changes would take up much less space on a point-and-figure chart than an active high flyer. On a conventional bar or line chart, both commodities would require the same amount of horizontal space because of the time factor. Point-and-figure charts may be relatively compressed or expanded, depending upon what price change the chartmaker has decided to utilize. A commodity chart showing 1¢ price changes, for example, will be more expansive and show more detail than a chart of the same commodity showing only 3¢ changes.

Cox, Houston A. "Point-and-Figure Charting." In his *Concepts on Profits in Commodity Futures Trading*, pp. 113–116. 1972.

> A general description of this type of charting. Point-and-figure work for commodity futures is said to be often useful, but time consuming. Small charts are used to illustrate eight kinds of tops and eight kinds of bottoms.

Gold, Gerald. "Point and Figure Charts." In his *Modern Commodity Futures Trading*, 6th ed., pp. 173–178. 1971.

> Detailed instructions for making a point-and-figure chart are presented in an easy-to-understand manner. Point-and-figure "reversal charts" are also covered.

Hart, John K. "The Use of Price Charts in Price Forecasting." In *Commodity Year Book 1948*, pp. 63–66. 1948.

> Detailed instructions are given for the construction of point-and-figure charts. A one and one-half point reversal chart of 1947 Chicago oats is used as an example.

Kroll, Stanley, and Shishko, Irwin. "Point-and-Figure Analysis." In their *Commodity Futures Market Guide*, pp. 148–154. 1973.

> Point-and-figure charts provide the market technician with great flexibility in that the technician is free to decide in each case whether a given

commodity future will be "scrutinized in minute detail or in summarized broad perspective." Congestion area analysis, trend analysis, support and resistance, chart formations, price objectives, and trading tactics are each briefly considered. In conclusion, Alexander H. Wheelan's six technical conditions are listed that comprise the "ideal buying point" for point-and-figure chartists. These conditions are written in point-and-figure language, such as "A catapult occurs coincidentally with the penetration of a downtrend line established within the fulcrum or from a previous top made tangent with the mid-fulcrum rally point."

Reinach, Anthony M. "Recording the Action." In his *The Fastest Game in Town*, pp. 46–50. 1973.

The construction of point-and-figure charts is explained in detail, but no opinion is given as to their predictive value.

Shaw, John E. B. "How to Use Point-and-Figure Charting." In his *A Professional Guide to Commodity Speculation*, pp. 98–106. 1972.

Even though Shaw states that moving from bar charts to point-and-figure is "a little like being graduated from Witchcraft I to Witchcraft II," he describes the point-and-figure method carefully and apparently believes that it is at least as useful as bar charting.

Wheelan, Alexander H. "Point-and-Figure Procedure in Commodity Market Analysis." In *Guide to Commodity Price Forecasting*, ed. by Harry Jiler and George B. Parker, pp. 33–47. 1965. (An earlier version of this article appears in the 1954 *Commodity Year Book*.)

Detailed instructions are given for the construction of point-and-figure price charts, which are said to be of great value in measuring speculator psychology in the commodity futures markets. Sample charts are used to illustrate the time flexibility of point-and-figure charting. For example, the same four days of price action in a cotton futures contract are shown in chart areas of $1/8'' \times 1/2''$, $1/2'' \times 1''$, and $5'' \times 2''$. The chart areas vary according to whether small or large price changes are being recorded; the smallest chart shows 10-point changes ($50 per contract of cotton), while the largest, designed for maximum detail, shows one-point changes ($5 per cotton contract). After his cotton illustrations, Wheelan goes on to discuss congestion area analysis, pattern identification, trends, support areas, and resistance areas. Eight patterns typical of market bottoms and eight typical tops are illustrated on a chart. Six specific buying points are defined.

PORK BELLIES, FROZEN (See *also* Pork Bellies, Frozen—Seasonal Price Trend)
The lower sides of a hog; the source of bacon. Frozen pork bellies are traded chiefly on the Chicago Mercantile Exchange.

Chicago Board of Trade. "Pork Commodities." In *Commodity Trading Manual*, pp. 173-177. 1973.

> Among the items discussed are feeding costs, production scheduling, supply considerations, and demand factors. Frozen pork belly futures trading details are given for the Chicago Mercantile Exchange, the Minneapolis Grain Exchange, and the International Commercial Exchange. For each exchange, delivery months, trading units, minimum price fluctuations, daily price move limits, position limits, delivery standards, and trading hours are listed.

Elberty, Mary. "Analyzing Hogs and Pork Bellies Price Trends." In *Commodity Year Book 1975*, pp. 13-23. 1975.

> While the great majority of this article is devoted to a discussion of hog production and the recurring hog price cycle, there is a brief consideration of "Pork Belly Demand." Demand for pork bellies is said to be relatively inelastic and prices relatively volatile. The point is made that people tend to think of bacon as a flavoring or condiment rather than as a meat. July pork belly futures prices are shown in chart form on a daily basis from 1969-1970 to 1974-1975.

Maduff, Michael L. "Forecasting Pork Belly Prices—The Fundamental Approach." In *Commodity Year Book 1970*, pp. 40-49. 1970.

> Emphasis is placed on the crop year, sliced bacon production, inventory levels, supplies in storage, and hog marketing patterns. At the end of his article, Maduff analyzes the pork belly marketing years from 1964 through 1967, with detailed explanations of how fundamentals predicted major price moves. (Although this is an article on fundamentals, Maduff states that even the most astute fundamentalist trader of pork bellies will find technical analysis helpful in timing.) Charts show daily futures prices for July pork bellies at Chicago from 1963 to 1970. A short discussion of sources of statistical information is included.

Shaw, John E. B. "Mechanical Method for Pork Bellies." In his *A Professional Guide to Commodity Speculation*, pp. 108-118. 1972.

> This pork belly system is Shaw's favorite mechanical trading method. It has worked well in recent years (1967-1971) but, like any automatic trading system, it cannot be guaranteed as to future results. The plan is fairly complicated, and is based on a ten-day moving average of the closing prices of a nearby pork belly futures contract. The seven rules necessary to follow the method are given, and nine pages of tabulation for the year 1967 are shown.

Stoken, Dick. "Forecasting Pork Belly Futures Prices." In *Commodity Year Book 1966*, pp. 17-27. 1966.

> The pork belly market is described as being an exciting place for futures speculators. To help the speculator make decisions, a simplified price

forecasting method for bellies is described, based on changes in supply-demand relationships. This method should be combined with a working knowledge of the strong seasonal and cyclical price patterns that often characterize pork bellies. Four cyclical patterns are therefore summarized for the trader. The annual highs and lows of cash pork belly prices are given from 1949–1950 to 1965–1966, with an indication of the months in which the annual highs or lows occurred. In 14 out of 17 years, highs took place during the July–September quarter and in 13 out of 17 years, lows occurred during the October-December quarter. Stoken mentions various information sources. Two statistical reports considered to be very important in evaluating the pork belly futures situation are quarterly pig crop reports and monthly cold storage figures. Carrying charges and the relationship between cash prices and futures are explained in some detail. Charts show futures versus cash prices on a daily basis for August pork bellies at Chicago from 1963 to 1966.

Teweles, Richard J., and others. "Frozen Pork Bellies." In their *The Commodity Futures Game*, pp. 423–437, 442. 1974.

The authors indicate that flexibility rather than stubbornness is a desirable trait for speculating in the volatile pork bellies market. Because daily price ranges tend to be broad, pork bellies are often used for day trading (transactions initiated and closed out within one day). Among the subjects covered by Teweles and co-authors are prices, information sources, supply, demand, seasonal trends, price spreads, and carrying charges.

PORK BELLIES, FROZEN—SEASONAL PRICE TREND

The marketing year for pork bellies normally begins in October. Low prices for the season typically occur in November or December, with highs sometime between the first of June and the end of August.

Teweles, Richard J., and others. "Seasonal Information." In their *The Commodity Futures Game*, pp. 433–436. 1974.

Although "pork belly supply and demand exhibit pronounced seasonal patterns ... speculators have all but eliminated the intrayear repetitive patterns." A chart shows "August pork bellies, seasonal: monthly mid-range price of August pork bellies as a percentage of average yearly price," with one line on the chart for each season from 1961–1962 to 1972–1973. The same data are also given in tabular form. Under the heading "Cyclical Variations in Price," a four-year cycle in the pig crop is described as being related to a similar cycle in pork belly cash prices.

POSITION MANAGEMENT. *See* Money Management

POTATOES

The tubers of the potato plant; a common, starchy vegetable. In addition to their direct use as a foodstuff, potatoes are used to make alcohol and starch. Russia is the leading potato grower, followed by Poland, Germany (East and West), and the United States. In the United States the crop is typically planted in the spring and harvested in late summer or early fall. Potato chips and frozen French fries are of growing importance as far as American consumption of potatoes is concerned. As is well known, Idaho and Maine are the big potato-producing states, although California and New York also have large crops. Maine potato futures are actively traded on the New York Mercantile Exchange and Idaho potatoes are less actively traded on the Chicago Mercantile Exchange.

Chicago Board of Trade. "Potatoes." In *Commodity Trading Manual*, pp. 235–238. 1973.

> Supply and demand factors are briefly discussed. A table shows "Utilization of Potatoes in the U.S." (11 separate uses) annually from 1961 to 1970. Potato futures trading details are shown for the New York Mercantile Exchange (Maine and Idaho potatoes) and for the Chicago Mercantile Exchange (Idaho russet potatoes). In each case, delivery months, trading units, minimum price fluctuations, daily price move limits, trading limits, position limits, delivery standards, and trading hours are listed.

Inkeles, David. "Understanding the Maine Potato Futures Market." In *Commodity Year Book 1969*, pp. 6–14. 1969.

> Potatoes are consistently a favorite with speculators. The relatively low value per futures contract (low margin requirement) appeals to small traders, as does the wide range of price fluctuations. Price changes of 50 to 100 percent are common during the life of a potato futures contract. Naturally, this increases the risk as well as the profit opportunities. Inkeles covers the fundamentals of the potato market, including merchandizing, processing, demand factors, price forecasting factors, and the importance of the May contract. The important government statistical reports are noted. Charts show daily futures prices for May potatoes at New York from 1954 to 1969.

Parker, George B. "How to Forecast Potato Futures Prices." In *Guide to Commodity Price Forecasting*, ed. by Harry Jiler and George B. Parker, pp. 133–143. 1965. (An earlier version of this article appears in the 1962 *Commodity Year Book*.)

> "As the demand for potatoes is relatively inelastic, the supply of potatoes is the most important factor influencing market prices." Production, harvesting, storage, transportation, utilization, and the relationship between cash and futures prices are discussed. A chart shows "Spot vs. May Futures Potato Prices" from 1955 to 1962. There are also charts showing daily potato futures prices for the May delivery from 1954 to 1965. Each potato season from 1956–1957 to 1963–1964 is briefly described.

118 COMMODITY FUTURES TRADING

Teweles, Richard J., and others. "Potatoes." In their *The Commodity Futures Game*, pp. 577-591. 1974.

> Because of small margin requirements, potatoes are popular with small traders, many of whom fail to take proper cognizance of market volatility. The authors cover price factors, information sources, nature of production, utilization, economic relationships, and seasonal tendencies. "Although erratic, the price of potatoes does exhibit some seasonal characteristics." A graph shows "Maine May potatoes, seasonal: monthly midrange price of May potatoes as a percentage of average yearly rate." There is one line for each season from 1961-1962 to 1972-1973. Another graph shows "Potatoes: monthly open interest and volume as a percentage of average monthly open interest and volume for the years 1962-1971 at the New York Mercantile Exchange (10-year, 1955-1964, average)." A table gives "Monthly midrange price of Maine May potatoes and percent of average yearly price" from 1960-1961 to 1972-1973. The authors call attention to the fact that potato prices tend to move sharply in one direction or another after the month of February.

POULTRY. See Iced Broilers

PREMIUM MARKET

A commodity market situation in which futures contracts for more recent months sell at a higher price than (at a premium to) the distant months of the same crop year. In a "normal" or carrying charge market, the distant months are more expensive than the closer months.

Williams, Larry R. "The First Indication of a Million Dollar Trade." In his *How I Made One Million Dollars in the Commodity Market Last Year*, pp. 41-51. 1973.

> An explanation of how to make profitable use of the general principle that premium markets tend to be bullish and discount or carrying charge markets tend to be bearish. Twelve charts are used as illustrations.

PREMIUM SPREADS. See Spreads

PRESIDENTIAL ELECTON YEARS AND COMMODITY PRICES

The tendency of stock prices to go up in presidential election years is well known, but not much has been written about commodities in this respect.

Commodity Research Bureau. "Commodity and Security Prices in Presidential Election Years." In *Commodity Year Book 1948*, pp. 16-18. 1948.

> Twelve small charts show the monthly wholesale commodity price index compared with the Dow Jones industrial stock average for each presidential election year from 1900 to 1944. For purposes of analysis, the textual material classifies the election years into three groups: war years (1916, 1940, 1944), postwar years (1900, 1920), and peace years (1904-

1912, 1924–1936). One of the conclusions reached is that commodity prices tend to go up during presidential election years, even though postwar years are likely to be exceptions.

PRICE-DIFFERENCE METHOD. See Oscillator Method

PRICE FORECASTING. See Fundamental Analysis; Random Walk Theory; Technical Analysis

PRICE INDEX OF COMMODITY FUTURES. See Dow-Jones Commodity Futures Index

PSYCHOLOGY (See also Trading Rules)
The emotional and behavioral characteristics of speculators. Control of the emotions is very important in commodity futures trading, as the assumption of risk subjects the psyche to a certain amount of stress.

Angrist, Stanley W. "Epilogue." In his *Sensible Speculating in Commodities,* pp. 196–197. 1972.

> In which the author deals with fear and greed—two feelings that are well known to just about every commodity speculator. Angrist manages to end on a positive note, however, by quoting Kierkegaard, and by stating that commodity trading is a sure way to gain self-knowledge and perhaps even some money.

Belveal, L. Dee. "Short-Term Trading Tactics." In his *Commodity Speculation with Profits in Mind,* pp. 91–102. 1967.

> Successful commodity speculation is said to require information, perspective, "and above all, great patience." Speculators from among the general public are designated as "weak hands" in the commodity markets and professional or commercial interests are called "strong hands." The tendency of the "weak hands" to abandon commodity positions quickly and all at the same time results in exaggerated price fluctuations. According to Belveal, "Speculation is not an exercise in lucky guesses. It is an activity which depends on knowledge, courage, and financial ability."

Belveal, L. Dee. "Understanding Your Market Competition." In his *Charting Commodity Price Behavior,* pp. 37–47. 1969.

> The characteristic trading behavior of "Small Public Traders," "Large Speculators," and "Hedgers—Commercial Interests" are described. Small traders are said to prefer the long (buying) side of the market. They are reluctant to sell short and reluctant to take losses. Large traders, on the other hand, are as willing to be short as long, and try to take losses promptly while letting profits run as far as possible. Large traders generally have definite levels in mind at which to initiate trades and will not "chase prices." Commercial hedgers are perhaps the most knowledge-

able participants in the commodity markets. Because of the tremendous market power of commercial interests, the small speculator should generally attempt to be on the same side of the market as the big hedgers, according to Belveal.

Gardner, Robert L. "If You Aren't Sure, Stay Clear." In his *How to Make Money in the Commodity Market*, pp. 178–180. 1961.

Moderation, coolness, decision-making powers, boldness, self-confidence, sound knowledge, hard work, courage, determination, good judgment, and good luck are mentioned as being necessary for success in commodity futures trading.

Glick, Ira O. *A Social Psychological Study of Futures Trading*. 1957. 267 pp.

A unique, interesting study of the emotions and operating styles of professional commodity traders. Glick's father was a member of the Chicago Mercantile Exchange who provided his son with a background in the "activities and problems of traders." Then I. O. Glick himself became a member of the Exchange and was active there for over two years, during which time "general impressions, occurrences, and conversations with fellow members were recorded." Glick held many in-depth interviews with traders, and their hopes and fears, as well as their attitudes about various matters ranging from chart trading to life in general, are quoted. Commodity trading as a career could perhaps be considered the main topic of this dissertation, with attention given to both successful and unsuccessful careers. In addition, Glick submitted 30 statements about futures trading to 28 of the professionals and asked them to place each statement into one of eight categories ranging from most true to least true. The statement rated as most true said that the successful trader must be able to change his mind very quickly and, therefore, his position in the market. The statement rated as second most true said that one must never be afraid to take a loss.

Hayden, Jack J. *What Makes You a Winner or a Loser in the Stock and Commodity Markets?* 1967. 64 pp.

An exposition of the theory that all investors (speculators) can be classified by their willingness to accept risk, as well as by their inherent optimism or pessimism. Those who are very much afraid of risk will not enter a market until there is a great deal of "information redundancy" (everything must look rosy), while those who are willing to accept a high degree of risk will take positions at the first sign of a turn for the better. As an additional factor, those who are naturally optimistic are happiest when buying, while those who are pessimistic by nature are most pleased when selling short. According to Hayden, one's willingness and ability to accept risk are much more important to investment success than good technique or knowledge. Those who accept risk easily (low risk averters), if otherwise intelligent, take early advantage of important market moves.

Those who are easily frightened by risk (high risk averters), regardless of intelligence or other admirable qualities, are typically not convinced that a market move can be taken advantage of until the move is just about over. Hayden tends to regard the average speculator as overly emotional and a born loser. "In speculative markets the emotions are nearly all that count . . . the markets are primordial jungles requiring elemental survival characteristics." The amateur trader has practically no chance at all of success over the long run unless he develops extraordinary self-discipline. (At the end of his book, on pages 49 to 63, Hayden presents mathematical models of his risk-aversion theory.)

Hieronymus, Thomas A. "Should You Trade?" In his *Economics of Futures Trading*, pp. 258–261. 1971.

The personality traits said to be necessary for successful speculation are a high degree of discipline, a willingness to work hard, and the right combination of cowardice and courage. The commodity speculator must have the nerve to take a position, but he must also be willing to turn tail and run if his position deteriorates. "Objectives must be established, trading plans developed, and markets continuously and carefully studied."

Keltner, Chester W. "Adopting a Definite Trading Plan." In his *How to Make Money in Commodities*, pp. 41–42. 1960.

The single most important thing a speculator must do, Keltner asserts, is to adopt a specific trading plan based on personal preferences and circumstances. Some traders will wish to use a technical plan in which price movements themselves are analyzed, while others will prefer the fundamental analysis of supply, demand, seasonal trends, and other crop factors.

Kroll, Stanley, and Shishko, Irwin. "On Seeking Profits in Commodities." In their *Commodity Futures Market Guide*, pp. 77–88. 1973.

"Many are called by the lure of high-leverage in commodity markets. Few are chosen to reap the glittering rewards." Kroll and Shishko, in this chapter of their book, present a general background to the frustrations of commodity trading. The problems of price prediction, insider information, sources of advice, and speculative philosophy are considered. The behavioral tendencies of winners and losers are shown in side-by-side columns on page 86 and 87 of the Kroll-Shishko volume.

Longstreet, Roy W. *Viewpoints of a Commodity Trader.* 147 pp. 1968.

This small volume is filled with homey advice for commodity speculators, with such chapter headings as "Look Before You Leap," "Do You Lie to Yourself?," and "Playing the Big One." Longstreet mentions self-reliance, good judgment, courage, prudence, pliability, perseverance, and humility as qualities that commodity traders should have. He emphasizes, ominously enough, a stiff-upper-lip policy: "Let us be among those who learn from tragedies and turn adversity into opportunities and advantages to ourselves."

Merrill Lynch, Pierce, Fenner & Smith, Inc. *Do You Have What It Takes to Be a Successful Commodity Futures Speculator?* No date (leaflet). 4 pp.

A ten-question quick quiz is presented to enable the prospective commodity trader to determine if he or she has the personal qualities necessary for success in speculation. Some of the characteristics thought to be desirable are aggressiveness, resiliency, the temperamental and financial ability to accept risk, the ability to stick with a trading plan, orderliness in thinking, objectivity, courage to act, patience, and freedom from the urge to gamble.

Teweles, Richard J., and others. "Behavioral Skills." In their *The Commodity Futures Game*, pp. 308-314. 1974.

"The behavior of the trader should move toward the kind of behavior necessary to survive." After a discussion of the studies by Ira O. Glick and Seymour Smidt on the subjects of trader behavior and amateur speculation, the concept of transactional analysis is applied to commodity futures speculation. Parent, adult, and child roles in trading operations are considered. In the final analysis, they say, "it may be as rewarding to travel as to arrive," which is somewhat the same as saying that commodity futures trading is a classy way to lose money.

Teweles, Richard J., and others. "The Commodity School for Losers." In their *The Commodity Futures Game*, pp. 277-286. 1974.

A hilarious but painful (to commodity traders and extraders) account of the activities of various characters who are currently attending "The Commodity School for Losers." The names and failings of these unfortunates are as follows: Herbert Hoyle (naive methodology—fancy "filter" rules); Gary Gullible (naive methodology—moving averages); Fred Fantasy (postponing losses by turning straight positions into spreads); William Wilde (overtrading); Marcus Mule (attempting to profit by taking delivery); Ivan Bentaken (blaming the broker); Eric Von Director (oversensitivity to how the market is "acting"—failure to use stop orders or price objectives); Deposit N. Withdrawal (poor money management); Oscar Ostrich (naive optimism—failure to use stop-loss orders); Wheeler Bandini (delusions and dishonesty); Barry Brass (unreasonable demands of brokers); Benjamin Franklin Bartlett (dependence on maxims).

Teweles, Richard J., and others. "Mistakes." In their *The Commodity Futures Game*, pp 249-250. 1974.

The greatest mistake, according to the authors, is neglecting to have some kind of plan for trading. Even a mediocre plan is better than no plan at all, because unplanned, haphazard speculation will often result in the trader sticking with a losing position to the bitter end ("I'm locked in"). Another big mistake discussed by the authors is having a plan and not following it.

Teweles, Richard J., and others. "Should You Speculate?" In their *The Commodity Futures Game*, pp. 20-21. 1974.

States that the personal nature of a commodity speculator is probably more important than the amount of his capital. The speculator must be able to take losses promptly, and to let profits run. "Each person must... decide whether he wishes to risk part of what he has to try to gain more."

Watling, T. F., and Morley, J. "Market Psychology: The Great Factor." In their *Successful Commodity Futures Trading*, pp. 75-87. 1974.

The authors state that at least a couple of trading rules are invariably right, but most are open to interpretation. However, even the unquestionable rules "are broken with monotonous regularity" because of the human emotions of speculators. Emotional reactions to the following trading rules are discussed: (1) never go against the price trend; (2) be patient; (3) cut losses short; (4) do not be afraid to sell short; (5) ignore tips on the market; (6) do not overemphasize news events; (7) don't anticipate price moves.

Williams, Larry R. "How Transactional Analysis Helped Make My Million Dollars." In his *How I Made One Million Dollars in the Commodity Market Last Year*, pp. 100-105. 1973.

The usual statement is made that virtually all public speculators are losers in the commodity market. Williams places the figures at 95 percent losers and a minuscule 5 percent winners, and says that similar data have been quoted since the turn of the century. His point is that, despite all the work on market theories, fundamental analysis, technical analysis, and so forth, the great majority of commodity traders are losing their shirts, just as they always have. Williams states that the two main problems are that everyday logic does not work in speculative markets and that people try to play games when trading, as in the "Dumb Broker" game, the "Dumb Client" game, the "Help Me..." game, and the "Let Me Rest" game. In "How to Become a Winner," Williams tells how to use transactional analysis and how to develop the essential factor of self-discipline.

PUBLIC SPECULATION. See Amateur Speculation

PUBLICATIONS. See Advisory Services; Bibliographies; Periodicals

PUTS AND CALLS. See Commodity Options

124 COMMODITY FUTURES TRADING

PYRAMIDING (*See also* Leverage; Margin)
The use of paper profits (excess margin) to make additions to an existing position in commodity futures. While modest pyramiding is generally looked upon as a reasonable procedure, pyramiding to the fullest extent possible in a volatile commodity results in enormous risk.

Belveal, L. Dee. "Adding to a Profitable Position." In his *Commodity Speculation with Profits in Mind*, pp. 191–204. 1967.

> Detailed advice is given on intelligent pyramiding. Belveal states that speculative positions should not be added to (pyramided) without stop-loss orders being moved to provide additional protection. He believes that commodity speculators often use poor judgment in pyramiding because of a tendency to overtrade. Also, "the prudent public speculator will limit his market forays to those situations which show the best opportunities for profit."

Gould, Bruce G. "Adding to a Winning Position." In his *Dow Jones-Irwin Guide to Commodities Trading*, pp. 288–241. 1973.

> The various techniques of adding to a previously established commodity position are discussed in some detail. The importance of moving stop losses as profits increase is emphasized. "Pure" pyramiding in which excess margin is always used to finance as many futures contracts as possible is said to be a sure way to lose. As to when to finally close out a trade: "Only the market knows how far it can go, and it doesn't know until it gets there."

Shulman, Morton. "Commodity Futures—The Ideal Gamble." In his *Anyone Can Still Make a Million*, pp. 133–134. 1973.

> Two types of pyramiding are discussed. In the first, additional futures contracts are purchased only as paper profits make such purchases possible—no additional cash is deposited with the broker. In the second, greater risk is assumed by depositing and using additional margin capital as prices move favorably.

RANDOM WALK THEORY (*See also* Mechanical Trading Systems; Technical Analysis)
The hypothesis that price changes are independent of each other and are therefore nonpredictive (prices move randomly, in other words). This is in direct contrast to the belief held by commodity and stock market technicians or technical analysts that profitable forecasts can be made from observation, charting, and analysis of price trends or patterns. For that matter, a strict random walk theoretician would not think much of price forecasts made by means of "fundamental" supply-demand analysis.

Cargill, Thomas F., and Rausser, Gordon C. "Temporal Price Behavior in Commodity Futures Markets." *Journal of Finance*, vol. 30, September 1975, pp. 1043–1053.

> Previous studies have determined that simple, mechanical filter rules used in commodity futures trading can produce substantial profits, even after commissions. Cargill and Rausser demonstrate that mechanical trading rules also produce theoretically profitable results with computer-generated random prices. In "Monte Carlo Results from the Application of a g-Per Cent Filter to a Random Walk Process," with ten filters from 1 to 10 percent, it is shown that 1, 3, and 10 percent filters were quite profitable, while 4, 7, and 8 percent filters produced either a loss or a very small profit. (Of course, the same filters would be expected to produce different results with a different set of randomly generated prices, emphasizing the difficulty of selecting profitable filters for trading in real life.) As filter tests are difficult to interpret statistically, the authors applied six tests of serial correlation to 464 actual futures contracts in seven commodities, generally from 1960 through 1972. (Data were from magnetic tapes supplied by Dunn & Hargitt, 124 W. State St., West Lafayette, Ind. 47902). The conclusion arrived at was as follows: "It clearly appears that the random walk model must be rejected as a realistic description of commodity markets." The authors are careful to point out that this conclusion does not necessarily imply a rejection of the efficient market process. Thirty-three references are given to the literature of the random walk hypothesis, statistical theory, and commodity markets.

Gould, Bruce G. "The Random Nature of Market Price." In his *Dow Jones-Irwin Guide to Commodities Trading*, pp. 227–235. 1973.

> "The net effect of market discounting is that price in an efficient, discounted market has at all times an exactly equal chance of going the same distance in either direction." Gould goes on, however, to point out six conditions or factors that may cause flaws (profit opportunities) in the otherwise perfect and randomly moving futures markets: (1) Biased supply-demand balance because of seasonal or other influences. (2) Time lags in the dissemination of information. (3) Nonrandom price factors, such as governmental price floors. (4) Fundamental price factors that are unusually obscure. (5) Self-fulfilling prophecies, sometimes resulting from large groups of stop-loss orders at certain price points. (6) On a personal basis, a trader may be able to beat 50–50 possibilities by cutting losses short and letting profits run. Gould's discussion of market behavior and the random walk theory is interesting and should be of practical value to the commodity futures speculator.

Labys, Walter C., and Granger, C. W. J. "The Random Behavior of Commodity Prices." In their *Speculation, Hedging and Commodity Price Forecasts*, pp. 63–87. 1970.

> While the random nature of commodity price movement is considered throughout the volume by Labys and Granger, the chapter above is used

specifically to introduce the random walk theory. Mathematical formulas are given, and "Previous Work on the Random Walk Model" is discussed. In their own investigation, using the sophisticated technique of spectral analysis, Labys and Granger found that seasonal and other components in commodity price movements were not particularly obvious, with the possible exception of a seasonal bulge in cash wheat prices. "The contribution of each component to the total variance in price... is in the vicinity of 1%." The authors present a random walk model that they say fits all commodity price change series very well.

Leuthold, Raymond M. "Random Walk and Price Trends: The Live Cattle Future Market." *Journal of Finance*, vol. 27, September 1972, pp. 879-889.

Filter rules of 1, 2, 3, 4, 5, and 10 percent were used to test mechanical trading results from 30 live cattle futures, ranging from the April 1965 contract to the February 1970 contract. Gross returns from all six filter rules were positive, but commissions threw net results from the 1 percent and the 5 percent filters into the minus column. Best results were obtained with the 3 percent filter (buy on a 3 percent price rise and sell short on a 3 percent price drop). Leuthold is careful to point out, however, that "no probabilistic statement can be given as to the chances of... any filter rule continuing to be profitable" over the years. Nevertheless, the results obtained "cast serious doubt that cattle futures prices behave randomly." Leuthold includes formulas, tables, footnotes, and a bibliography of 18 items.

Powers, Mark J. "Random Walk." In his *Getting Started in Commodity Futures Trading*, pp. 85-88. 1973.

The background of the random walk theory is briefly described. "... the random walk model is probably not descriptive of most commodities markets, although it is probably descriptive of some markets for selected periods of time." Reasons given for commodity prices not necessarily being random are: (1) Producers and consumers are active in commodity markets, in addition to the purely speculative element. (2) Both production and demand for many commodities are highly seasonal in nature. (3) Some commodity markets are relatively unknown and undeveloped.

Stevenson, Richard A., and Bear, Robert M. "Commodity Futures: Trends or Random Walks?" *Journal of Finance*, vol. 25, March 1970, pp. 65-81.

With regard to the random walk hypothesis, Stevenson and Bear claim their study casts "considerable doubt on the applicability of this hypothesis to the market for commodity futures." One and a half percent, 3 percent, and 5 percent filters were used by the authors in their tests of July corn and July soybeans from 1957 through 1968. The most profitable trading technique for both corn and soybeans was that of taking a position with the market whenever a price trend of 5 percent up or down occurred (buy if the market has moved up 5 percent; sell short if the market has moved down 5 percent). Trailing stop-loss orders were maintained at a distance of 5 percent. This simple filter technique produced profits in July corn seven years out of twelve and profits in July soybeans eight years out of twelve, after commission costs. The 3 percent filter produced mediocre results and the 1.5 percent filter consistently produced losses. Other trading techniques were also tested. Formulas, tables, footnotes, and a good bibliography (22 items) are provided.

Teweles, Richard J., and others. "The Behavior of Commodity Futures Prices." In their *The Commodity Futures Game*, pp. 75-105. 1974.

> The theory of the random walk is explained in detail, including an enlightening discussion of how price trends can exist without invalidating the theory. Some important studies of the random walk hypothesis, such as those by Seymour Smidt and Hendrik Houthakker, are described. Among the trading ideas tested were moving averages, negative correlation (buy when the price drops), positive correlation (buy when the price goes up), and stop orders. Test results were generally inconclusive, but it is pointed out that study of the random walk literature by commodity traders will at least disabuse them of any notion of making "easy money" in the futures markets. This is true, even though most speculators "feel they have 25 trading rules that will bring them riches beyond the dreams of avarice."

RESISTANCE LEVELS. See Support and Resistance Levels

REVERSAL CHARTS. See Point-and-Figure Charts

REVERSE CRUSH SPREAD. See Soybean Oil-Soybean Meal-Soybeans Spread

RISK FACTORS. See Losses; Money Management; Psychology; Trading Rules

RUBBER

In this case, the product obtained from the milky sap of the rubber tree—natural rubber. Inflation of synthetic rubber costs has resulted in a renewed interest in natural rubber in recent years. The countries that produce the natural product in greatest quantity are the Far Eastern nations of Malaysia, Indonesia, and Thailand. While inactive for a number of years, natural rubber futures contracts are now being traded on the New York Cocoa Exchange.

Figgis, T. S. E. "Rubber." In *Getting Started in London Commodities*, ed. by C. W. J. Granger, pp. 52-57. 1975.

> Production, consumption, and quality grades are discussed with reference to the British natural rubber market. Futures contract and trading information is given for the Rubber Trade Association of London, with the monthly range of cash rubber prices at London shown in chart form for the years 1966 to early 1975. The author mentions that, in earlier times (1918 to about 1930), rubber and cotton were probably the two most popular speculative commodities.

128 COMMODITY FUTURES TRADING

Radhakrishnan, P. "Understanding the Natural Rubber Market." In *Commodity Year Book 1975*, pp. 44–49. 1975.

> Renewed interest in natural rubber was shown by the introduction of new futures contracts in late 1974 and early 1975. Rising synthetic rubber prices have made natural rubber more competitive. Natural rubber prices, as a result, have become volatile, increasing the need for commercial interests to be able to resort to the futures market for price protection. Radhakrishnan presents a good discussion of how and where natural rubber is produced and marketed. Among the topics considered are supply and demand factors, competition between natural and synthetic rubbers, marketing, price influences, and the futures markets in the United States and in London. A chart shows the "Index of Seasonal Variation in Production in West Malaysia (Estates and Smallholdings)" for the 12 months of the year, with the index based on production figures from 1956 to 1967.

Watling, T. F., and Morley, J. "Rubber." In their *Successful Commodity Futures Trading*, pp. 163–167. 1974.

> Rubber production and supply-demand factors are briefly discussed. Futures trading details are given for the Rubber Trade Association of London.

RULES FOR TRADING. See Trading Rules

RYE (*See also* Rye—Seasonal Price Trend; Wheat-Rye Spread)
An important cereal grain in cooler climates that is often used to make a dark, heavy bread. Rye malt is used for rye whiskey and Holland gin. Rye grows well in relatively poor soils and is, therefore, often used as a cover crop. The leading rye-producing countries are Russia, Poland, Germany (East and West), and the United States, with the Dakotas being the leading states for rye. Futures contracts for this grain are traded on the Winnipeg Commodity Exchange.

Keltner, Chester W. "Fundamental Analysis Applied to Rye Situations." In his *How to Make Money in Commodities*, pp. 167–174. 1960.

> The fundamental price analyses of rye and wheat are similar in that both are cash crops (they are sold by farmers for cash and not retained for use as feed), just as the analyses of the feed grains corn and oats are similar. Keltner mentions that rye prices are highly volatile and very sensitive to any changes in crop prospects or supply and demand balance. This is because rye crops are relatively small and supply is usually closely matched to demand. The inherent volatility of rye prices tends to make any seasonal trend less apparent than in the other grains. Fundamental analysis for rye is more difficult than for other grains, and the timing of speculative positions assumes great importance.

Parker, George B. "Factors That Affect Rye Prices." In *Guide to Commodity Price Forecasting*, ed. by Harry Jiler and George B. Parker, pp. 144–152. 1965. (An earlier version of this article appears in the 1963 *Commodity Year Book*.)

Rye is said to have price movements that are erratic, volatile, and difficult to forecast. The volatile rye market is a result of small crops, small trading volume, and a preponderance of small speculators in the market. Production factors, utilization, relationship between cash and futures prices, and seasonal trends are considered. Charts included with this article show daily rye futures prices for the Chicago May delivery from 1954 to 1965.

Teweles, Richard J., and others. "Rye." In their *The Commodity Futures Game*, pp. 598–602. 1974.

Supply and demand factors are discussed. (Sources of information about rye are listed on page 594 of the Teweles book.) Rye is said to be primarily a European crop, with a thin Canadian market dominated by a few traders. Liquidation could therefore be difficult under adverse conditions.

RYE—SEASONAL PRICE TREND

Marketing of the rye crop each year normally begins in July. Low prices for the season typically occur in August, with highs the following February.

Commodity Research Bureau. "Seasonal Trends in Grain Futures Prices." In *Commodity Year Book 1952*, pp. 17–19. 1952.

A price advance in May rye occurred after September 20 in every season from 1935–1936 to 1950–1951. The advance ranged from 3¢ to 147¢, or from about 4 to 106 percent. A table shows "May Rye Futures Prices: 1935–1936 to 1950–1951, Chicago Board of Trade; Price Advance from September 20 Low to Subsequent High (Cents per Bushel)." A chart shows "Monthly Seasonal Trend in Marketing of Rye (in Percent of Total Marketings), 10 Year Monthly Average, 1941–1950." The monthly percentages shown in the chart are related to rye receipts at principal markets. Other charts show daily futures prices for May rye at Chicago from 1935 to 1952.

Keltner, Chester W. "Chicago December Rye—Seasonal Price Advances Following the July-August Low in Past Years." In his *How to Make Money in Commodities*, p. 170. 1960.

This is a table showing loan rate, July-August low price, September high price, October high, November high, December high, and extreme price advance for each year from 1940 to 1959.

RYE-WHEAT SPREAD. *See* Wheat-Rye Spread

130 COMMODITY FUTURES TRADING

SEASONAL PRICE TREND (*See also* individual commodities, such as Wheat—Seasonal Price Trend)
The movement of commodity prices caused by recurring seasonal factors, such as the downward movement that may take place right after the harvest of a crop. The seasonal trend is more likely to be of importance in the analysis of a commodity with a definite growing and harvesting pattern, such as soybeans, than in the study of a commodity with year-round production, such as eggs.

Angrist, Stanley W. "Seasonal Price Tendencies." In his *Sensible Speculating in Commodities*, p. 84–95. 1972.

>In the analysis of commodity prices from the viewpoint of fundamentals, Angrist states that, for most commodities, seasonal price patterns or trends are next in importance to supply-demand considerations. Experienced speculators do not go against seasonal expectations without having very good reasons for doing so. Of course, as the author points out, there are many times that seasonal trends are erratic, and not many people attempt to speculate in commodity futures solely on the basis of seasonal fluctuations. Angrist includes charts showing the price trend of July corn "when there are sufficient supplies available to the commercial market" and in the quite different situation "when there is a deficit of supplies available to the commercial market." With regard to wheat, "The Voice from the Tomb" seasonal method is described, and with reference to soybeans, past profits are shown that would have been obtained from buying May soybean futures on October 1 each year and selling on the following January 31. To illustrate this seasonal trend, charts of daily prices of May beans are included for the years 1961 to 1971. A table for 14 different commodities shows seasonal price tendencies in the form of high months and low months.

Commodity Research Bureau. "Seasonal Influences on Commodity Futures Prices." In *Commodity Year Book 1951*, pp. 11–17. 1951.

>Seasonal trends for cotton, cold storage eggs, oats, and soybeans are discussed. Tables give seasonal price changes for March cotton from 1935 to 1951, October cold storage eggs from 1932 to 1950, May oats from 1936 to 1950, and March or May soybeans from 1937 to 1950. Charts show daily futures prices for March cotton (1935–1951), October cold storage eggs (1936–1951), and May oats (1936–1951).

Commodity Research Bureau. "Seasonal Patterns in Marketing Farm Products." In *Commodity Year Book 1952*, pp. 23–25. 1952.

>Brief discussions are given of seasonal marketing patterns for cotton, cottonseed oil, soybeans, soybean oil, lard, cocoa, eggs, butter, and potatoes. Eleven small line charts show "Monthly Seasonal Trends in Marketings of Commodities (in Percent of Total Marketings), 10 Year Monthly Averages, 1941–50" for all of the commodities named above, plus coffee and "All Commodities" (a composite chart).

Commodity Research Bureau. "Seasonal Trends in Grain Futures Prices." In *Commodity Year Book 1952*, pp. 13–22. 1952.

> Price tables and price charts are presented for corn, oats, rye, and wheat from the 1930s to 1951. It is demonstrated that "grain futures prices have followed a highly consistent pattern at certain times of the year."

Fink, Robert, and Turner, Dennis. "Seasonal and Cyclical Studies." In *Commodity Year Book 1973*, pp. 27–29. 1973.

> Three methods of using time-series analysis to establish seasonal indexes are described. (1) In the average percentage method, "the price of each month is expressed as a percentage of the average price for the season" or number of seasons. (2) The link relative method measures the percentage move of prices in one month relative to the previous month. (3) The ratio to moving average method is used to reduce irregularities in seasonal indexes caused by excessive price moves.

Gould, Bruce G. "Seasonals and Odds." In his *Dow Jones-Irwin Guide to Commodities Trading*, pp. 255–280. 1973.

> A unique and helpful approach to seasonal trends. Gould tells how to figure the probability (odds) that a particular cash or futures price will rise or fall during a certain time of the year. His advice is to "expect the usual, and you will usually be right." The importance of cash prices is emphasized, and the futures trader is advised to always be aware of the seasonal pattern of the cash commodity. Charts show the cash seasonal trend of prices for eggs (1955–1967 average), potatoes (1961–1967), corn (1956–1967), soybean meal (1955–1967), soybeans (1960–1970), and pork bellies (1949–1968). In addition, the average monthly highs and average monthly lows for the September soybean futures contrast are charted based on the period 1961–1962 to 1970–1971. Thirteen pages of futures price statistics are reprinted from the Chicago Board of Trade's *Statistical Annual 1970*. In these tables, the monthly price ranges for various futures contracts are shown for the past ten years. In easy-to-understand, question-and-answer form, Gould takes the speculator through the specific steps necessary to determine cash odds and futures odds. Some general advice is given under the heading "A Word About Playing the Odds" (p. 267).

Keltner, Chester W. "Seasonal Price Tendency" and "Normal Seasonal Price Tendencies." In his *How to Make Money in Commodities*, pp. 123–124, 128–129. 1960.

> Short, general discussions of seasonal price changes. Keltner believes that commodity speculators should keep normal seasonal price tendencies in mind, even though other factors will often be dominant. He states that it is often wise to avoid being long during the period of normal seasonal weakness for a particular commodity and to avoid being short during the time of normal strength. The seasonal trends for wheat, oats, rye, corn, and soybeans are briefly described.

132 COMMODITY FUTURES TRADING

Merrill Lynch, Pierce, Fenner & Smith, Inc. "Basic Facts About Other Important Commodity Futures." In their *How to Buy and Sell Commodities*, pp. 36–37. 1972.

> A handy table showing, among other things, the "Normal Seasonal Price Pattern" for 26 individual commodities. High and low months are indicated in each case, with the exception of the metals, which have no discernible seasonal patterns. (Seasonal trends for wheat and soybeans are shown separately in full-page charts on pages 35 and 39 of the Merrill Lynch booklet.)

Shaw, John E. B. "Profiting from Cyclical Markets." In his *A Professional Guide to Commodity Speculation*, pp. 63–69. 1972.

> Specific methods of taking advantage of price cycles in hog futures and egg futures are discussed in some detail. A two-year cycle in hog prices and a six-month cycle in eggs are considered.

Shaw, John E. B. "Profiting from Seasonal Markets." In his *A Professional Guide to Commodity Speculation*, pp. 56–62. 1972.

> Seasonal commodities are described as those that are harvested once a year and used primarily during the following 12 months. Examples are the grains, cotton, and cocoa. Other commodities, such as pork bellies and eggs, are said to be cyclical rather than seasonal. Still others, such as the metals, are neither seasonal nor cyclical. Shaw provides a very interesting discussion, complete with tables, of how the speculator can attempt to profit from seasonal price trends in wheat, corn, and soybeans. A fascinating correlation between flaxseed and soybean prices is cited. Potatoes and orange juice are given as examples of commodities that have seasonal "crop scare" opportunities.

Teweles, Richard J., and others. "Seasonal Price Movements." In their *The Commodity Futures Game*, pp. 200–204. 1974.

> A table shows "Seasonal Patterns of Spot Commodity Prices" for 20 different commodities. High and low months are indicated. The advantages of following seasonal price trends are said to be that seasonal information may help in sizing up risks and that an analysis of seasonal patterns will at least result in a better informed speculator. Disadvantages are that seasonal tendencies are subject to change without notice, that known seasonal patterns tend to disappear as more and more traders try to take advantage of them, and that there is a big problem of interim risk when holding a commodity futures position for a seasonal move.

SELF-DISCIPLINE. See Money Management; Psychology; Trading Rules

SERVICES, ADVISORY. See Advisory Services

SHORT SELLING

The selling of commodity futures contracts without first buying the contracts. While short selling is fairly complicated in the stock market (stock must be borrowed by the broker, for example), the process in the futures market is merely the reverse of buying. Traders sell short, in most cases, as easily as they buy. Orders to brokers are entered simply as sell orders, whether the purpose is to actually be short the commodity or to cancel (offset) an existing long position.

Angrist, Stanely W. "He Who Sells What Isn't His'n Must Buy It Back or Go to Prison." In his *Sensible Speculating in Commodities*, pp. 53–56. 1972.

> Despite the title of this section of his book, Angrist emphasizes that successful commodity traders are just as willing to be short as long and often make money faster on the short side. The simplicity of short selling in the commodity markets is pointed out, as is the fact that professional speculators are likely to be short sellers in a weakening market while the speculating public stays long. Short selling eventually serves as a support for the market, when offsetting purchases are made.

Donnelly, Richard A. "Commodities Corner." *Barron's*, vol. 54, July 15, 1974, p. 32.

> Most individual speculators are described as "compulsive bulls," even though there is frequently a great deal of profit to be made in commodity futures by selling short. While short selling theoretically entails more risk than buying (there is no ceiling on rising prices), substantial gains can often be made quickly on the short side because of the tendency for inflated prices to fall more rapidly than they went up. Prices that took a full year or so to reach a peak may fall back to their starting points in a couple of months or even weeks. Stop-loss orders are recommended by Donnelly when short selling.

Keltner, Chester W. "How Short Sales Are Made." In his *How to Make Money in Commodities*, pp. 26–27. 1960.

> Emphasizes the simplicity of short selling in commodity futures markets.

Longstreet, Roy W. "Declining Commodity Markets." In his *Viewpoints of a Commodity Trader*, pp. 82–83. 1968.

> An extolling of the merits of bear markets. Longstreet says, "I like the short side of the market because there is less company." The professional commodity trader is much more likely to be a short seller than the amateur speculator.

SILVER

A precious metal used extensively in photography, electronics, fine tableware, and jewelry. In previous decades, much silver was also used in coinage. The main silver-producing countries are Canada, Peru, Russia, Mexico, and the United

States, with Idaho and Arizona being the principal silver-mining states. Futures contracts for silver bars are traded on the Chicago Board of Trade, the Commodity Exchange, Inc. (New York), the American Board of Trade, the Mid-America Commodity Exchange, and the London Metal Exchange. Silver coins are traded on the New York Mercantile Exchange.

Carabini, Louis E., ed. *Everything You Need to Know Now About Gold and Silver.* 1974.

> A collection of question-and-answer interviews published originally in Carabini's *Gold and Silver Newsletter* (Carabini is also president of the Pacific Coast Coin Exchange). The interviews are mainly on the subject of how gold and silver prices will be affected by inflation, depression, devaluation, and other monetary matters. The persons interviewed include Franz Pick, Thomas J. Holt, Murray N. Rothbard, Harry Browne, and others with favorable attitudes toward investing in precious metals. A good bibliography is included.

Chicago Board of Trade. "Silver . . ." In *Commodity Trading Manual,* pp. 193–196. 1973.

> Supply considerations, federal policies, demand factors, major uses, substitutable commodities, and futures markets are discussed. Silver futures trading details are listed for the Chicago Board of Trade, the Commodity Exchange, Inc., and the Mid-America Commodity Exchange. The following are given for each exchange: delivery months, trading units, minimum price fluctuations, daily price move limits, position limits, delivery standards, and trading hours.

Inkeles, David M. "Understanding the Silver Futures Market." In *Commodity Year Book 1970,* pp. 26–32. 1970.

> Inkeles begins with a good history and summary of legislation affecting silver prices from 1871 to 1969. The supply of silver, "the speculative hoard," the production deficit, and industrial consumption are all discussed. A table shows the silver content of old and new U.S. coins. Inkeles gives an interesting summary of ways to trade in silver outside the futures market, such as the buying of physical quantities of silver dust or silver bullion. Then the organized silver futures markets are described and speculation in futures is explained, with emphasis on carrying charges. Charts show daily futures prices for March silver at New York from 1965 to 1970. A short bibliography (nine items) is included.

Ryan, J. Patrick. "The Long Term Outlook for Silver." In *Commodity Year Book 1968,* pp. 43–49. 1968.

> Price escalation is predicted as U.S. Treasury stocks of silver near depletion. However, large physical supplies exist that will become available at higher prices. Supply-demand factors are discussed, and India is mentioned as the largest potential source of silver, although most silver in India is closely held by individuals.

Smyth, David, and Stuntz, Laurance F. "Silver—The Hoarder's Metal." In their *The Speculator's Handbook*, pp. 78–91. 1974.

> A general discussion of the advantages of owning silver, including silver bullion, silver coins, silver futures, and silver coin futures. There is also a brief consideration of a spread position utilizing silver futures versus silver coin futures. Margin requirements are indicated for all examples.

Teweles, Richard J., and others. "Silver." In their *The Commodity Futures Game*, pp. 491–498. 1974.

> High volatility and relatively high margin requirements are said to characterize the silver futures market. The authors comment upon factors influencing prices, nature of production, utilization, and seasonal trends (probably none). Silver information sources are given on page 513 of the Teweles book.

Turner, Dennis, and Blinn, Stephen H. *Trading Silver—Profitably*. 1975. 190 pp.

> Twenty computer-tested methods or systems for trading silver are discussed, ranging in past profitableness from very good to very bad. The test period was relatively limited, however, covering only the years from 1968 to 1972. The systems are ranked in various ways, with the most suitable trading methods for silver said to be ones utilizing a 25-day and 8-day combined moving average, as well as closing-price channel systems using 9-day, 13-day, or 21-day periods.

Watling, T. F., and Morley, J. "Silver." In their *Successful Commodity Futures Trading*, pp. 185–188. 1974.

> Silver usage, hoarding, and supply-demand factors are briefly discussed. Futures trading details are given for silver on the London Bullion Dealer Market.

SMALL TRADERS. See Amateur Speculation

SOYBEAN CONVERSION SPREAD. See Soybean Oil-Soybean Meal-Soybeans Spread

SOYBEAN MEAL (See also Soybean Oil-Soybean Meal-Soybeans Spread; Soybeans)

The nation's most important protein meal, used extensively as livestock feed. Soybean meal is made by toasting and pulverizing the flakes and hulls that are the by-products of crushing soybeans for oil. Soybean meal futures contracts are traded on the Chicago Board of Trade.

Chicago Board of Trade. "Oil and Meal Commodities." In *Commodity Trading Manual*, pp. 159–162. 1973.

> Seventeen specific uses (animal feed, human food, and industrial) for soybean meal are listed. Processing methods, gross processing margin, the

reverse crush pattern, and exports are discussed. Soybean meal futures trading details are given for the Chicago Board of Trade. Delivery months, trading units, price fluctuation specifications, daily price limits, position limits, delivery standards, and trading hours are given.

Hieronymus, Thomas A. "Forecasting Soybean Meal Futures Prices." In *Commodity Year Book 1961*, pp. 20–31. 1961.

A review of the fundamentals of soybean meal prices. The forecasting of meal prices is said to require two steps: (1) Basic supply-demand factors must be analyzed to arrive at an estimate of average price for the season. (2) Seasonal variation for the particular year in question must be estimated. ". . . the contest is between the forecaster and the market." Exports, livestock production, and livestock prices are discussed as important influences on soybean meal prices. A multiple correlation analysis is given of prices from 1947–1948 to 1959–1960, with forecast errors included. Biggest misses occurred during the Korean War. Hieronymus points out that, while there are specific seasonal variations during individual years, meal prices are devoid of a regular seasonal pattern. Speculative discounting has eliminated the seasonal pattern that once existed. The relationship between soybean meal futures prices and cash prices is discussed at some length.

Hieronymus, Thomas A. "Forecasting Soybean Meal Prices." In *Guide to Commodity Price Forecasting*, ed. by Harry Jiler and George B. Parker, pp. 161–165, and 173–174. 1965.

Among the topics discussed are total supplies of soybean meal, domestic supplies, uses of soybean meal, the trend in demand for meal, and price analysis. Tables show "Supplies of High Protein Feeds Available for Feeding" from 1953 to 1963 and "Use of Soybean Meal by Various Kinds of Livestock, 1947–58, 1,000 Tons and Percent to Each." Charts show daily soybean meal futures prices for the July delivery from 1954 to 1965.

Houck, James P., and others. *Soybeans and Their Products.* 1972. 284 pp.

A complex econometric study of U.S. and world markets for soybeans, soybean oil, and soybean meal. Futures trading is mentioned only in passing. Part one, "The Markets," is worthwhile background reading for anyone who is interested in the total soybean situation.

Shane, Arthur F. "Price Characteristics of Soybean Meal Futures." In *Commodity Year Book 1967*, pp. 28–34. 1967.

States that soybean meal, like soybeans, is noted "for consistency of wide and sustained price movement." Sizable price swings have taken place in the soybean meal market every year since trading began on the Chicago Board of Trade in 1951. Six factors are explained as being responsible for the large price movements in soybean meal: (1) surpluses do not build up because demand keeps up with supply; (2) growth in the use of meal as a high protein animal feed; (3) relative inelasticity of demand; (4) soybean meal cannot be stored for long periods of time; (5) meal is manufactured and therefore not eligible for government price supports; (6) soybean crop scares influence meal prices. Seasonal price movements of soybean meal are discussed, with the point being made that meal futures prices often advance from late summer to the middle of winter. A table shows "March Soybean Meal—Net Change from Sept. 5 to Feb. 5 (Dollars per Ton)," for the 16 seasons from 1951-1952 to 1966-1967. The net change was positive in twelve seasons and negative in four. The reasons for the four negative changes are explained by Shane. It is also pointed out that soybean meal futures have a tendency to have price advances in late spring. A second table shows "July Soybean Meal—Net Change from May 1 to July 1," from 1956-1957 to 1965-1966. There were six gains and four losses, with a tendency for the losses to occur "when the July delivery has already undergone an uninterrupted rise of major proportion. . . ." Shane concludes by saying that the market growth prospects for soybean meal are definitely favorable. (Daily basis price charts with this article show March soybean meal futures from 1951-1952 to 1966-1967 and July futures from 1956-1957 to 1965-1966.)

Teweles, Richard J., and others. "Soybeans, Soybean Oil, and Soybean Meal." In their *The Commodity Futures Game*, pp. 349-354. 1974.

Supply, demand, exports, and the domestic market are discussed. The demand for soybean meal is said to be elastic relative to price: price has a big effect on how much is bought by end users. Price changes for soybean meal may be easier to forecast than for soybean oil. A graph (on page 359 of the Teweles book) shows "Soybean meal: monthly open interest and volume as a percentage of average monthly open interest and volume for the years 1962-1971 at the Chicago Board of Trade" (page 359).

SOYBEAN MEAL—SOYBEAN OIL-SOYBEANS SPREAD. See Soybean Oil-Soybean Meal-Soybeans Spread

SOYBEAN MEAL SPREAD

Usually, the buying of July soybean meal with the simultaneous selling short of September soybean meal. Because of seasonal strength, the July contract has a tendency to gain in price relative to the September contract from about March to expiration in July.

Angrist, Stanley W. "Intracommodity Spreads." In his *Sensible Speculating in Commodities*, pp. 164-165. 1972.

Mentions that the margin requirement for going long (buying) one contract of July soybean meal at the same time as selling short one contract of September soybean meal ranges from about $100 to $250, depending on the broker. Specialized commodity brokers are said to offer lower margin requirements for spreads than stock brokers having commodities as a sideline. Angrist believes that the soybean meal spread is more suitable (less risky) than some others for the beginning commodity speculator.

SOYBEAN OIL (See also Soybean Oil-Soybean Meal-Soybeans Spread; Soybeans) The most important vegetable oil in the United States, used not only in edible products (the principal use) but also in the manufacture of paint, soap, printing ink, and other items. Crushed soybeans yield about 20 percent of their weight in oil. Soybean oil futures contracts are traded on the Chicago Board of Trade.

Chicago Board of Trade. "Oil and Meal Commodities." In *Commodity Trading Manual*, pp. 159–162. 1973.

> Twenty specific uses for soybean oil (both food and nonfood) are listed. Processing methods, gross processing margin, the reverse crush pattern, and exports are considered. Soybean oil futures trading details are given for the Chicago Board of Trade. Delivery months, trading units, price fluctuation specifications, daily price limits, position limits, delivery standards, and trading hours are listed.

Emery, Walter L. "Understanding the Soybean Oil Market." In *Commodity Year Book 1974*, pp. 16–21. 1974.

> As soybean meal is relatively more valuable than soybean oil, and as both products are produced when soybeans are crushed, the demand for soybean meal has a great influence on soybean oil supplies and prices. Emery discusses the domestic market for soybean oil, interchangeability among fats and oils, import threats (mainly palm oil from Malaysia and Indonesia), crushing margins, exports, and the importance of concessional sales through Public Law 480 to less developed countries. Daily basis price charts of May soybean oil futures at Chicago are shown from 1969 to 1974.

Hieronymus, Thomas A. "Forecasting Soybean Oil Prices." In *Guide to Commodity Price Forecasting*, ed. by Harry Jiler and George B. Parker, pp. 156–161, 171–172. 1965.

> Domestic supply and use, fats and oils exports, the world fats and oils market, and the price of oil are all considered in this forecasting summary. Two large tables show "Beginning Stocks, Production, Exports, Domestic Disappearance, and Ending Stocks, Principal United States Food Fat and Oils, Crop Years 1956–62, Millions of Pounds" and "World Production, Exports, and Retained Consumption, Principal Edible Fats and Oils (Fat Content), Thousands of Short Tons, 1956–63." Charts show daily soybean oil futures prices for the July delivery from 1954 to 1965.

Houck, James P., and others. *Soybeans and Their Products*. 1972. 284 pp.

> A complex econometric study of U.S. and world markets for soybeans, soybean oil, and soybean meal. Futures trading is mentioned only in passing. Part one, "The Markets," is worthwhile background reading for anyone who is interested in the total soybean situation.

Teweles, Richard J., and others. "Soybeans, Soybean Oil, and Soybean Meal." In their *The Commodity Futures Game*, pp. 347–348, 353–359. 1974.

> Describes the domestic soybean oil market, as well as soybean oil exports. The "incredibly complex world market" is said to be the main determinant of the price of fats and oils. Soybean processors' profit margins are discussed. A graph shows "Soybean oil: monthly open interest and volume as a percentage of average monthly open interest and volume for the years 1962–1971 at the Chicago Board of Trade."

Watling, T. F., and Morley, J. "Soybean Oil." In their *Successful Commodity Futures Trading*, pp. 189–191. 1974.

> After a short general discussion of soyabean, or soybean, oil, futures trading details are given for the London Vegetable Oil Terminal Market Association.

SOYBEAN OIL-SOYBEAN MEAL-SOYBEANS SPREAD

The buying of soybean products (meal and oil) with the simultaneous selling short of soybeans themselves, if one believes that the products are underpriced relative to the basic crop. This is called a reverse crush spread because it is the reverse of what soybean processors usually do (buy soybeans for processing and sell oil and meal). Of course, the speculator can also buy soybeans and sell oil and meal short as a spread position if he believes that the products are overpriced relative to beans. The soybean product represented by one futures contract for oil (60,000 pounds) plus one contract for meal (100 tons) is reasonably close to the actual amounts that can be processed from the 5,000 bushels of beans covered by one contract. Therefore, a typical reverse crush spread involves one meal contract plus one oil contract bought and one soybeans contract sold short.

Angrist, Stanley W. "Intercommodity Spreads." In his *Sensible Speculating in Commodities*, pp. 161–162. 1972.

> States that the margin requirement for going long (buying) one contract of soybean meal and one contract of soybean oil at the same time as selling short one contract of soybeans is about $1,000. Angrist says that the soybean products spread is one of the most popular intercommodity spreads, and he describes the arithmetic of the "gross processing margin," a vital factor in this commodity operation.

Belveal, L. Dee. "Inter-Commodity Spreads." In his *Commodity Speculation with Profits in Mind*, pp. 232–234. 1967.

> The equation is given that shows the normal value relationship between soybeans and soybean products (oil and meal). The speculator who is interested in a spreading or arbitrage operation can use this equation to determine if soybeans are overpriced or underpriced relative to oil and meal. If soybeans appeared to be overpriced, a reverse crush spread would be assumed, in which soybeans are sold short at the same time that a combination of oil and meal is bought. If soybeans are apparently under-

priced, a crush spread (no reverse) might be assumed, in which oil and meal are sold short at the same time that beans are bought. Belveal says that these spreads have provided attractive profit opportunities in the past.

Chicago Board of Trade. "Putting on the Crush" and "Reverse Crush Spread." In *Commodity Trading Manual*, pp. 121–123. 1973.

A good, general discussion of "putting on the crush," in which soybean processors take a hedge position to protect gross processing margin (GPM) against price fluctuation within the soybean complex. If the GPM really deteriorates, the processors will reduce operations and resort to the reverse crush spread to put pressure on soybean prices relative to oil and meal prices. (Further on in the Board of Trade's manual, pages 160–161, there is a clear explanation of the soybean industry's gross processing margin, with an example of how it is computed.)

Hieronymus, Thomas A. "Soybean Processors." In his *Economics of Futures Trading*, pp. 224–230. 1971.

Any speculator interested in the soybean products spread should read Hieronymus' illuminating account of how things are from the point of view of the soybean processors (those who convert soybeans into oil and meal). The processing margin of profit is discussed at some length. Processors are said to be "continuously matching wits with merchants, product buyers, and with the market."

Kallard, Thomas. "Raw Materials vs. Product Spreads." In his *Make Money in Commodity Spreads!*, pp. 17–23. 1974.

The conversion or crush spread and the reverse conversion spread are discussed separately. Kallard states that variations in the cost of crushing make acceptable processing margins difficult to determine, although there is some agreement that processors must have a margin of from 20¢ to 25¢ per bushel of soybeans in order to show a profit. When the value of soybeans rises above the combined value of soybean oil and meal (per bushel of soybeans), processors tend to sell soybeans and buy oil and meal, thus engaging in a reverse conversion or reverse crush spread. Kallard explains the circumstances that are favorable for speculating in reverse spreads. He regards the January contracts as the most dependable for spreading, and presents a line chart showing "January Soybeans vs. Meal and Oil" for each year from 1967 to 1975. Also included is a point-and-figure chart showing January 1974 soybeans versus soybean meal and oil.

McHale, James E. "Spreads Between Prices of Soybeans and Soybean Meal and Oil." In *Guide to Commodity Price Forecasting*, ed. by Harry Jiler and George B. Parker, pp. 235–249. 1965. (An earlier version of this article appears in the 1963 *Commodity Year Book*.)

A comprehensive discussion of the relationship between the price of soybeans and the price of soybean end products (oil and meal). The "cents-per-bushel-margin" method and the "contract-dollar-difference" method of calculating board conversion spread differences are described. The difficult problem of deciding when to put on or take off a soybean products spread is considered. Influences on this particular spreading operation are classified as external factors, seasonal influences, internal factors, and crush yields. Charts show daily premiums of soybean meal and oil over soybeans at Chicago from 1957 to 1962. There are separate groups of charts for these years for four delivery months: January, March, July, and September. McHale includes "Observations on Trends That Are Depicted on Futures Spread Charts."

Shaw, John E. B. "How to Use Conversion and Substitution." In his *A Professional Guide to Commodity Speculation*, pp. 81–86. 1972.

>The soybean reverse conversion spread (buy oil and meal, sell beans) is examined in detail. Some reasons why the spread may not work out profitably are given.

Teweles, Richard J., and others. "The Reverse Crush Spread." In their *The Commodity Futures Game*, pp. 354–355. 1974.

>Some factors influencing the crushing margin (processors' gross margin of profit) are discussed in relation to the reverse crush spread.

SOYBEAN PRODUCTS SPREAD. See Soybean Oil-Soybean Meal-Soybeans Spread

SOYBEANS (See also Soybean Meal; Soybean Oil; Soybeans—Seasonal Price Trend)
America's leading source of vegetable oil and livestock feed protein; a member of the pea, peanut, and bean family (Leguminosae). Soybeans are crushed or processed to obtain the two soybean products, oil and meal. The main soybean-producing states are Illinois, Iowa, Indiana, Arkansas, Missouri, and Minnesota, with planting taking place in the spring and harvesting in the fall. In futures trading, soybeans are often loosely classified as one of the "grains," along with wheat, corn, oats, and rye. Soybean futures are very actively traded on the Chicago Board of Trade, and are noted for wide price fluctuations.

Arthur, Henry B. "The Soybean Complex." In his *Commodity Futures as a Business Management Tool*, pp. 180–210. 1971.

>General description of the soybean and soybean product market, with the emphasis on commercial hedging rather than speculation. Special attention is given to soybean growers, crushers, and dealers. The hedging operations of Central Soya Co., Archer Daniels Midland Co., and Swift & Co., are described in detail.

Chicago Board of Trade, "The Soybean Complex." In *Commodity Trading Manual*, pp. 157–163. 1973.

>A brief history of the soybean industry is given, followed by discussions of production, carryover, federal programs, demand factors (50 uses are listed

for soybeans and soybean products), processing, and exports. Soybean futures trading details are given for the Chicago Board of Trade and the Mid-america Commodity Exchange (formerly the Chicago Open Board of Trade). Delivery months, trading units, price fluctuation specifications, daily price limits, position limits, delivery standards, and trading hours are summarized for each exchange.

Cramer, Scott E. "How to Analyze the Soybean Futures Complex." In *Commodity Year Book 1973*, pp. 16-23. 1973.

Soybean production grew from 5 million bushels in 1925 to over 1,200 million bushels in 1972, with 1,800 million bushels projected as a minimum for 1980. This growth is occurring because soybean meal and soybean oil are high quality products in great demand. Volume of trading in soybean futures at Chicago increased about 300 percent from 1967 to 1972. After discussing the phenomenal growth in soybean production and trading, Cramer devotes the major part of his article to a consideration of the advantage that hedging has for soybean processors. The concept of processing margin (gross profit margin for soybean crushers) is explained, as is futures "board conversion" (the relationship between the price of soybeans and the equivalent, combined value of soybean oil meal). Nine important market factors are listed for soybeans, 15 for soybean meal, and 10 for soybean oil. A special chart shows "January Soybeans vs. Combined Value of January Soybean Oil and Soybean Meal on a Bushel Basis" daily for the period 1970-1973 (also labeled "Premium of Soybean Meal and Soybean Oil Over Soybeans"). Other charts show daily futures prices for March soybeans, soybean oil, and soybean meal at Chicago from 1968 to 1973. Also charted on a weekly basis is the "Spread Between Cash Soybeans and January Soybean Futures," August-September, 1969-1973.

Emery, Walter L. "How to Analyze the Soybean Futures Market." In *Commodity Year Book 1971*, pp. 21-29. 1971.

Covers the fundamentals of the soybean futures market, including general characteristics of the commodity, export factors, general price influences, supply and demand factors, seasonal characteristics, conversion spread factors, and crushing margins. A comprehensive "Check List of Important Statistical Data" is arranged according to whether statistics are issued daily, weekly, monthly, quarterly, or yearly. Charts show daily futures prices at Chicago for May soybeans from 1960 to 1971.

Goldberg, Ray A. *The Soybean Industry*. 1952. 186 pp.

Even though Goldberg's volume is over 20 years old, it may still be of interest to commodity traders who wish to learn as much as possible about soybeans and the soybean crushing industry, including historical background. Production, utilization, and processing are covered in detail, but futures trading as such is not discussed. Tables in an appendix provide soybean acreage, yield, and production statistics for the years 1924 through

1950. Soybean oil production, trade, and stocks are shown in tabular form, 1910 through 1950. An extensive bibliography is included.

Goldberg, Ray A. "Soybeans." In his *Agribusiness Coordination*, pp. 101-145. 1968.

> A scholarly look at the fundamentals of the soybean market, in three parts: "The Dynamics of the Soybean System" (utilization, exports, processing, marketing), "The Structure of the Soybean System" (farms, processing firms, the futures market, government activities), and "Behavioral and Performance Patterns in the Soybean Economy" (storage, consumption, price stability). Goldberg's book features a systems approach to the soybean complex.

Hieronymus, Thomas A. "Forecasting Soybean and Soybean Product Prices." In *Guide to Commodity Price Forecasting*, ed. by Harry Jiler and George B. Parker, pp. 153-174. 1965. (An earlier version of this article appears in the 1961 *Commodity Year Book*.)

> The price of soybeans is said to depend on the value of soybean oil and soybean meal. Estimates of soybean prices can be computed from forecasts of oil and meal prices. Hieronymus discusses the supply of soybeans for processing soybean exports, forecasting the price of soybean oil, forecasting the price of meal, forecasting soybean prices, and the relationship between cash and futures prices. Charts show daily soybean futures prices for the July delivery from 1954 to 1965. Daily soybean oil and soybean meal futures prices are shown for the same period.

Houck, James P., and others. *Soybeans and Their Products*. 1972. 284 pp.

> Most of this is the report of a complex econometric study of the total soybean market from 1946 to 1967, with speculation in futures mentioned only in passing. However, serious-minded soybean traders will find part one ("The Markets") to be a valuable review of the general characteristics of U.S. and world markets for soybeans and soybean products.

Keltner, Chester W. "Fundamental Analysis Applied to Soybean Situations." In his *How to Make Money in Commodities*, pp. 175-181. 1960.

> States that there had been no sizable surplus accumulation of soybeans in the United States despite an increase in the annual crop from 187 million bushels in 1947-1948 to 538 million bushels in 1959-1960. Because scarcity was the dominant market factor, soybeans "acquired a reputation for being extremely volatile and . . . staging almost unbelievable bull moves." This situation was expected by Keltner to continue. He explains the relationship of soybean prices to demand for soybean products (oil and meal) and tells about processing margins and seasonal price tendencies. Tables show soybean supplies, disappearance, free surplus, impoundings, Chicago loan rate, and seasonal price advances for each crop year from 1947-1948 to 1959-1960. (Daily price charts of Chicago May soybeans from 1950-1951 to 1959-1960 are shown separately on pages 210 to 217 of Keltner's book.)

Lowell, Fred R. *Profits in Soybeans.* 1966. 316 pp.

> Section one of Lowell's book contains a detailed discussion of each soybean marketing season from 1950–1951 to 1965–1966. Section two consists of 48 statistical tables concerning soybeans, with an explanation and discussion of each table. The tables cover the years 1950 to 1965. In Section three, Lowell presents a group of price charts showing daily prices for May, July, and November soybean futures contracts from 1950 to 1966. Studying Lowell's presentations and comments is a good way for soybean speculators to learn about factors that have been important price influences.

Teweles, Richard J., and others. "Soybeans, Soybean Oil, and Soybean Meal." In their *The Commodity Futures Game,* pp. 337–346, 355–359. 1974.

> These subjects are covered: factors influencing prices, information sources, supply, demand, exports, and seasonal tendencies. Graphs show "May soybeans, seasonal: monthly midrange price of May soybeans as a percentage of average yearly price" and "Soybeans: monthly open interest and volume as a percentage of average monthly open interest and volume for the years 1962–1971 at the Chicago Board of Trade." In "Notes from a Trader" (pp. 355–359), the authors observe that soybeans are especially responsive to weather during the late summer and that the one "moment of truth" in the soybean market may be the report of January 1 stocks in all positions.

SOYBEANS—SEASONAL PRICE TREND

Marketing of new soybeans normally begins in September. Low prices for the season typically occur in October, with highs the following May.

Commodity Research Bureau. "Seasonal Influences on Commodity Futures Prices." In *Commodity Year Book 1951,* pp. 16–17. 1951.

> "Trading in soybean futures began in 1936, was discontinued during some of the war and postwar years and resumed in 1947." Soybean prices are said to have a pronounced tendency to advance each season after October 15. A table shows "Soybean Futures Prices—1936–37 to 1949–50, Price Advances from October 15 Low to November–January High." March or May deliveries are quoted.

Lowell, Fred R. "A Season by Season Review of Past Soybean Situations." In his *Profits in Soybeans,* pp. 7–133. 1966.

> Several pages of discussion are devoted to each of the soybean seasons (October of one year to September of the next) from 1950–1951 to 1965–1966. Headlines at the beginning of each season's review summarize what happened during that crop year, such as "Acute Shortage and a Phenomenal Bull Move" (1953–54) or "Excessive Supply and a Narrow Market" (1957–58). Accompanying each season's discussion is a chart showing total trading volume at Chicago on a daily basis, total open interest on a daily basis, and daily prices for the July and November futures contracts. The

Chicago equivalent soybean loan rate (farm loan plus 20¢) is also indicated for each year. Further data on soybean seasonal tendencies are given in 48 statistical tables, such as the one on page 164 of Lowell's book, covering 1950 to 1965, and showing "Season's Highs and Lows for Chicago May, July, and November Futures Contracts; Also Months in Which Highs and Lows Were Established."

Teweles, Richard J., and others. "Seasonal Information and Carrying Charges." In their *The Commodity Futures Game*, pp. 355–357. 1974.

The statement is made that speculative activity has virtually eliminated the seasonal characteristics of soybean prices, except for carrying charges. The same is said to be true for other well-developed markets. This lack of seasonable price trend in soybeans is illustrated by means of a chart showing the monthly midrange price (average of monthly high and low) as a percent of the average yearly price for May soybeans, with a separate chart line for each year from 1961 to 1973, June to May. The random movements of the lines are apparent, although there are a couple of years (1961 and 1973) with exceptional price trends. The same information is also given in a table.

SOYBEANS SPREAD (See also Soybean Oil-Soybean Meal-Soybeans Spread)

Typically, the simultaneous buying of July soybean futures and selling short of September soybean futures in an attempt to profit from the alleged tendency of the July contract to gain on September toward the end of the soybean marketing season.

Anderson, Hilding. "Soybean July-September Futures Price Spread." In *Guide to Commodity Price Forecasting*, ed. by Harry Jiler and George B. Parker, pp. 230–234. 1965. (An earlier version of this article appears in the 1964 *Commodity Year Book*.)

"The trend of the July-September soybean straddle seems to depend upon whether or not a short supply is in prospect." Anderson provides an interesting discussion of the pattern of soybean prices in seasons of short supply and also in seasons of medium to large supply. Charts show the daily spread of July soybeans over September at Chicago from 1953 to 1964.

Greenberg, Stephen. "July-September Soybean Spread." In *Guide to Commodity Price Forecasting*, ed. by Harry Jiler and George B. Parker, pp. 223, 226–227. 1965. (An earlier version of this article appears in the 1960 *Commodity Year Book*.)

July soybeans are said to have shown a reasonably consistent tendency to gain in relative price over September soybeans during winter or early spring. This relative gain has been caused by the rapid growth of the soybean industry and the resulting fear of processors of being short of supplies as the marketing year draws to a close. A table shows "Premium of July Over September (cents per bu.)—Gains from March 31 to Widest Point

146   COMMODITY FUTURES TRADING

Reached in Following 3 Months." Charts show the daily spread of July soybeans over September at Chicago from 1956 to 1964.

SPECULATION BY AMATEURS. See Amateur Speculation

SPOT COMMODITY. See Cash Commodity

SPREADS (See *also* names of individual spreads, such as Wheat-Corn Spread)

Trading positions in which the commodity speculator is deliberately long (bought) and short (sold short) at the same time, the plan being to profit from a change in the difference or spread between the prices of the different contracts involved. While the prices of the long and short contracts may move in the same direction, the trader hopes that his long position, for example, will move up at a faster rate or fall at a slower rate than his short position. Spreads may be set up between different delivery months of the same commodity or between different commodities. However, a spread implies that the differing commodities are related, as in the fact that oats and corn are both used as feed. Intracommodity spreads are between different months of the same commodity, intercommodity spreads are between different but related commodities, intramarket spreads are between commodities traded on the same exchange, and intermarket spreads are between commodities traded on different exchanges.

Angrist, Stanley W. "Spreads." In his *Sensible Speculating in Commodities*, pp. 155–173. 1972.

>In this chapter on spreads, the author is careful to point out that commodity speculators can often lose money just about as fast in spread positions as by being simply long or short. However, as he mentions, some spreads do reduce risk (and profits—the other side of the coin), along with having the undeniable appeal of greatly reduced margin requirements. The example used by Angrist quotes the margin requirement on one soybean contract as $750, while a soybean spread would only require from $150 to $350, depending on the individual broker. Herein lies a paradox. At the same time that the speculator is theoretically reducing his risk by spreading, he is sorely tempted by extremely low margin requirements to overtrade (too many contracts) and thus greatly *increase* his personal risk. Angrist discusses various kinds of intracommodity, intercommodity, and intermarket spreads, with special attention being given to the intercommodity spreads of soybean oil-soybean meal, wheat-corn, and oats-corn and the intermarket spread of Kansas City wheat-Chicago wheat. Charts and tables are used to illustrate. In his conclusion, the author stresses the importance of not overtrading, always using stop-loss orders, and never using a spread to attempt to bail out of a losing long or short position. "When Not to Spread" is considered at some length.

Belveal, L. Dee. "Speculation in Price Relationships." In his *Commodity Speculation with Profits in Mind*, pp. 225–236. 1967.

    Spreads in both normal and inverted markets are discussed. The soybean product "reverse-crush spread" and "crush spread" are explained as examples of intercommodity spreads. Belveal points out that, "The opportunities for spreading are limited by little except the ingenuity of the trader." He warns that, although spreads usually are less risky than straight trades, this is not always the case, and spreading opportunities should be approached with caution.

Chicago Board of Trade. "Spreading in Commodity markets." In *Commodity Trading Manual*, pp. 113–124. 1973.

    The four major types of spreads are described: interdelivery (intracommodity), intermarket, intercommodity, and commodity versus product. Detailed illustrations are given of the intracommodity spread in both carrying charge ("normal") markets and inverted markets. Spreads involving soybeans versus soybean products are used as examples of commodity product spreads. In the hedging spread known as "putting on the crush," the soybean processor buys soybean futures and sells soybean oil and meal futures, thus protecting his gross processing margin (GPM). The "reverse crush spread" is the opposite position to "putting on the crush," and is used when soybean prices are too high relative to oil and meal. The Board of Trade concludes that, "Although spreading offers attractive leverage, it is a sophisticated technique and is not recommended for the beginning commodity trader." Successful spreading is said to require careful analysis of supply and demand factors within a historical and seasonal context.

Commodity Research Bureau. "Commodity Spreads and Straddles." In *Commodity Year Book 1948*, pp. 38–48. 1948.

    A well-thought-out spread can bring a reduction in risk to the commodity speculator. After a general discussion of spreads, this article proceeds to a detailed consideration of the July-October cotton spread, the cottonseed oil-lard spread (obsolete), the May-June wheat spread, and the July-September wheat spread. "Seasonal Factors in Wheat Spreads" are discussed.

Clifton, Frederick T. "Carrying Charge Spreads and Premium Spreads in Commodity Futures." In *Commodity Year Book 1966*, pp. 38–47. 1966.

    A warning that "traditional" spread positions based on carrying charges are not always of low risk. These traditional spreads, on the occasions that they are available, are not as suitable for inexperienced commodity speculators as is commonly believed. That is, such spreads are often "agonizingly slow in realization," Clifton says, tempting the neophyte to take impetuous action out of frustration. (Impetuousness in the commodity futures markets invariably results in loss.) Clifton tells how to operate with negative, discount, carrying charge, bear market spreads and also with positive, premium, bull market spreads. That is, in bull markets the near futures sell at a premium over distant futures, while in bear markets, the carrying charge factor results in near futures selling at a discount. This article states, however, that the small speculator may be better off simply to take outright positions and avoid spreads because the prospective gains relative to available margin capital are often greater in straight trades. This is often true, despite lower margin requirements for spreads. Clifton examines some of the more popular spreads: March-May wheat, May-July soybeans, and July-September corn.

Clifton, Frederick T. "Intercrop Grain and Soybean Spreads." In *Commodity Year Book 1965*, pp. 6–18. 1965.

Intercrop spreads utilize the "differences between one crop and the next crop of the same grain or oilseed." One crop may be in its marketing period, while the other may not even be planted. (July 1, incidentally, is set somewhat arbitrarily as the beginning date of the crop year or marketing season for wheat, oats, and rye, while October 1 is used as the starting date for corn and soybeans.) Clifton presents a handy "Schematic of Simultaneous Futures Trading Periods: Intercrop Spreads (Approximate Dates)." The schematic shows the periods of time that old-new crop combinations may be used for spreads. Then demand factors for the nearer half of grain spread times, beginning late summer or fall, are discussed, as are supply factors for the latter half of spread periods, ending in May. Particular attention is given to the May-July wheat spreads, July-December corn spreads, May-July oats, May-July rye, and July-November soybeans. Five pages of price charts on a daily basis show all of these spreads from 1956 to 1964. Clifton's final word is that spreads can on occasion be as dangerous as outright long or short positions. Therefore, "a sensible trading plan is necessary."

Clifton, Frederick T. "Old and New Factors in Popular Commodity Spreads." In *Commodity Year Book 1973*, pp. 41–47. 1973.

Traditional spread patterns have been broken by recent dynamic price moves in commodity futures, but new opportunities for "sophisticated" spreads have arisen. Clifton says that his aim is "to define and enumerate, in depth, fundamental and 'technical' forces operating in active and interesting spreads." He gives an excellent summary of general spreading principles and techniques. Wise money (margin) management, correct timing, and use of a sensible trading plan are emphasized. Overtrading and not cutting losses are the cardinal sins; letting profits run is the principal virtue. Clifton lists 22 different types of spreads or spread concepts and defines 17 colloquial terms, such as "dead leg" spreads, "straddle-up" spreads, and "suicide" spreads. Examples of initial capital requirements are given for 14 spread situations, with the amounts ranging from $200 to $2,000. Finally, there are brief but informative discussions of over a dozen specific spreads, such as September-November soybeans, May-July wheat, and July-December corn. Clifton's article is above average in its usefulness to the small speculator.

Clifton, Frederick T. "Trading the Dynamic Futures Spreads." In *Commodity Year Book 1972*, pp. 36–42. 1972.

The "dynamic" futures spreads are said to be such trades as frozen pork bellies versus live hogs or one month of frozen concentrated orange juice versus another month. These spreads or others of the "dynamic" variety are said to often offer better speculative opportunities than the "classic" spreads, such as wheat versus corn or the soybean products spread. In any event, much of Clifton's article is devoted to some very good, sensible advice on strategy and money management for speculators interested in spread positions. In view of low margin requirements for spreads, over-trading is especially to be avoided. The charts provided in this article show the "Premium of May Pork Bellies Over June Hog Futures" from 1968 to 1972, the premium of "Old Crop July Soybean Futures Over New Crop November Soybeans" from 1968 to 1972, and "Orange Juice—January Over/Under November" from 1967 to 1972. These are line charts on a weekly basis.

Dobson, Edward D. *Commodity Spreads: A Historical Chart Perspective*. 1975. 78 pp.

Sixty-seven different commodity spreads are charted here, covering 16 major commodities from 1965 through 1974. Most of the spreads involve different months of a single commodity (intracommodity) in a single market (intramarket), although Chicago wheat versus Kansas City is included, as well as the popular soybean product intercommodity spreads. A good bibliography covering all aspects of commodity spreads and a glossary are included.

Gardner, Robert L. "Spreads and Straddles." In his *How to Make Money in the Commodity Market*, pp. 170–172. 1961.

Concentrates on limited-risk spreads in normal markets wherein near months of a particular commodity are bought and distant months are sold short. The risk is limited because the carrying charge factor will limit the premium of the distant months over the near months. So far as potential profit is concerned, there is no limit to the premium of a near month over a distant month. The catch is that everyone is aware of this situation; when demand for commodities is strong, normal markets become inverted, thereby increasing the possible loss from spread positions. Gardner states, "though in theory a successful straddle can bring unlimited profits . . . changes in prices between delivery months are rarely spectacular or rapid."

Gold, Gerald, "Premiums and Discounts." In his *Modern Commodity Futures Trading*, 6th ed., pp. 28–34. 1971.

A very good, clear explanation of why different delivery months of a particular commodity have varying prices. So-called "normal markets" and "inverted markets" are discussed. Premiums or discounts on distant delivery months are said to depend on various factors, such as available supply, traders' opinions of future price movements, and carrying costs. Speaking of selling near months at big premiums and buying distant months (a spread position in an inverted market), Gold says, "There is no point at which the speculator or general trader can enter the market with an automatic profit possibility." In other words, there is always the possibility of a big premium on a nearby month becoming even bigger.

Gold, Gerald. "Spreads and Straddles—A Method of Commodity Speculation." In his *Modern Commodity Futures Trading*, 6th ed., pp. 227–236. 1971.

"The Limited Risk Spread" is discussed, in which the nearer month of a particular commodity is bought at a discount at the same time that the more distant month is sold at a premium. Risk is limited by the carrying charge factor, while profit potential is not limited. Unfortunately, as Gold points out, "inverted" markets lately have been the rule, making limited risk hedging impossible. Therefore, Gold explains the hedge in which the near month is sold and the distant month bought. Trading on news events or by charts is said to be common for hedges in inverted markets. As risk is not limited, the use of stop-loss orders is essential. Line charts as an aid in spreading, margin requirements, straddles in two different commodities, and tax straddles are briefly considered.

Greenberg, Stephen. "Commodity Spreads and Straddles." In *Guide to Commodity Price Forecasting*, ed. by Harry Jiler and George B. Parker, pp. 213–229. 1965. (An earlier version of this article appears in the 1960 *Commodity Year Book*.)

Intramarket, intermarket, and intercommodity spreads may be either seasonal or statistical. Seasonal spreads attempt to capitalize on seasonal price tendencies for profit, while statistical spreads are based on the hope that one market will tend to deviate from another in relative price. Greenberg emphasizes, as do other writers, that spread positions reduce overall risk only if proper money management is used. That is, the small margin requirements for spreads should not be used as an "excuse" for trading in larger quantities than one ordinarily would. The specific spreads discussed in detail by Greenberg are May-July wheat (intramarket), December wheat-December corn (intercommodity), December corn-December oats (intercommodity), July-September soybeans (intramarket), and May wheat-May rye (intercommodity). Daily price charts covering all of these spreads are shown for a number of years.

Kallard, Thomas. *Make Money in Commodity Spreads!* 1974. 190 pp.

About one fourth of the Kallard book is textual matter discussing various types of commodity spreads: interdelivery, intermarket, intercommodity, raw material versus product, "money," limited risk, dynamic, and tax. Interdelivery (intracommodity) spreads are discussed with regard to both carrying charge markets and inverse markets. The conversion spread and the reverse conversion spread (soybean products) are elaborated upon as examples of raw materials versus products. About three quarters of the Kallard volume consists of charts of spread positions in many different commodities. Most of the charts cover a year or so.

Kroll, Stanley, and Shishko, Irwin. "Straddles and Spreads." In their *Commodity Futures Market Guide*, pp. 237–257. 1973.

To locate profitable spreads, the authors recommend the study of commodities in depth, the review of past behavior of spread situations, the use of price difference charts, the search for seasonal regularities, and the careful estimation of possible gain as opposed to possible loss. Kroll and Shishko cover many different kinds of spreads, including the "Intracrop Spread—Low-Risk Variety" (buying a nearby contract, while shorting a distant contract of the same commodity that is trading close to a premium over carrying charges), the "Intercrop Spread—High-Risk Variety" (shorting a nearby contract, while buying a distant contract of the same commodity, but in the next crop year), the "Location Straddle" (long or short a commodity in one location, with the opposite position being taken in the same commodity in a different location), the "Multicommodity Straddle" (opposite positions in different but related commodities, such as long in one of the grains, but short in another), and the "Processor's Straddle" (mainly the soybean conversion spread, but also fresh eggs versus frozen eggs). Kroll and Shishko conclude with the assertion that one must play the straddles game objectively, not impulsively.

Longstreet, Roy W. "Spread Trading." In his *Viewpoints of a Commodity Trader*, pp. 86–87. 1968.

States that most of the successful, experienced commodity professionals engage in the trading of spreads. Spreads should be entered into deliberately; it is usually a mistake to attempt to rectify an error in a net long or short position by spreading (assuming another position opposite to the original, without canceling the original). Converting net positions into spreads in this manner is usually a sign of confusion on the part of the speculator. Longstreet is definitely in favor of spreading as a technique, if trades are started as spreads and closed in the same way, because spreads are often more predictable than net positions. Also, margin requirements are usually smaller and spreads can work out profitably in either advancing or declining markets. The spreader is oftentimes neither a bull nor a bear.

Powers, Mark J. "Fact and Fiction About Spreads." In his *Getting Started in Commodity Futures Trading*, pp. 133–146. 1973.

The point is made that spreading can be riskier than straight trading because of the reduced margin requirements for spreads and the opportunity for overtrading. This is apt to be especially true in the case of perishable commodities, such as eggs. Powers discusses various kinds of spreads,

152 COMMODITY FUTURES TRADING

arriving at a seven-point conclusion: (1) Spreads based upon normal price relationships (time, quality, location) can be both reasonably profitable and reasonably safe. (2) Perishable commodity spreads can be very risky. (3) Commercial traders sometimes take delivery when closing out a spread, but public speculators should generally avoid delivery. (4) Spread positions offer an opportunity to overtrade. (5) Dollar amounts on both sides of a spread should be approximately the same. (6) Never convert a losing, outright position to a spread. (7) Spread positions for tax purposes should be attempted only in consultation with a tax expert.

Shaw, John E. B. "The Advantages of Spreading." In his *A Professional Guide to Commodity Speculation*, pp. 70–78. 1972.

Methods of profiting from the following spreads are discussed: buy March wheat and sell March corn; sell two contracts of May oats and buy one contract of May corn; buy Kansas City September wheat and sell Chicago September wheat; buy December rye and sell March corn; buy December wheat and sell January soybeans. Records of profit and loss for each spread are given, along with ways to try to improve results.

Teweles, Richard J., and others. "Spreads." In their *The Commodity Futures Game*, pp. 216–227. 1974.

Intracommodity spreads, intercommodity spreads, intermarket spreads, "no-risk" spreads, and tax spreads are covered. The authors emphasize that the so-called "no-risk" spread, involving a full carrying charge difference in a normal market (distant months selling higher than near months), is quite rare, and when such a spread situation does occur, the virtual absence of risk is often accompanied by a very low possibility of worthwhile profit. There is no free lunch. Under the heading "Mistakes," the authors give some unpleasant examples of how careless or inexperienced commodity traders go about losing money with spreads. Nevertheless, the conclusion of this chapter is that "For a new trader, spreads provide an opportunity to enter the commodity markets with minimum capital and risk."

SPREADS, TAX. See Tax Considerations

STATISTICS SOURCES (*See also* Advisory Services; Bibliographies)

Noted here are recommendations of statistical information sources made by various authors writing on the subject of commodity futures. (A list of government reports and periodicals of interest to commodity traders will be found at the back of the present volume.)

Angrist, Stanley W. "Sources of Statistical Information." In his *Sensible Speculating in Commodities*, pp. 207–209. 1972.

A descriptive listing of 15 standard sources of data about farm products. Some of the sources are privately published, such as the *Commodity Year*

STATISTICS SOURCES 153

Book and the *Chicago Mercantile Exchange Year Book*, while others are government publications, such as *The Feed Situation* and the *USDA Crop Production Report*.

Chicago Board of Trade. "Periodic Reports." In *Commodity Trading Manual*, pp. 154, 170, 183, 191, 209, 216, 226, 250, 263. 1973.

> These are convenient lists of crop news reports and statistics sources, mainly those issued by the U.S. Agricultural Marketing Service, the U.S. Crop Reporting Board, the U.S. Economic Research Service, and other federal agencies. Topics covered individually are the grains, oil and meal, livestock, poultry and eggs, metals, forest products, textiles, foodstuffs, and foreign currencies.

Gold, Gerald. "Sources of Commodity Information." In his *Modern Commodity Futures Trading*, 6th ed., pp. 51–53. 1971.

> Briefly covers government reports, publications of commodity exchanges, newspapers, services, and brokerage houses as sources of information about commodity futures.

Gould, Bruce G. "Government Reports." In his *Dow Jones-Irwin Guide to Commodities Trading*, pp. 122–131. 1973.

> The commodity *Situation Reports* and other U.S. Department of Agriculture statistics sources are described. Sample pages from various reports are used as illustrations.

Gould, Bruce G. "Primary Agricultural Reports Distributed Free of Charge by the U.S. Department of Agriculture." In his *Dow Jones-Irwin Guide to Commodities Trading*, pp. 304–305. 1973.

> A convenient list of 42 commodity situation and production reports that are available free of charge from the U.S. Department of Agriculture.

Powers, Mark J. "What to Look for—And Where to Find It." In his *Getting Started in Commodity Futures Trading*, pp. 147–158. 1973.

> From 10 to 15 statistical reports and periodicals are listed, with complete address information, for each of the following commodities or groups of commodities: grains, potatoes, metals, eggs, hogs, beef cattle, pork bellies, soybeans, lumber, and feeder cattle. Short- and long-lerm supply and demand factors are also listed for each commodity.

Shaw, John E. B. "How to Find Additional Information." In his *A Professional Guide to Commodity Speculation*, pp. 159–162. 1972.

> A good discussion of how the U.S. Department of Agriculture goes about gathering crop information and issuing statistical reports. Voluntary mail samplings and the famous "lockup" routine are considered in some detail.

154 COMMODITY FUTURES TRADING

Teweles, Richard J., and others. "Choosing the Game (Markets)." In their *The Commodity Futures Game*, pp. 335–610. 1974.

> Under the uniform heading, "Sources of Information," the authors list and discuss important data sources for each of some 30 different commodities. The chapter on cocoa, for example, includes "Sources of Information" for that commodity.

STATISTICS SOURCES (LONDON MARKETS)

Parker, George B. "Sources of Information." In *Commodity Year Book 1971*, pp. 46–47. 1971.

> A short discussion of where the American commodity trader can get statistical information about commodity futures traded in London. Detailed price quotations are said to be relatively difficult to obtain.

Watling, T. F., and Morley, J. "Commodity Information." In their *Successful Commodity Futures Trading*, pp. 55–63. 1974.

> British sources of information are discussed, including London newspapers.

STATISTICS SOURCES (SOYBEANS)

Emery, Walter L. "A Check List of Important Statistical Data." In *Commodity Year Book 1971*, pp. 26–27. 1971.

> For those interested in the soybean market, this is a comprehensive annotated list of government and Chicago Board of Trade data sources. The arrangement is according to frequency of publication—daily, weekly, monthly, quarterly, and yearly.

STOCK PRICES AND COMMODITY PRICES

The relationships between stock market prices and commodity market prices are complex and not easy to follow.

Commodity Research Bureau. "The Relationship Between Stock Prices and Commodity Prices." *Commodity Year Book 1939*, pp. 21–26. 1939.

> The statement is made that short-term stock prices and commodity prices often move in opposite directions, despite an overall tendency for commodity and stock prices to follow the same long-term trends. Basic industry stock groups (copper companies, for example) are the most likely to have prices that parallel commodity markets. Five charts compare various stock and commodity price indexes from 1909 to 1938.

Labys, Walter C., and Granger, C. W. J. "Stock Markets and Commodity Markets." In their *Speculation, Hedging and Commodity Price Forecasts*, pp. 268–270. 1970.

> Five similarities in price behavior between stock prices and commodity prices are mentioned: (1) The random walk model fits both sets of prices

very well. (2) Using hindsight, variables can be found to explain prices for both (for example, earnings or dividends for stocks and supply-demand factors for commodities), but using the same variables to forecast does not provide results in either case that are better than those obtained from a random walk model. (3) Price changes for both stock and commodity markets continue even when the markets are closed (things happen overnight or during weekends). (4) Stock prices of companies in the same industry move together, and futures prices of commodities in the same "industry" (for example, soybean oil and cottonseed oil) tend to move together. (5) Neither stock nor commodity prices appear to be significantly related to the economy in general, except over the very long run. Four differences in behavior between stock and commodity prices are mentioned by Labys and Granger: (1) Excess speculation can be roughly measured for commodities, but not for stocks. (2) Supply-demand factors for commodities are vital and would exist with or without speculation. On the other hand, most stock trading is merely the passing of stock certificates back and forth from one holder to another. (3) There is a clear relationship between volume of trading and the extent of price changes in stocks, but not so for commodities. (4) The commodity market is almost a perfect auction, while the stock market is flawed by the presence of floor specialists.

STOP-LOSS ORDERS (See also Orders to Brokers)

A standing order left with a broker to offset a commodity futures contract if the price reaches a certain unfavorable level, the purpose being to cancel out the position before loss becomes too great. Unfortunately, if the price is moving fast in the wrong direction, or worse, if there are limit moves in the wrong direction, the loss may be extended before the broker can execute the stop-loss order.

Gardner, Robert L. "The Stop-Loss Order." In his *How to Make Money in the Commodity Market*, pp. 162–165. 1961.

> Several ways to use the stop-loss order are described. Gardner states that the stop-loss device is indispensable, even though it may not work too well in a thin market with rapidly changing prices. How far away from the market price should a stop-loss be placed? This question is briefly discussed, with the conclusion that each situation has so many variables that no specific rules can be offered.

Gold, Gerald. "The Stop-Loss Order and Its Use in Chart Trading." In his *Modern Commodity Futures Trading*, 6th ed., pp. 193–196. 1971.

> Chart traders can have losses on half or even more of their trades and still make money, so long as losses are taken promptly and kept small. The stop-loss order is a convenient and widely used means of keeping losses small. The stop-loss procedure can also be used to protect profits on previously established positions and to initiate new positions.

156 COMMODITY FUTURES TRADING

Gould, Bruce G. "Stop Orders." In his *Dow Jones-Irwin Guide to Commodities Trading*, pp. 284-288. 1973.

> An excellent discussion of the strategy of stop-loss orders. Gould tells in detail how to go about setting stop losses close enough to afford protection from unreasonable losses, but not so close as to be activated by "noise" (random fluctuations).

Teweles, Richard J., and others. "Stops." In their *The Commodity Futures Game*, pp. 241-243. 1974.

> Stop orders are recommended both for taking profits and for limiting losses. The stop-loss point may be determined by chart analysis, by percentage of margin, or simply by the amount of money the trader is willing to lose. Even well-disciplined speculators "seldom gain by not having ... orders entered in advance."

STRADDLES. See Spreads

STRATEGY. See Money Management; Psychology; Trading Rules

STUD LUMBER. See Lumber and Plywood

SUGAR

The major food sweetener, obtained primarily from sugar cane and sugar beets, and known technically as sucrose. (There is no difference between refined cane sugar and refined beet sugar in taste or appearance.) Most of the sugar consumption in the United States is through soft drinks, baked goods, candy, jelly, and other sweetened food products. A certain amount of sugar is also used in nonfood products, such as chemical plasticizers. Russia is the leading sugar producer (beet sugar), followed by Brazil (cane), Cuba (cane), India (cane), and the United States (beet and cane). Because of high consumption, the United States must import large amounts of sugar each year. Both domestic and world sugar futures contracts are traded on the New York Coffee and Sugar Exchange, but the United Sugar Terminal Market Association in London is also an important futures market.

Chicago Board of Trade. "Sugar." In *Commodity Trading Manual*, pp. 229-232. 1973.

> Sugar supply and demand considerations are summarized. Sugar futures trading details are given for the New York Coffee and Sugar Exchange (sugar futures are also traded actively in London). The following are listed for New York: delivery months, trading units, minimum price fluctuations, daily price move limits, position limits, delivery standards, and trading hours. "World Production of Sugar (Centrifugal Sugar, Raw Value)" is quoted in thousands of short tons for each of ten countries annually from

1962-1963 to 1971-1972. Sugar imports in metric tons are quoted for ten countries from 1962 to 1970. Exports for each country are also given.

Davies, M. E. T. "Sugar." In *Getting Started in London Commodities*, ed. by C. W. J. Granger, pp. 37-40. 1975.

> A British view of sugar trading, beginning with a brief history and background of the commodity. Today's London sugar futures market is described, including contract and trading details for the United Sugar Terminal Market Association. Sugar is said to have "more complicated factors" than cocoa and, therefore, sugar is favored by professional traders and cocoa by amateur speculators. A table shows London sugar futures transactions in long tons from 1959 to 1974, while the monthly range of London spot prices is shown in chart form for the years 1966 to early 1975.

Inkeles, David M. "How to Analyze the World Sugar Futures Market," In *Commodity Year Book 1968*, pp. 6-14, 1968.

> The author states that his purpose is twofold: (1) to present background information on the sugar industry and sugar futures and (2) to give suggestions as to how sugar price analysis should be approached. Inkeles begins with a discussion of the 1963-1964 bull market in sugar in which a margin deposit of $500 could have yielded a profit of $12,800 without pyramiding, assuming that one was so brilliant as to buy a futures contract at the bottom of the initial price move and sell it at the top. The sugar market in various countries of the world is considered, followed by outlines of the crop characteristics of both cane sugar and beet sugar. Legislation affecting sugar, consumption factors, statistics sources, carryover, and the technical aspects of open interest are all discussed. Speculators are urged to act dispassionately and not get carried away by visions of 10¢ price moves.

Shishko, Irwin. "Forecasting Sugar Prices with the Aid of Econometric Techniques." In *Guide to Commodity Price Forecasting*, ed. by Harry Jiler and George B. Parker, pp. 175-182. 1965. (An earlier version of this article appears in the 1963 *Commodity Year Book*.)

> This is an article devoted to the disciplined analysis (largely mathematical) of the factors that cause sugar prices to change. The fundamentals of the sugar market are carefully described in the first part of the article, with the second part given over to "The Econometric Approach in Sugar." Instructions are given for the use of various equations in the study of sugar price trends. Charts show daily sugar futures prices for the July "no. 7" contract from 1962 to 1965 and the July "no. 8" contract from 1960 to 1965.

Teweles, Richard J., and others. "Sugar: World and Domestic," In their *The Commodity Futures Game*, pp. 514-522, 534. 1974.

> A very good summary of the fundamentals of sugar price determination. History, factors influencing markets, information sources, production,

158 COMMODITY FUTURES TRADING

utilization, political aspects, and seasonal tendencies (if any) are discussed. In "Notes from a Trader" the possibility of a spread position between New York and London is mentioned, although fluctuation in currency values is said to be a complicating factor. Because of government controls on domestic sugar, world sugar is the primary speculative vehicle.

Watling, T. F., and Morley, J. "Sugar." In their *Successful Commodity Futures Trading*, pp. 157–162. 1974.

>An "ugly trading triangle" is mentioned in which London merchants bought slaves at low prices in Africa and sold them to planters in the West Indies, who used the slaves to produce sugar, which was in turn sold to England and other wealthy countries at high prices. Sugar production and supply-demand factors are briefly discussed. Complete futures trading details are given for the United Terminal Sugar Market Association in London.

SUPPLY-DEMAND FACTORS. See Fundamental Analysis

SUPPORT AND RESISTANCE LEVELS (See *also* Charts)
A support level is a price level that a commodity has difficulty in breaking through on the downside, and a resistance level is the same on the upside. Buying activity increases at support levels and selling pressure increases at resistance levels. The terms support and resistance are used especially by followers of commodity futures price charts.

Cox, Houston A. "Support and Resistance in Commodities." In his *Concepts on Profits in Commodity Futures Trading*, pp. 106–109. 1972.

>Monthly futures charts of oats and cocoa are used to show that "resistance levels tend to be near previous highs" and "support levels tend to be near previous lows." "The measured move," a method of estimating how far a trend will progress, is briefly discussed.

Gold, Gerald. "Support and Resistance Areas." In his *Modern Commodity Futures Trading*, 6th ed., pp. 189–192. 1971.

>A consideration of the reasons, psychological or otherwise, for the development of support and resistance levels in price charts.

Kroll, Stanley, and Shishko, Irwin. "Support and Resistance: The Congestion Area." In their *Commodity Futures Market Guide*, pp. 120–127. 1973.

>Support and resistance levels help the speculator in determining (1) whether or not a trend will continue, (2) price objectives, and (3) logical points of purchases and sale. The Kroll-Shishko discussion of these levels is unusually complete and intelligently written. After an explanation of why congestion areas exist, the authors consider the validity factor, and tell how to anticipate the direction of a price breakout from a congestion area. The well-known tendency of prices to retrace from 40 to 50 percent of a previous move is mentioned.

Reinach, Anthony M. "Congestion Area Action." In his *The Fastest Game in Town*, pp. 74–100. 1973.

> Commodity price chart congestion areas are categorized as follows: (1) areas of distribution (tops), (2) areas of redistribution (downward consolidation), (3) areas of accumulation (bottoms), and (4) areas of reaccumulation (upward consolidation). Congestion areas are generally defined as having "sidewise price action within a trading range," and more specifically as temporary trend interruptions (consolidations) or final trend terminations (tops or bottoms). "End runs," "bull traps," and "bear traps" are illustrated by means of charts. Four characteristics of congestion areas are said to be important in determining if a top or a bottom exists: (1) location within recent historical price range, (2) breadth or time duration, (3) price change activity, and (4) volume of trading. Reinach explains all four factors in detail. He also states that the four major price reversal patterns are triangles, saucers, V-shapes, and platforms. These are all discussed, including the simple platform bottom, the compound platform bottom, the delayed ending platform bottom, the duplex horizontal platform bottom, and the delayed V ending bottom. The famous head-and-shoulders formation is thoroughly examined and shown in various charts.

SWING CHARTS. See Trend Following

SYSTEMS OF TRADING. See Mechanical Trading Systems; Moving Average; Trading Rules; Trend Following

TACTICS OF TRADING. See Psychology; Trading Rules

TAX CONSIDERATIONS

While taxation of ordinary, speculative, short-term or long-term profits or losses in commodity futures is essentially the same as for stocks, complications arise when trades are for hedging rather than speculation or when futures are deliberately used as a device to reduce taxes.

Arthur, Henry B. "Tax Status of Commodity Futures Operations." In his *Commodity Futures as a Business Management Tool*, pp. 38–44. 1971.

> Speaking of the complex matter of taxation of futures transactions, Arthur states that "Certain pragmatic rulings have been affirmed. . . ." He then summarizes these rulings as to speculation on the long side, speculation on the short side, and commercial hedging operations. A table shows "Tax Treatment of Commodity Futures Contract Results" for both open and closed contracts in the following four situations: "Speculator Gains on Long Positions," "Speculator Losses on Long Positions," "Speculator Gains or Losses on Short Positions," "Gains and Losses from Futures Contracts Qualified as Hedging."

Briloff, Abraham J. "Straw Into Gold? Commodity Straddles Turn Short-Term Capital Gains Long." *Barron's*, vol. 54, March 25, 1974, pp. 5, 12.

>Eleven "ground rules" are outlined with respect to the use of commodity straddles solely to gain a capital gains tax advantage (a straddle in this context is not expected to generate any trading profit—only a tax advantage). To work well, Briloff states, this plan should involve the use of a volatile commodity. Unfortunately, there are risks caused by the possibility of the relationship between the buy and sell sides of the tax straddle not remaining uniform. That the plan "is anything but risk-free should be abundantly clear from the caveats strewn along the way."

Kallard, Thomas. "Tax Spreads." In his *Make Money in Commodity Spreads!*, pp. 39–41. 1974.

>The use of commodity futures spreads as tax devices is said to be a technique suitable mainly for those in the upper tax brackets. The task of the tax spreader is to find spread situations in which high risk is absent but in which there is at least some change of making a capital gain (apart from the tax advantage to be gained). Spreads between different crop years, different commodities, or different markets are definitely to be avoided, according to Kallard. Also, never engage in a "bear spread" (short the near months and long the distant) for tax purposes, as this kind of spread may turn a tax problem into a loss-of-capital problem. Kallard uses March and May pork bellies to give an example and an explanation of a suitable tax spread.

Nevans, Ronald. "'Straddling' the Years to Cut Your Taxes; Commodity Straddles Can Help Push Profits into Next Year." *Financial World*, vol. 142, November 27, 1974, pp. 20–22.

>Describes the use of commodity straddles to defer taxes on short-term capital gains. The idea is to take a spread position (long one month and short another in the same commodity) with the intent of closing out the losing side in the current tax year and the plus side in the next tax year. Various ramifications of this are considered.

Reinach, Anthony M. "Taxes and Commodity Futures." In his *The Fastest Game in Town*, pp. 138–143. 1973.

>Tax straddles making use of silver futures contracts are emphasized. These straddles are used to move short-term capital gains forward into the next tax year, or to attempt to convert short-term gains to long term. Reinach recommends consultation with an accountant or tax adviser before processing with a tax straddle program.

Shaw, John E. B. "How to Find Tax and Tax Straddles Advantages." In his *A Professional Guide to Commodity Speculation*, pp. 152–158. 1972.

>Tells about tax straddles, which are merely spread positions taken in an attempt to negate previous short-term capital gains and turn them into

long-term gains. Shaw states that, in his experience, tax straddles work out as expected about half the time. Sometimes the tax-conscious trader is in the position of having paid a considerable sum in commissions to engage in straddles that yielded little or no tax advantage. Shaw gives ten rules that should be followed by anyone who is about to set up tax straddles.

Teweles, Richard J., and others. "Tax Considerations." In their *The Commodity Futures Game*, pp. 70–74. 1974.

A very good summary of the tax treatment of commodity futures trading. The difference between speculative and hedge positions is emphasized, in that true hedging results in business expense or profit, while speculators have capital losses or gains. Wash-sale ambiguity is mentioned, and a most skeptical view is taken of commodity futures spreads as tax devices. "Spread trading for tax purposes is no area for the amateur."

TAX SPREADS. See Tax Considerations

TECHNICAL ANALYSIS (*See also* Charts; Computer Analysis; Mechanical Trading Systems; Moving Average; Random Walk Theory; Trend Following)

The study of price movements themselves, often in chart form, as an aid in forecasting, and in contrast to "fundamental" analysis of supply and demand factors.

Angrist, Stanley W. "Technical Trading I: Basic Chart Reading" (pp. 103–118), "Technical Trading II: Charts with Open Interest and Volume Data" (pp. 119–134), and "Technical Trading III: Moving Averages" (pp. 135–154). In his *Sensible Speculating in Commodities*, pp. 103–154. 1972.

With regard to the "perfect" trading system, Angrist remarks that, "The idea is as intriguing as it is elusive." He says that such a system falls into the same class of fanciful creation as the perpetual motion machine. Perpetual motion is impossible according to the laws of thermodynamics, and the perfect trading system is impossible in a free market. Angrist states that trading systems should be based on past results over ten years or so and should be based on sound principles. Even so, the dangers of "whipsawing" are always present, as when the market moves up and down within relatively narrow limits. The author discusses the basic bar chart patterns, such as the head and shoulders and double tops and bottoms. He emphasizes that the use of charts as price forecasters "should be tempered by fundamental information as much as possible, and with a little common sense thrown in to boot." Charting open interest and volume of trading, as well as price movements, is strongly recommended by Angrist. The various combinations of open interest and price are considered at some length, such as prices rising with open interest increasing, prices rising with open interest falling, and so forth. Finally, moving averages and weighted moving averages are viewed as to their usefulness in following price trends. Angrist concludes that moving averages can be profitable for trading commodity futures if the averages are chosen carefully and used in a consistent manner. These chapters offer an excellent short course in charting and technical analysis.

Belveal, L. Dee. "Introduction to Technical Trading." In his *Charting Commodity Market Price Behavior*, pp. 13–24. 1969.

States that that the three points of reference necessary for the intelligent judging of commodity prices, from the technical point of view, are as follows: (1) the standard, recognized chart patterns; (2) open interest; (3) and volume of trading. Belveal is of the opinion that charts (technical analysis) are not very reliable for medium- or long-term price forecasting, but they can be "priceless when used *in combination*, as dependable and consistent warning signs to alert you against *short-term* hazards...." By "in combination," the author means that one technical factor alone should not be relied upon too heavily. Several charts are used as illustrations of the main points of the text.

Chicago Board of Trade. "The Technical Approach." In *Commodity Trading Manual*, pp. 84–100. 1973.

Even those who are concerned primarily with supply-demand factors (the fundamentals of the market) should not overlook technical considerations (price trends). Bar charts, moving average charts, point-and-figure charts, volume, open interest, trader commitments, and contrary opinion are all covered in the Board of Trade's *Manual*. As an important caveat, it is pointed out that stop-loss orders placed by hundreds of chartists at almost identical prices can produce "false signals." Also, "...the cumulative effect of...similar actions...creates price fluctuations which may destroy much of the validity of the whole chart technique."

Clifton, Frederick T. "How to Adjust Trading and Hedging Methods to the Volatile Markets of the Seventies." In *Commodity Year Book 1974*, pp. 40–50. 1974.

Clifton refers to recent commodity futures markets as "V-type markets," because extreme price moves within limited periods of time cause many "V" formations to appear on price charts. Traditional, fundamental methods of market analysis should be supplemented by a technical, chart-oriented approach if these volatile markets are to be followed effectively. Under "Technical Methods for Timing Entrance and Exits in Commodity Markets," seven techniques are listed: (1) simple chart reading, (2) seasonal pattern spotting, (3) writing-in fundamental factors on price charts, (4) moving averages, (5) zone trading, (6) computer analysis, and (7) volume of trading and open interest analysis. "...an automatic entry/exit futures trigger will save a lot of indecisive waiting and attendant monetary woe, in the abrupt markets we view for this decade."

TECHNICAL ANALYSIS

Clifton, Frederick T. "Price-Making Factors and 'Technical Conditions' in Commodity Futures." In *Commodity Year Book 1971*, pp. 30–35. 1971.

> Market technicians (chartists) should be aware of (1) seasonal patterns; (2) price breakouts into new high or low areas; (3) the importance of timing by trend lines, moving averages, chart patterns, or other methods; (4) the use of volume data; (5) the use of open-interest figures; and (6) how computers can be used to test market strategies or theories. Technicians need a trading plan, philosophy, or strategy that attempts to keep the risk factor as low as possible and the profit objective high. The "technical condition" of the market should not be used as an excuse for failure.

Gould, Bruce G. "Limits of Technical Forecasting." In his *Dow Jones-Irwin Guide to Commodities Trading*, pp. 253–254.

> An interesting discussion in which Gould points out that random walk theorists do acknowledge that price trends exist in actual commodity markets. However, these trends are said to exist only through hindsight and are no more predictable than the trends obtained through the flipping of a coin. On the other hand, some academicians have found "meaningful nonrandom elements in commodity prices," as in studies by Arnold Larson and Sidney Alexander.

Hieronymus, Thomas A. "Technical Versus Fundamental." In his *Economics of Futures Trading*, pp. 269–271. 1971.

> A mildly critical view of technical analysis of commodity price movements. Hieronymus regards conflict between technicians and fundamentalists as unfortunate. He states that chart followers are usually well aware of fundamentals when trading, and fundamentalists are generally conscious of price patterns.

Keltner, Chester W. "The Price Movement Analysis, or Technical, Approach." In his *How to Make Money in Commodities*, pp. 44–46.

> A philosophical discussion of the technical analysis of commodity price trends. Keltner believes that the average trader without much knowledge of fundamental market factors will do well to adopt a technical trading system. However, he believes that greater profit is possible for the speculator who studies commodity fundamentals and trades conservatively.

Kroll, Stanley, and Shishko, Irwin. "Introduction to Technical Analysis." In their *Commodity Futures Market Guide*, pp. 89–106, 1973.

> Fifteen technical approaches to commodity trading are listed, although they are not mutually exclusive (trend following is, of course, basic to many of the approaches). Short discussions are given of tape reading, chart analysis, computers in technical analysis, the testing of trading theories, line charts, point-and-figure charts, and moving average charts.

Powers, Mark J. "Technical Analysis." In his *Getting Started in Commodity Futures Trading*, pp. 67–78. 1973.

> Bar charts, point-and-figure charts, chart interpretation, trend definition, and common chart formations are briefly discussed.

Teweles, Richard J., and others. "The Technical Approach." In their *The Commodity Futures Game*, pp. 165–215. 1974.

> An unusually complete review of the so-called "technical" methods of price-movement analysis, including bar charts, point-and-figure charts, "old-time price patterns," moving averages, swing charts, oscillators, volume-open-interest analysis, on-balance volume, tape reading, contrary opinion, seasonal price trends, time cycles, and the Elliott wave theory. The advantages and disadvantages of each method are discussed. While the pitfalls of technical analysis are many, "The rewards are great and they are attainable," but only if the trader can control his impatience and stick with a sound method. The enemies are said to be greed, hope, and fear.

TIME CYCLES (*See also* Elliott Wave Principle)
Fluctuation patterns in commodity prices according to hour of the day, day of the week, week of the month, month of the year, year within a decade, or some other element of time. Much effort has been expended by statisticians in attempts to determine if commodity prices do indeed have cyclical tendencies.

Teweles, Richard J., and others. "Time Cycles." In their *The Commodity Futures Game*, pp. 204–208. 1974.

> Most commodity-price time cycles fall into three categories: (1) Major highs and lows spaced by regular, distinct intervals, such as the 67 and one-third month cycle in cash corn prices. (2) Brief but powerful price moves at regular intervals, sometimes known as "kick in the pants" cycles. An example is given in the form of a chart of world sugar futures prices from 1937 to 1971 showing very clearly the strong upward move that occurs in sugar prices at six-year intervals. (3) Mathematical models. The advantages of using time cycles are said to be that these cycles are probably real and not fantasies, and that the trader will gain valuable insight into price movements by studying cycles. Disadvantages are that no absolute mathematical proof exists to prove the validity of time cycles, that there is a great deal about cycles that is simply not known, that time cycle studies are mainly for cash prices instead of futures, and that unforeseen events can throw previously well-established time cycles off the track.

TOPS AND BOTTOMS, DOUBLE. *See* Double Tops and Bottoms

TRADERS, SMALL. *See* Amateur Speculation

TRADING BUDGET. See Money Management

TRADING PHILOSOPHY. See Money Management; Psychology; Trading Rules

TRADING RULES (See *also* Mechanical Trading Systems; Money Management; Psychology)

Admonitions to speculators in commodity futures are very common. Lists of rules, warnings, do's and don'ts, and nostrums in general are forever appearing in the popular literature of commodity trading.

Angrist, Stanley W. "The Eight Commandments of Sensible Speculation in Commodities." In his *Sensible Speculating in Commodities*, pp. 183-195. 1972.

> "I have tried to make clear that commodity trading is a risky business...," Angrist says in his preamble to his eight commandments. His trading rules, each of which he explains, are on the following subjects: (1) Follow a trading plan. (2) Do not overtrade (keep capital in reserve). (3) Set limits to risk. (4) Always use stop-loss orders. (5) Diversify. (6) Usually, do not pyramid. (7) Ignore irrelevant advice. (8) If profits are made, part of them should be used for something other than commodity trading.

Bache & Co., Inc. *Money Management Concepts for Commodity Traders*. No date. 10 pp. (pamphlet).

> Six very important rules are stated and briefly explained to help keep the amateur commodity futures trader from going broke in a hurry. Bache states that successful commodity speculation requires self-discipline, planning, correct diagnosis of market conditions, and a knowledge of how to make the best use of available capital. The following six rules are discussed: (1) set aside a specific amount of capital for futures trading; (2) never enter a trade before choosing both a stop-loss point and an initial profit objective; (3) be sure that your net potential profit/potential loss ratio is at least 2 to 1; (4) risk no more than 10 percent of your trading capital on any single position, and no more than 30 percent on all positions combined; (5) do not take a position unless your profit objective is at least 8-10 times your commission; and (6) remember that margin requirements are irrelevant to profit and loss objectives. Bache points out the often overlooked fact that commodity prices are not especially volatile; it is the small margin required that makes them seem that way to traders. Commodities would seem tame indeed, most of the time, if traded on a 100 percent margin basis. According to how he employs his capital, each speculator sets his own level of conservatism or recklessness.

Belveal, L. Dee. "Launching a Program in Commodity Speculation." In his *Commodity Speculation with Profits in Mind*, pp. 119-130. 1967.

> "...the speculative plains are literally strewn with the bleached bones of courageous, inexperienced speculators...." To help the beginning trader avoid financial disaster, Belveal offers an excellent program of

practice trades. This pretesting of abilities should be done very carefully in a series of "paper trades" before actually committing speculative capital in the real market. The following practice rules for the beginner are discussed: (1) Select an active commodity and read about it; learn the crop fundamentals. (2) Study historical price behavior, trading volume, open interest, and seasonal trends. (3) Begin to follow daily price fluctuations of the commodity and try to develop an understanding of why price trends occur. (4) Start a chart of daily prices, including a ten-day moving average. (5) Prepare a supply of practice "trading cards" (Belveal shows the form to use). (6) Prepare a "recap sheet" to give a running summary of practice trade results (Belveal shows a sample form). Finally, Belveal emphasizes the importance of being scrupulous in maintaining records of practice trades—losses as well as profits. Also, assumed capital must be at a realistic level.

Belveal, L. Dee. "Speculative Pitfalls." In his *Commodity Speculation with Profits in Mind*, pp. 263-287. 1967.

States that most of the *serious* losses sustained by amateur commodity speculators are avoidable for those speculators who do not become stubborn, who adopt a definite strategy, and who take small losses with alacrity. Belveal believes that a trader can make money by being correct in price trend forecasting in as few as one third of positions assumed, but only with good strategy and proper money management. The following rules of trading are purposefully explained: (1) Do not overtrade. (2) Never answer a margin call. (3) Never move a stop-loss order in the direction of a greater loss. (4) Never average down ("speculative madness"). (5) Averaging up may be done if certain rules are followed. (6) Do not close out a winning position prematurely. (7) Use stop-loss orders. (8) Do not guess as to the occurrence of market tops or bottoms; that is, do not argue with the market. (9) Do not trade markets that are moving sideways (no trend). (10) Do not trade according to current events or news happenings. (11) Stay informed. (12) Generally, never carry an open position, long or short, into a major crop report. Surprises can be ruinous. (13) Beware of trading on the opening or close of a session. (14) Avoid the last days of contract life. (15) Dull markets are often followed by significant price reversals. (16) Active markets are the best trading markets.

Business Week. "Why Commodities Lure More and More Investors." *Business Week*, December 23, 1972, pp. 100-102.

". . . studies have shown that upward of 75 percent of commodities speculators lose money in the long run. . . ." Nevertheless, a "winning strategy" outlined by "experts" includes the following suggestions: (1) Set aside no more than 10 to 20 percent of investment capital for the purpose of trading commodity futures. This 10 to 20 percent should be regarded as risk capital. (2) A reserve of speculative capital should be maintained at all times; that is, don't bet everything on one trade. (3) Diversify by trading in several commodities at one time. (4) Sell short, if that appears to be the profitable thing to do. (5) Have a careful game plan and by all means stick to it. (6) Use stop-loss orders.

Chicago Board of Trade. "Trading Strategy." In *Commodity Trading Manual*, pp. 105–106. 1973.

Eight guidelines are listed, based on the trading experience of successful speculators: (1) Analyze markets carefully (avoid tips and rumors). (2) Do not trade if doubtful about price forecast. (3) Follow the market trend. (4) Do not attempt to forecast exact price reversal points. (5) Be just as willing to sell short as to buy. (6) Potential profit should be large, relative to the risk involved. (7) Be prepared to take numerous small losses, but profits must be allowed to accumulate. (8) Have a well-developed trading plan before entering the market. Always keep some speculative capital in reserve.

Cox, Houston A. "Consistency, Money Management, and Profits." In his *Concepts on Profits in Commodity Futures Trading*, pp. 169–171. 1972.

"Three consistency resolutions" (have a logical plan and stick with it) and "the five success rules of money management" (do not overtrade) are quoted. Cox's rules for money management in futures trading are quite specific regarding the amounts of capital that should be utilized in individual situations.

Cox, Houston A. "The Keys to Successful and Profitable Commodity Trading." In his *Concepts on Profits in Commodity Futures Trading*, pp. 168–169. 1972.

Five major rules are given that deal mainly with the strategy of trend following. Seventeen subrules cover the prerequisites for a major trend, the conditions for a trend reversal, when to increase position size, and when to liquidate.

Gardner, Robert L. "Seven Keys to Success for the Beginning Trader." In his *How to Make Money in the Commodity Market*, pp. 173–180. 1961.

(1) Cut losses; let profits accumulate. (2) Do not overtrade. (3) Do not seek the very bottom or the very top of the market. (4) Do not go against the trend of the market. (5) Know the fundamentals of commodities traded in. (6) Liquidate position if a margin call is received. (7) If uncertain, do not trade. After discussing each of his seven rules, Gardner indicates that profitable commodity speculation requires hard work, courage, and determination.

Gold, Gerald. "Some Speculators Make Money—Rules for Speculative Trading." In his *Modern Commodity Futures Trading*, 6th ed., pp. 237–245. 1971.

Ten trading rules for successful commodity speculation are discussed. Gold admits that the rules are not unique, "but have been developed by many people out of past experience." (1) Do not hesitate to sell short where indicated. (2) Limit losses, but let profits accumulate. (3) Profit potential should be considerably greater than potential loss. Try to have a profit objective. (4) Do not assume a larger position than you can financially feel comfortable with. Overtrading warps judgment and makes one cross and irritable. (5) When in doubt, stay out of the market. (6) Do not trade against the trend. (7) Chart traders should have a knowledge of the fundamentals of the particular commodity being traded in. Charts should not be used indiscriminately. (8) Never meet a margin call. Liquidate your position. (9) Never assume a spread position to avoid taking a loss. (10) Develop a logical trading procedure or strategy through study, time, and effort.

Gould, Bruce G. "Program (Have One)." In his *Dow Jones-Irwin Guide to Commodities Trading*, pp. 282–284. 1973.

Each speculator should have a trading program to cover all possible contingencies. Seven other recommendations by Gould are: (1) Do not answer margin calls. Close out positions instead. (2) Avoid thin, erratic markets, as an unfavorable position may be difficult to close out except at great loss. (3) Use stop-loss orders at all times, because "mental stops" do not work. (4) Do not close out a position until a signal is received from the market itself. (5) Do not average down. (6) Do not assume a straddle position in an attempt to avoid a loss. (7) Do not hesitate to remove winnings (money) from a commodity account. "Take the money and run."

Hammonds, T. M. "Trading Rules." In his *The Commodity Futures Market from an Agricultural Producer's Point of View*, pp. 65–67. 1972.

Hammonds' rules are intended primarily for the producer (farmer) who is using the commodity futures market for hedging: (1) Use stop orders. (2) Sophisticated orders may be used to enter the market, but simple market orders are best for closing out a position. Trying for those last few pennies of profit is poor procedure. (3) Never assume a futures position that is so large as to make one emotionally uncomfortable. One must be able to stay with a rational plan of operation. (4) Reevaluate market positions when necessary, and take small losses rather than large ones. (5) Do not hedge routinely. There is no point in hedging when prices are improving, although stop orders may be used to automatically establish a hedge if prices fall. (6) Do not rely too much on price formations on charts. (7) Never "average down"—do not add to a position that is moving in the wrong direction. Take the loss while it is still small.

Hieronymus, Thomas A. "Allocation of Capital and the Selection of Trades." In his *Economics of Futures Trading*, pp. 272–275. 1971.

Four steps the speculator should take before beginning to trade are (1) establish profit goals, (2) decide what proportion of available capital will be committed at any one time, (3) determine whether relatively long-term or relatively short-term price moves are to be sought, and (4) decide on what level of risk (how big a loss) will be acceptable. In addition, five conditions for closing out a trade are given: if time runs out, if the profit objective is reached, if loss potential increases too much, if unrealized loss becomes too great, or if a more attractive trade appears.

Keltner, Chester W. "Rules You Must Observe—If You Hope to Trade Successfully." In his *How to Make Money in Commodities*, pp. 197–203. 1960.

Four basic rules are explained in full: Follow a definite trading plan. Trade conservatively in regard to available capital. Do not risk all capital on one situation. Do not depend on commodity trading profits for living expenses.

Kroll, Stanley, and Shishko, Irwin. "The 'Don'ts' of Trading." In their *Commodity Futures Market Guide*, p. 236. 1973.

The nine "don'ts" may be summarized as follows: (1) Don't let losses run. (2) Don't straddle a losing position. (3) Don't trade without a plan. (4) Don't overlook either technical or fundamental factors. (5) Don't ignore persistent seasonal patterns. (6) Don't become overconfident after successful trades. (7) Don't trade on "tips." (8) Don't always go with the crowd. (9) Don't fight the trend of the market.

Kroll, Stanley. "Epilogue." In his *The Professional Commodity Trader*, pp. 151–155. 1974.

A review of what it takes to be a winner instead of a loser when speculating in commodity futures: (1) Realism. There is no "easy money" in futures trading; all the homework must be done. (2) Emotional stability. Patience, objectivity, determination, and courage are all necessary to a high degree. (3) The ability to sit still and let big gains accumulate. (4) Being able to identify major and minor price trends. (5) The ability to time trades well after identifying correct market trend. (6) Simplicity. A sense of the dominant price trend is much more important than access to elaborate market studies. Kroll discusses each of these six desirable qualities.

Kroll, Stanley, and Shishko, Irwin. "The Folklore of Wall Street." In their *Commodity Futures Market Guide*, pp. 82–83.

A "critical but not unfriendly view" of four of the commonly accepted Wall Street maxims: (1) Follow the market trend. (2) Let profits run, but cut losses short. (3) Expect a turn in the market when everyone appears to be on the same side. (4) Be patient; wait for situations with high profit potential. The essence of the criticism by Kroll and Shishko is that these rules are obvious and very much easier to state than to follow. The problem is not "what," but "how."

Kroll, Stanley, and Shishko, Irwin. "Trading Concepts." In their *Commodity Futures Market Guide*, pp. 228–230. 1973.

> Four rules for identifying trades, six absolute tactical rules, and nine conditional tactical rules are presented. The six absolutes are: (1) Never go against the major or minor trend. (2) Always place a limit on losses. (3) Take part of profits when price objective is reached and use stops to protect balance of position. (4) Enter scale orders in advance. (5) Be patient; do not trade merely out of boredom. (6) Diversify rather than increase the size of a profitable position.

Kroll, Stanley, and Shishko, Irwin. "Who Wins and Who Loses in Commodity Speculation?" In their *Commodity Futures Market Guide*, pp. 86–87. 1973.

> "Winners tend to" and "Losers tend to." Under these headings, the tendencies of winners and losers are lined up for all to see. The nine typical actions of winners can be taken as positive trading rules and the nine habits of losers as negative rules.

Merrill Lynch, Pierce, Fenner & Smith, Inc. "Mistakes That Speculators Make." In *How to Buy and Sell Commodities*, pp. 19–24. 1972.

> Merrill Lynch's commodity specialists found that the following six errors were commonly made by commodity traders: (1) Amounts traded were too large. (2) Small profits were taken, but losses were allowed to grow. (3) Trades were made on the basis of "hot tips." (4) Trades were made too frequently. (5) Trades were made in commodities that had not been studied in advance. (6) The fact that there are two sides to every price question was ignored. The Merrill Lynch booklet discusses each of these six major mistakes.

Merrill Lynch, Pierce, Fenner & Smith, Inc. "9 Rules Followed by Professional Speculators." In *Do You Have What It Takes to Be a Successful Commodity Futures Speculator?*, p. 4. No date (leaflet).

> The statement is made that by cutting losses short and letting profits run, it is possible for "successful speculators" to come out substantially ahead, even though losses are taken on 75 percent of trades. Merrill Lynch has formulated nine rules for commodity traders, based on experience over the years: (1) Profit objective and maximum loss should both be clearly in mind for each trade. (2) Study the market; never trade on tips or rumors. (3) Profit objective should generally be at least three times greater than potential loss. (4) Don't fight the market; trade with the trend. (5) Don't take small profits; stay with the trend. (6) Be conservative in adding commitments to original positions. (7) Be prepared for many small losses; be patient. (8) As a general rule, do not risk more than 5 to 8 percent of available trading capital on any one trade. (9) Inexperienced speculators should trade only in active markets and should make use of stop orders to protect positions against changes in trend.

Shaw, John E. B. "How to Get Into the Commodity Markets." In his *A Professional Guide to Commodity Speculation*, pp. 26–29. 1972.

> Eight general rules for trading commodity futures are listed and discussed on page 29 of Shaw's book: (1) Use mental stops only. (2) Know your broker. (3) Use a broker experienced in commodities. (4) Use only one half of your speculative capital at any one time. (5) Deal only in active commodities. (6) Do not trade on foreign commodity exchanges. (7) Work out a trading plan on paper before starting actual trading. (8) Be an independent thinker.

Sherwood, Hugh C. "Cardinal Errors of Investing in Commodities." *Industry Week*, vol. 178, September 17, 1973, p. 52.

> Advice from Daniel G. Kelly of the Kelly Grain Co. is presented in the form of eight crucial mistakes that are sometimes made by commodity speculators: (1) improper pyramiding (overbuying as profits increase); (2) trading only on the long side; (3) failing to cut losses short; (4) putting up more money for margin calls; (5) trading too often (overactivity); (6) trading to the full extent of available speculative capital (over trading); (7) trading in too many commodities (overdiversification); (8) trading in the near months. These eight vital principles may, of course, also be stated in a positive manner: (1) pyramid by buying smaller and smaller amounts as the price rises; (2) sell short if a favorable opportunity to do so presents itself; (3) take many small losses and a few very large profits; (4) never meet a margin call; close out the losing position; (5) trade only when there appears to be a good opportunity to make a large profit; (6) two thirds of available speculative capital should always be kept in reserve; (7) learn a lot about just a few commodities and then trade only in those; (8) the distant months of a particular commodity are generally to be preferred.

Shulman, Morton. "Commodity Futures—The Ideal Gamble." In his *Anyone Can Still make a Million*, p. 137. 1973.

> Five rules for commodity trading are given: (1) Select active commodities that have big open interest. (2) Trade in only one or two commodities. (3) Use stop-loss orders. (4) Do not put up additional margin money if a trade goes bad. (5) Use profits (if any) to pyramid. Shulman also states that one basic rule exists for all commodity futures trading: "cut your losses and let your profits ride. Never average down."

Teweles, Richard J., and others. "The Broad Plan." In their *The Commodity Futures Game*, pp. 231–233. 1974.

> Traders must have a plan or rules for taking care of the three possibilities that exist after a position is initiated: loss, profit, no change. (1) Loss. Teweles and co-authors strongly recommend using stop orders to prevent small losses from becoming big ones. Disaster is predicted for those who do not use stops when initiating trades. (2) Profit. There is said to be no clearly preferable method of taking profits, although the trader should

always have one plan or another in mind. The price objective system may be used, an indicator of some kind may be used, or the winning trade may simply be closed out after a specified period of time has elapsed. (3) No change or little change. Either establish an arbitrary time limit or wait until the delivery month approaches.

Teweles, Richard J., and others. "Maxims: Good and Bad." In their *The Commodity Futures Game*, pp. 287-294. 1974.

"There is some old saying that will justify almost any action or lack of action." The authors emphasize the fact that many maxims or trading rules are contradictory, as in "Don't put all your eggs in one basket" versus "Put all your eggs in one basket and watch the basket." Adages are discussed by broad category, as to whether they are concerned with selection of commodities to be traded, opinions of others, timing of trades, or character of the market. Teweles and co-authors close their chapter on maxims by quoting a most distressing saying: "A speculator who dies rich has died before his time."

Thackray, John. "The Perilous Present for Commodity Futures." *Money*, vol. 2, August 1973, pp. 28-31.

Eight "golden rules for survival" are given for those who insist on speculating in commodity futures: (1) Use only capital that you can afford to lose. (2) Have a logical trading plan and stick with it. (3) Start with enough capital—at least $10,000. (4) Diversify; do not put more than one third of speculative capital into a single position. (5) Any pyramiding must be done with restraint. (6) Don't trade too actively; be patient. (7) Trade only in active commodities. (8) "Follow several commodities continuously," although probably only a couple will be worth speculating in at a given moment.

Watling, T. F., and Morley, J. "Market Psychology: The Great Factor." In their *Successful Commodity Futures Trading*, pp. 75-87. 1974.

Some rules from British authors that are very similar to those from American writers: (1) Never buck a trend (trade with the major price trend). (2) Be patient. (3) Don't run losses (cut losses short). (4) Don't be afraid to short the markets (sell short when necessary). (5) Don't listen to tips. (6) Try to learn what news is significant and what is not. (7) Don't anticipate a directional move (don't anticipate chart movements). Each rule is thoroughly explained.

TRADING SYSTEMS See Mechanical Trading Systems; Moving Average; Trading Rules; Trend Following

TRADING TACTICS. See Psychology; Trading Rules

TRADING VOLUME. See Volume of Trading

TREND FOLLOWING (*See also* Mechanical Trading Systems; Moving Average) Various methods of speculating in commodity futures that are based on the tendency of prices to display inertia and to continue for a while in a previously established direction.

Angrist, Stanley W. "Trend Lines." In his *Sensible Speculating in Commodities,* pp. 107–109. 1972.

>Basic trend lines on a commodity bar chart are shown, and there is a brief discussion of trading with the trend.

Cox, Houston A. "The Keys to Successful and Profitable Commodity Trading." In his *Concepts on Profits in Commodity Futures Trading,* pp. 168–169. 1972.

>The strategy of trend following is covered by five major rules and various subrules for finding a major trend, recognizing trend reversals, increasing position size, and knowing when to liquidate positions.

Cox, Houston A. "Trendline Analysis . . ." In his *Concepts on Profits in Commodity Futures Trading,* pp. 118–122. 1972.

>Trend analysis is based on the premise that a trend, once established (up or down), will continue. Cox states that this concept is "Simple, usually true, but not infallible." Trends do end. Two rather elaborate illustrations, one for downtrends and the other for uptrends, are used to explain trend lines and channels. The "little-understood fan-line variation" is explained as being a combination of three trend lines. Charts of daily sugar futures (July 1968) and monthly coffee futures (1935–1967) are used to show actual trend lines.

Donchian, Richard D. "Trend Following Methods in Commodity Price Analysis." In *Guide to Commodity Price Forecasting,* ed. by Harry Jiler and George B. Parker, pp. 48–60. 1965. (An earlier version of this article appears in the *1957 Commodity Year Book.*)

>General review of trend-following techniques in commodity futures trading. Examples are given for the following commodities: soybeans, cotton, rubber, wheat, and corn. The main advantage to trend following is said to be that profits are allowed to run as far as they will go, while losses are cut short. The chief disadvantage is that one may be caught in a trend that quickly changes direction several times in succession, resulting in a string of small but painful losses. Donchian states that three particular methods of following commodity price trends are "introduced, illustrated, and briefly discussed" in his article: the moving average, "swings," and relative strength. Detailed instructions for constructing tables and charts for each technique are given. The only relatively long-range results that are shown are for a ten-week moving average of weekly closing prices for May and November soybeans from 1952 to 1956. Results were good for this particular moving average of soybeans during this particular period, with a total gain of 204¢ being taken, exclusive of commissions. It must be

pointed out, however, that 98¢ of this profit resulted from a single trade (there were 24 transactions in all). Results are based on always being in the market, either long or short a single contract. Favorable results are also shown for a ten-day moving average in December 1956 cotton. The "swing" method is illustrated for December 1956 rubber, and this method might best be described as being based on short-term support and resistance points. Results were good with "50 point swings" (half-cent swings), but were even better with "100 point swings" (full-cent swings). Donchian then says that, "Grains tend to fluctuate more erratically than cotton or imported commodities." He recommends some specific swing amounts for various grains and illustrates one and a half cent swings for December 1956 wheat. Moving on to relative strength techniques, Donchian charts ratio lines showing the price strength of March 1957 wheat and March 1957 corn relative to the Dow Jones Commodity Futures Index. In the closing part of his article, he wisely recommends that technical trend-following techniques not be followed blindly, but be combined with a consideration of crop fundamentals.

Gold, Gerald. "Trade with the Trend—Not Against It." In his *Modern Commodity Futures Trading*, 6th ed., pp. 239-242. 1971.

Points out that all kinds of money can be lost by trying to guess where a trend will reverse before it actually does reverse. Gold states that one should never sell short just because the market seems "too high," nor buy because the market appears to be "low enough." Always go with the trend, for the market often proceeds further in one direction than would seem logical or reasonable.

Gold, Gerald. "The Trend Line." In his *Modern Commodity Futures Trading*, 6th ed., pp. 197-201. 1971.

The correct drawing of uptrend and downtrend lines is described and illustrated. A practical method of trading by using trend lines on commodity futures price charts is discussed.

Keltner, Chester W. "The Minor Trend Rule." In his *How to Make Money in Commodities*, pp. 52-54, 61-64, 68-72, 77-81. 1960.

The emphasis here is on the word "minor." In a trendless, narrowly fluctuating market, the minor trend rule will put the trader in and out of positions at a rapid rate, with many small losses. In a market with trends that persist for even a few weeks, the rule should work well. The speculator's buying and selling actions are dictated by minor price swings. A buy signal is given when the price of a commodity rises above the nearest previous price peak, regardless of the size of the peak, and a sell signal is flashed when the price falls below the nearest previous price dip or valley. On page 61 of his book, Keltner illustrates the minor trend rule with both a bar and a line chart for November 1959 soybeans (other trend following rules are also charted on this page). Pages 62-64 contain tabular price data for November 1959 soybeans, with minor trend rule buying and selling points indicated. On pages 68–72, there are itemized lists of trades made in wheat and soybeans, based on the continuous application of the minor trend rule from 1950 through 1959. A summary of profits and losses for each of the ten years is given. In "The Theoretically Perfect Mechanical Rule" (pp. 77–81), Keltner tells of the virtues of the minor trend rule for patient traders. Patience is required because there are years in which the rule will produce a net annual loss, as in 1951, 1952, 1955, 1957, and 1958 in May and December wheat. For the trader with strong nerves, however, the good years should more than make up for the bad ones.

Keltner, Chester W. "Trading Rule No. 19." In his *How to Make Money in Commodities*, pp. 54–58, 61–64, 73–77. 1960.

This mechanical trading rule utilizes a somewhat complicated system of "down-trend key days" and "up-trend key days." Keltner states that, "Trading Rule 19 was first published in January of 1935 and got its name... from a numbering system under which rules qualifying for a cash prize were identified." The rule worked very well for Chicago wheat futures from 1928 through 1934, but failed in later years, illustrating the point that it is impossible to tell in advance just how long a mechanical rule will be profitable. The fact that any mechanical system can stop working well at any time puts a great strain on the emotions of a commodity speculator who relies on such a system.

Kroll, Stanley, and Shishko, Irwin. "The Trend of the Market." In their *Commodity Futures Market Guide*, pp. 107–120. 1973.

The trend line, the trend channel, wave theory, mathematical trends, and trend reversal are discussed. The authors state that a trend that is "lean and steep" is more likely to endure and have significant momentum than a trend that is "broad and shallow." Four hypotheses on trend validity are presented, although, as the authors admit, the hypotheses have been derived from the folklore of Wall Street. Five elements that are characteristic of the reversal of an uptrend are listed.

Reinach, Anthony M. "Basic Types of Action." In his *The Fastest Game in Town*, pp. 70–73. 1973.

Theoretical price trend action is illustrated. Lengths of trends are designated as follows: mini-term (a few days), short-term (a week to a month), medium-term (from one to three months), long-term (three months to a year), and maxi-term (over a year).

Reinach, Anthony M. "Trend Action." In his *The Fastest Game in Town*, pp. 101–125. 1973.

A major trend is characterized by a price rise of 50 percent or over or a price drop of 33 percent or more. An intermediate trend will have a price increase of from 10 to 50 percent or a decrease of 10 to 33 percent. Minor trends show price changes of from 3 to 10 percent, while nominal trends involve changes of less than 3 percent. Eight popular methods of attempting to profit from commodity price trends are explained: (1) anticipating or "bucking" the trend; (2) taking a position during a trend consolidation; (3) attempting to buy during the formation of a bottom or sell during the formation of a top; (4) buying or selling when prices break out of congestion areas; (5) buying or selling "upon the breaking of the first minor counter trend after a breakout from a bottom or a top"; (6) taking a position just as soon as a trend is perceived; (7) taking clues from price gaps—common, breakaway, runaway, or exhaustion; and (8) using moving averages. Reinach discusses each of these eight procedures.

Teweles, Richard J., and others. "Trend-Following Methods." In their *The Commodity Futures Game*, pp. 176–182. 1974.

> Moving averages and swing charts are covered. The advantages of trend following are said to be objectivity, clearly defined action points, and the automatic following of big price moves. Disadvantages are whipsawing, late trades, the great danger of trendless markets, and the sad fact that a system that worked very well during one period of time may fail during another period.

TRIANGLES (COILS)

Progressively smaller or larger price formations resulting in triangular or coil-shaped areas on commodity price charts. Commodity market technical analysts believe these patterns are significant, although difficult to interpret.

Gold, Gerald. "Triangles, Coils, Flags and Pennants." In his *Modern Commodity Futures Trading*, 6th ed. pp. 207–210. 1971.

> An ascending triangle, a descending triangle, a symmetrical triangle, and a "flag" are pictured (price chart formations) and described. The logical placement of stop-loss orders is discussed in relation to chart formations.

U.S. DEPARTMENT OF AGRICULTURE SOURCES. See Statistics Sources

VERTICAL LINE CHARTS. See Charts

"THE VOICE FROM THE TOMB"

Seasonal dates for buying and selling corn and wheat, supposedly revealed from a search of the papers of a dead commodity speculator who had become wealthy by trading in futures according to these dates.

Belveal, L. Dee. "Voice from the Tomb." In his *Commodity Speculation with Profits in Mind*, pp. 151–152. 1967.

> Buying and selling dates for corn and wheat are given, according to the "Voice." "The story is told that an old and highly successful speculator lay on his deathbed"—and so forth. Belveal says that the phantasmal dates conform well enough to seasonal price behavior to deserve consideration.

Gold, Gerald. "The Voice from the Tomb." In his *Modern Commodity Futures Trading*, 6th ed., p. 65. 1971.

> The ghostly trading dates are set forth, with the remark that they are still believed to be used by some speculators as guides. The dates are, of course, based on well-known seasonal tendencies for corn and wheat, making them earthly rather than otherworldly.

Newsweek. "Voice from the Tomb." *Newsweek*, vol. 21, March 29, 1943, p. 50.

> Edward A. Driver was a relatively small grain speculator in Chicago who baffled his colleagues as to why he was so consistently on the winning side. Then Driver died (February 5, 1904) and his secret formula was found among his papers. His plan called for the buying or selling of corn and wheat on ten different dates, as follows: buy wheat on February 21, July 1, and November 28; sell wheat on January 10, May 10, and September 10; buy corn on March 1 and June 25; sell corn on May 20 and August 10. Driver gave a logical explanation for the choice of each date. For example, buy wheat on July 1 because the movement of winter wheat to market is well under way and prices should be dropping; sell wheat on September 10 because this will close the trader out of his position before spring wheat marketing starts to drive prices down. This system worked very well until governmental crop controls, price supports, and commodity loans began to distort normal seasonal factors.

VOLUME OF TRADING (*See also* Open Interest)
Total buying and selling of a commodity futures contract or contracts during a specified period of time, as during a day, week, or year. As the number of purchases is, of course, the same as the number of sales, volume data are given as "total sales." Technicians and price chartists usually attach importance to noticeable changes in volume.

Belveal, L. Dee. "Understanding Trade Volume as a Measurement of Urgency." In his *Charting Commodity Price Behavior*, pp. 101-124. 1969.

> Volume of trading is stated to be a neutral factor so long as it remains fairly constant. However, sharp changes in volume should be regarded by speculators as being of high significance. Belveal says that "volume is a sphinx *most* of the time," in that weeks and months may pass with no particular change in the volume level of a certain commodity. Various volume patterns and their relationship to price changes are considered.

Gold, Gerald. "Volume of Trading." In his *Modern Commodity Futures Trading*, 6th ed., pp. 211-224. 1971.

> If volume of trading for all delivery months combined of a particular commodity is rising at the same time that prices are rising, the upward price trend is likely to continue. On the other hand, if volume increases while prices fall, the downtrend will probably be maintained. Gold uses a full-page chart to illustrate volume, open interest, and trend of prices.

178 COMMODITY FUTURES TRADING

Kroll, Stanley, and Shishko, Irwin. "Seasonally Adjusted Open Interest and Volume Charts." In their *Commodity Futures Market Guide*, pp. 348–352. 1973.

> Charts show seasonal trends of open interest and volume for 15 different commodities. Volume is charted monthly, January through December, based on a ten-year, 1955–1964, average. The data plotted represent monthly totals as percentages of the ten-year average.

Kroll, Stanley, and Shishko, Irwin. "What Do Volume and Open Interest Show?" In their *Commodity Futures Market Guide*, pp. 137–148. 1973.

> Price changes accompanied by high volume are apt to be more significant than price changes accompanied by low volume. For the most part, the Kroll-Shishko discussion of volume of trading is combined with a consideration of open interest.

Reinach, Anthony M. "Volume Action—Secret of the Pros." In his *The Fastest Game in Town*, pp. 126–137. 1973.

> Commodity futures trading volume is classified as being either "attendant" (generally anticipated, and therefore of little predictive value) or "prognostic" (unexpected, and therefore of definite predictive value). The forecasting value of volume changes as prices move into or out of congestion areas is especially elaborated upon. Reinach states that commodity volume action is not so capricious as it seems, but such action must be analyzed in a logical manner.

Shaw, John E. B. "How to Use Trading Volume." In his *A Professional Guide to Commodity Speculation*, pp. 137–140. 1972.

> A mechanical trading method is described in which daily price changes are multiplied by daily volume of trading. Calculations are shown on a daily basis for the May 1969 pork belly contract during January and February 1969.

Teweles, Richard J., and others. "On Balance Volume." In their *The Commodity Futures Game*, pp. 188–191. 1974.

> "On balance" volume is a running total of cumulative volume to which volume on price-up days is added and volume on price-down days is subtracted. The absolute level of the cumulative volume is not important; only the direction or shape of the plotted curve is significant. The advantages of "on balance" volume analysis are said to be that an awareness of the activity of large traders is provided, and that it is important to know if prices are rising or falling on big volume. The disadvantages are that this kind of analysis may be too long term in nature, that there are no objective rules for interpretation, and that the calculation itself may be too simplistic.

WAR AND COMMODITY PRICES

Because of shortages that develop, wars have a great influence on commodity prices.

Commodity Research Bureau. "War and Commodities." In *Commodities in Industry; the 1940 Commodity Year Book*, pp. 2–14. 1940.

> "The most violent rises in commodity prices have always occurred during times of war." The major factors affecting prices during a war are inflation, civilian production restrictions, destruction of facilities, hoarding, rationing, and transportation problems. These factors are discussed in the text of this *Commodity Year Book* article, and various charts are presented. The "Yearly Average Price of Wheat in England" is charted from 1500 to 1940 in U.S. cents per bushel, with war periods indicated. Fifteen other, small charts show the prices of many different commodities during the World War I period (1914–1920).

Commodity Research Bureau. "War and Commodities." In *Commodity Year Book 1939*, pp. 27–35. 1939.

> A discussion from a historical viewpoint of the manner in which wars or war scares affect commodity prices. A long-term price chart of two pages shows the wholesale commodity price index from 1720 to 1938, with 1910–1914 equaling 100.

Commodity Research Bureau. "War and Commodity Prices." In *Commodity Year Book 1941*, pp. 42–54. 1941.

> "...major, protracted wars breed higher commodity prices." Topics discussed include inflation, commodity demand dislocation, wartime production limitations or expansions, transportation problems, and inflation controls. Fourteen small charts show cash prices for various commodities for 1914 to 1920. Eleven larger charts show cash prices from 1914 to 1919, with monthly price movements from 1939 to early 1941 plotted directly under prices from 1914 to early 1916.

WAVE THEORY. See Elliott Wave Principle

WEATHER MARKET

As the weather has a great influence on crop prospects, the weather has a great influence on commodity futures prices.

Belveal, L. Dee. "Weather Markets." In his *Commodity Speculation with Profits in Mind*, pp. 283–285. 1967.

> Speculators tend to become emotional about weather prospects for any particular commodity, and therefore tend to overbuy if the weather news seems bad and oversell if conditions seem favorable. Changeable, erratic weather will, as a result of these feelings on the part of traders,

produce sharp fluctuations in commodity futures prices. Belveal says that prices in weather markets are always fickle, but produce "exciting and profitable speculative opportunities." The speculator must be prepared to take small losses while waiting to establish a position in a major move.

WHEAT (See also Wheat—Seasonal Price Trend; Wheat Spread; Wheat-Corn Spread; Wheat-Rye Spread)

The seed or kernel of the wheat plant, the most important source of grain in the world. Most wheat is ground into flour of various kinds that is used chiefly by commercial bakeries, but some wheat is also used for breakfast foods, macaroni products, animal feed, and other purposes. The two main categories are winter wheat, which is planted in the fall and harvested in the early summer, and spring wheat, which is planted in the spring and harvested later in the summer of the same year. Total production of winter wheat in the United States is roughly three times that of spring wheat. The leading wheat-growing countries are Russia and the United States, and the principal wheat-growing states are Kansas (winter wheat) and North Dakota (spring wheat). Both winter and spring wheat are traded on the futures market of the Chicago Board of Trade; winter wheat is traded on the Kansas City Board of Trade; spring wheat is traded on the Minneapolis Grain Exchange; and domestic feed wheat is traded on the Winnipeg Commodity Exchange.

Arthur, Henry B. "Wheat and Flour Milling." In his *Commodity Futures as a Business Management Tool*, pp. 141–179. 1971.

> General description of the wheat market, with emphasis on the activities of farm managers, grain elevator operators, and grain dealers. The hedging operations of three companies—Continental Grain Co., Pillsbury Co., and Bay State Milling Co.—are described at some length.

Chicago Board of Trade. "Grain Commodities." In *Commodity Trading Manual*, pp. 137–142. 1973.

> Information is given regarding varieties of wheat (hard red winter, soft red winter, hard red spring, durum, and white), supply factors, the federal wheat program, and consumption factors. Futures trading details for wheat are given for the Chicago Board of Trade, Kansas City Board of Trade, Minneapolis Grain Exchange, and Mid-America Commodity Exchange (formerly the Chicago Open Board of Trade). Delivery months, trading units, price fluctuation specifications, daily price limits, position limits, delivery standards, and trading hours are summarized for each exchange. The history of wheat is also briefly discussed.

Chicago Board of Trade. *Introduction to the Wheat Futures Market*. No date. 38 pp.

> Wheat markets at Chicago, Kansas City, and Minneapolis are covered. Grain price structure, the forecasting of price trends in wheat, the loan

rate, supply and demand, exports, and seasonal price influences are among the topics included. The advantages of spreading operations between the three major markets are briefly considered and examples of hedging transactions are given. Two charts show the Chicago-Kansas City December wheat spread from 1965 to 1968 and the Chicago-Minneapolis December wheat spread for the same time period.

Emery, Walter L. "Understanding the Wheat Futures Markets." In *Commodity Year Book 1967*, pp. 6-18. 1967.

"It is the purpose... to bring the major classes of wheat and their distribution pattern into focus...." Section one covers the Kansas City wheat market, section two is on Chicago wheat, section three deals with Minneapolis wheat, and section four presents "A Method of Procedure in Evaluating Price Prospects." Production, exports, price structure, and the futures market are discussed for Kansas City (hard red winter wheat), Chicago (soft red winter wheat), and Minneapolis (hard red spring wheat). Soft white wheat, grown in Washington state, and durum wheat (North Dakota) are briefly discussed. Section four of Emery's article is a discourse on wheat supply and demand. Although total supply may equal carryover plus production, serious disruptions can be caused by bad weather delaying the harvest, farmers holding back wheat, boxcar shortages, rail strikes, and other events. Estimates of wheat production and stocks are sometimes subject to sizable revision. On the demand side, exports receive more attention than domestic business because exports are subject to great fluctuation. "On balance one must bear in mind that markets tend to move on anticipation rather than realization...." (Daily basis price charts are included with this article, showing May wheat futures at Chicago from 1960 to 1967.)

Goldberg, Ray A. "Wheat." In his *Agribusiness Coordination*, pp. 19-99, 1968.

A scholarly look at the fundamentals of the wheat market, in three parts: "The Dynamics of the Wheat Economy" (consumption, production, processing, and transportation), "The Wheat Complex" (distribution, ownership, the futures market, government activities), and "Behavioral and Performance Patterns of the Wheat System" (inventory, pricing, wheat users). A systems approach is used by Goldberg to describe the wheat economy.

Keltner, Chester W. "Fundamental Analysis Applied to Wheat Situations Since 1940." In his *How to Make Money in Commodities*, pp. 131-154, 1960.

This is a detailed, fundamental analysis of the supply and demand situation in wheat from 1940 to 1960. Each of the 20 crop years is individually described and analyzed. Tables show supplies, disappearance, free surplus, impoundings, Chicago loan rate, and seasonal price advances for each year. Keltner devotes pages 150-154 to a general discussion of the fundamental analysis of wheat prices. Supply and demand, the price level, and seasonal price tendencies are emphasized. (Daily price charts of Chicago May wheat from 1950–1951 to 1959–1960 are shown separately on pages 205 to 209 of Keltner's book.)

Lowell, Fred R. *The Wheat Market*. 1968. 473 pp.

After a detailed discussion of each wheat marketing season from 1930–1931 to 1967–1968, Lowell reviews wheat legislation, export programs, intermarket (Chicago versus Kansas City) spreads, and intracommodity (carrying charge) spreads. Twenty-eight statistical tables are shown to "provide a statistical record of basic factors and prices with respect to wheat for the 1930-31 through 1966-67 period." Each of the 28 tables is explained. Finally, a section of price charts shows Chicago May wheat on a daily basis from 1930 to 1968, Chicago July wheat on a daily basis from 1930 to 1968, and Chicago December wheat on a daily basis from 1930 to 1967. This is an important volume for commodity traders who are seriously interested in the wheat futures market.

Merrill Lynch, Pierce, Fenner & Smith, Inc. "Questions and Answers About Wheat." In *How to Buy and Sell Commodities*, pp. 28–35. 1972.

A series of 30 questions and answers provides an excellent summary of the basic facts about wheat futures trading. A clear, full-page chart shows the "Seasonal Trend of Wheat Price" for farm prices, May futures, and December futures. The chart covers the 12-month season from the beginning of July to the end of June.

Schruben, Leonard W., and Clifton, Ruth E. "How to Forecast Wheat Prices." In *Guide to Commodity Price Forecasting*, ed. by Harry Jiler and George B. Parker, pp. 183–200. 1965. (An earlier version of this article appears in the 1961 *Commodity Year Book*.)

States that anyone who is good with words is capable of turning out a commodity forecast that reads well and seems logical. Whether or not the forecast actually has any value is, of course, another matter. "There are no short cuts to hard work and hard experience." After considering supply-demand balance and price supports, the authors devote most of their article to a detailed examination of seasonal variations in wheat prices. Charts show daily wheat futures prices for the July Chicago contract from 1956 to 1965.

Teweles, Richard J., and others. "Wheat." In their *The Commodity Futures Game*, pp. 360–375. 1974.

Factors influencing prices, sources of information, supply and demand, government programs, seasonal trends, and carrying charges are all covered. Results of the wheat-corn spread in which a trader is long December wheat and short December corn are given from 1949 through 1973. Results of the opposite spread, short December wheat and long December corn, are also given for the same years. A graph shows "Wheat: monthly open interest and volume as a percentage of average monthly open interest and volume for the years 1962-1971 at the Chicago Board of Trade."

Watling, T. F., and Morley, J. "Grains." In their *Successful Commodity Futures Trading*, pp. 189-190. 1974.

Futures trading details for "home-grown wheat" (British) are given as traded by the London Corn Trade Association.

WHEAT—SEASONAL PRICE TREND (*See also* "The Voice from the Tomb")

Marketing of the annual wheat harvest normally begins in May with winter wheat from southern regions (Southwest) and ends in the fall with spring wheat from the Dakotas. Low prices for the season typically occur in July or August, with highs the following winter or early spring.

Commodity Research Bureau. "Seasonal Trends in Grain Futures Prices." In *Commodity Year Book 1952*, pp. 20-22. 1952.

A price advance in May wheat occurred after August 15 in every season from 1938-1939 to 1950-1951. The advance ranged from 11¢ to 93¢ or from about five to 74 percent. A table shows "May Wheat Delivery: Closing Prices August 15, Subsequent Highs and Advances Thereafter, 1938-39 to 1950-51 (Cents per Bushel)." A chart shows "Monthly Seasonal Trend in Marketing of Wheat (in Percent of Total Marketings), 10 Year Monthly Average, 1941-50." The monthly percentages shown in the chart are related to wheat receipts at primary markets. Other charts show daily futures prices for May wheat at Chicago from 1939 to 1952. The government loan rate at Chicago is also indicated on each chart.

Keltner, Chester W. "Chicago December Wheat—Seasonal Price Advances Following the July-August Low in Past Years." In his *How to Make Money in Commodities*, p. 134. 1960.

This is a table showing loan rate, July-August low price, September high price, October high, November high, December high, and extreme price advance for each year from 1940 to 1959.

Lowell, Fred R. "A Season by Season Review of Past Wheat Situations." In his *The Wheat Market*, pp. 9-209. 1968.

Several pages of discussion are devoted to each of the wheat seasons (July of one year to June of the next year) form 1930-1931 to 1967-1968. Headlines at the beginning of each season's review summarize what happened during that crop year, such as "Futures Prices Weaken Again Despite Drouth Disaster" (1934-1935) or "Large Impoundings and Higher Loan Lead to a Broad Price Advance" (1955-1956). Accompanying each season's discussion is a chart showing total trading volume at Chicago on a daily basis, total open interest on a daily basis, and daily prices for the May and July Chicago futures contracts. The Chicago wheat loan rate is also indicated for each year. (Those who wish further data on the seasonal tendencies of wheat should consult the tables at the back of Lowell's book, where he gives such handy compilations as the one on page 342, covering 1930 to 1967, and showing "Season's Highs and Lows for Chicago May, July and December Futures Contracts; Also Months in Which Highs and Lows Were Established.")

Schruben, Leonard W., and Clifton, Ruth E. "Seasonal Price Fluctuations." In *Guide to Commodity Price Forecasting*, ed. by Harry Jiler and George B. Parker, pp. 191–198. 1965.

> Wheat prices are said to follow a distinct seasonal pattern, with low prices occurring during the summer harvest season and high prices the following winter or spring. A chart is provided showing two indexes of the seasonal variation of Kansas farm wheat prices. One index line represents the average seasonal pattern of wheat prices during the years from 1910 to 1937, while the other index line represents 1938 to 1960 (federal government support of wheat prices started in 1938). Three very interesting tables show the percent of years that the midmonth Kansas farm wheat price increased, stayed the same, or declined from any given month (base month) to any subsequent month within the next 12 months. The period of time covered is from 1910 to 1964. For example, during 81 percent of the crop years covered, farm wheat prices increased from July to the following May. During 80 percent of the crop years, farm wheat prices declined from March to July. Three additional tables give the same information for the years from 1938 to 1963. The percent of regularity of seasonal changes was greater from 1938 to 1963 than from 1910 to 1964.

WHEAT SPREAD (*See also* Intermarket Wheat Spread)
Buying one month of wheat futures and selling another on the same market (in this case) in an attempt to profit from changes in the price relationship or spread.

Commodity Research Bureau. "Commodity Spreads and Straddles." In *Commodity Year Book 1948*, pp. 46–47. 1948.

> The May-July and the July-September wheat spreads are discussed. "Seasonal Factors in Wheat Spreads" are briefly considered.

Greenberg, Stephen. "Illustration of Intra Market and Statistical Straddle—the May-July Wheat Spread." In *Guide to Commodity Price Forecasting*, ed. by Harry Jiler and George B. Parker, pp. 214–219. 1965. (An earlier version of this article appears in the 1960 *Commodity Year Book*.)

> The May-July wheat spread is said to be an operation that attempts to take advantage of variations in price between old crop futures (May) and new crop futures (July). Greenberg discusses three major factors influencing May wheat and three factors affecting July wheat. While there is no clear seasonal pattern to the May-July wheat spread, success-

ful analysis of the various factors can result in large profits. Charts show the daily "May over July" futures spread at Chicago from 1948 to 1965.

Lowell, Fred R. "Carrying Charge Relationships." In his *The Wheat Market*, pp. 297–312. 1968.

"Successful spreading operations involving carrying charge relationships require a carefully acquired background knowledge.... An understanding of the general theory ... is by no means sufficient knowledge to insure successful trading operations." Lowell emphasizes that the average commodity speculator should understand that carrying charge relationships are complex and may be, at any one time, meaningful or virtually meaningless. Many considerations are involved. Pages 303–312 of Lowell's book are devoted to reproductions of charts showing the March over December spread and the May over March spread for Chicago wheat prices from the 1957–1958 season to 1966–1967.

Vannerson, Frank. "May-July Wheat Spread at Chicago." In *Commodity Year Book 1969*, pp. 43–48. 1969.

Volatility is what makes the May-July wheat spread of particular interest to traders. In recent years, the price spread of the May futures contract over the July contract has been, for example, about 48¢ in February 1964 and an unusual minus 4¢ in April 1968, to give two extreme examples. The May-July wheat spread is said to frequently offer excellent speculative opportunities. The only catch is the usual one—timing. Wheat carryover figures are not easy to predict, but they must be predicted early in the crop year (*correctly* predicted, that is) if major spread moves are to be taken advantage of. Vannerson gives detailed instructions to help the speculator make valid forecasts. Charts show the spread of May wheat over July wheat on a daily basis at Chicago from 1954 to 1969.

WHEAT-CORN SPREAD

Usually, the buying of December wheat with the simultaneous selling short of December corn. When instituted about the first of June, seasonal tendencies work for the trader in that wheat prices should be low (and ready to rise) during June harvest, while corn prices should be high prior to falling during the autumn harvest.

Angrist, Stanley W. "Intercommodity Spreads." In his *Sensible Speculating in Commodities*, pp. 165–167. 1972.

Angrist says that the margin needed for this spread would probably be the same as the margin required for the higher priced of the two commodities (wheat, normally). He includes a table, "The Long December Wheat-Short December Corn Spread," showing the results that would have been obtained from this spread from June to November of each year from 1962 to 1971. The author mentions that the December wheat-

December corn spread is one of the more popular operations and that, unfortunately, being popular can lessen a spread's profitability.

Clifton, Frederick T. "Spreads Between Wheat and Corn." In *Guide to Commodity Price Forecasting*, ed. by Harry Jiler and George B. Parker, pp. 263–275. (An earlier version of this article appears in the 1964 *Commodity Year Book*.)

Fundamentals of the wheat-corn spread are discussed, with emphasis on seasonal considerations. The following are treated in some detail: long wheat-short corn; the March wheat-March corn spread; long corn-short wheat (spreading the Julys). Spreaders are told to work hard at timing, to stay in tune with price trends, to take advantage of supply-demand factors, to get out quickly if something goes wrong, and to stay out of the market "if things don't look right." Charts show the March wheat-March corn price spread on a daily basis from 1957 to 1964 and the July wheat-July corn spread for the same years.

Greenberg, Stephen. "Seasonal and Inter Commodity Straddle—December Wheat and December Corn Spread." In *Guide to Commodity Price Forecasting*, ed. by Harry Jiler and George B. Parker, pp. 219–222. 1965. (An earlier version of this article appears in the 1960 *Commodity Year Book*.)

There are two definite seasonal tendencies to keep in mind when analyzing the December wheat over December corn spread: (1) December wheat often loses ground to December corn between March and June and (2) December corn typically loses to December wheat between June and November. A table shows "Premium December Wheat Over December Corn (Cents per Bushel)" for the dates March 1 and June 1 from 1949 to 1964. Another table gives the same data for June 1 and November 1 from 1949 to 1964. Charts show the daily "Wheat vs. Corn" futures spread at Chicago from 1949 to 1964.

Teweles, Richard J., and others. "Seasonal Information." In their *The Commodity Futures Game*, pp. 371–372. 1974.

The traditional long wheat and short corn spread is described as having been profitable in recent years (although unprofitable in 1962, 1964, and 1966–1968). A table shows "Results of Spread, Long December wheat—Short December Corn: Position Initiated on June 1 and Closed on November 1, 1949–1973." The table shows 17 winning years and 8 losing years. Another table shows results of the reverse position, in which wheat is sold short and corn bought, with positions initiated in March and closed out in June. In this case, there were 19 winning years and only 6 losing, although profits were quite limited in seven of the winning years.

WHEAT-RYE SPREAD

Typically, the buying of May wheat while selling May rye short. The logic here is that rye tends to be marketed in quantity in the spring, while large supplies of wheat do not generally appear on the market until summer harvest. Therefore, in the months just prior to harvest, there is a tendency for wheat prices to be strong relative to rye.

Greenberg, Stephen. "The May Wheat-May Rye Spread." In *Guide to Commodity Price Forecasting*, ed. by Harry Jiler and George B. Parker, pp. 223, 226, 228. 1965.

> Greenberg states that the potential risks in this straddle cannot be overlooked (it works part of the time, in other words). He mentions the following "sobering points" that may contribute to strength in rye prices and thus contribute to the failure of the wheat-rye spread (assuming that wheat is bought and rye sold short): a small decrease in rye production can result in a large increase in rye prices, because of relatively thin markets; rye exports may increase and tighten available supplies. A table shows "Premium of May Wheat Over May Rye, August 1, the Following April 1 and Net Change from August 1 to April 1, 1948-49 Through 1963-64 (Cents Per Bushel)." Charts show the daily spread of May wheat over May rye at Chicago from 1956 to 1964.

WOMEN AS COMMODITY TRADERS

There has evidently been a tendency on the part of some commodity brokers to regard women as too "emotional" for the rigors of commodity speculation and to try to put restrictions on trading by women.

Angrist, Stanley W. "Women Commodity Traders." In his *Sensible Speculating in Commodities*, pp. 50-52. 1972.

> In which the author tells of certain commodity firms (not named) that will not open accounts for women unless their husbands agree to be responsible for any losses. On the other hand, many brokers accept women clients on the same basis as men. Angrist recommends that any woman who comes across a discriminatory broker should file a complaint with her state attorney general.

WOOD PRODUCTS. See Lumber and Plywood

WOOL

The fleecy, resilient hair from sheep, used to make cloth, carpeting, and other products. Australia, Russia, and New Zealand are the leading wool-producing countries. U.S. wool production is relatively small. Wool futures are traded on the New York Cotton Exchange, the Sydney Greasy Wool Futures Exchange Ltd. of Australia, and the London Wool Terminal Market.

Baldwin, Gedney H. "How to Forecast Wool Futures Prices." In *Guide to Commodity Price Forecasting*, ed. by Harry Jiler and George B. Parker, pp. 201-

212. 1965. (An earlier version of this article appears in the 1962 *Commodity Year Book*.)

> Wool is said to be a complex commodity that is difficult to approach from the normal supply-demand standpoint. For example, there are over 3,000 commercial wool types that are produced in varying amounts all over the world. Other complicating factors are foreign exchange fluctuations, late statistics, and synthetic wool substitutes. Baldwin discusses factors influencing wool prices in both the United States and world markets. A long-term chart shows grease wool futures prices weekly from 1953 to 1965. Other charts show daily grease wool futures prices for the December delivery (New York) from 1954 to 1965.

Chicago Board of Trade. "Wool." In *Commodity Trading Manual*, pp. 222-225. 1973.

> Wool supply and demand factors are briefly considered. Wool futures trading details are given for the New York Cotton Exchange Wool Associates (wool is also traded in Sydney, Australia, and London, England). The following are listed for the Wool Associates of the New York Cotton Exchange: delivery months, trading, units, minimum price fluctuations, daily price move limits, position limits, delivery standards, and trading hours. "World Production of Wool, Millions of Pounds (Greasy Basis)" is quoted for each of ten countries annually from 1963 to 1971. "U.S. Mill Consumption of Raw Wool, Scoured Basis" is given for apparel wool and carpet wool from 1963 to 1972.

Davies, M. E. T. "Wool." In *Getting Started in London Commodities*, ed. by C. W. J. Granger, pp. 48-50. 1975.

> A British view of wool trading, including contract and trading details for the London Commodity Exchange. Volume of trading has dropped greatly in recent years because of competition from synthetic fibers and the transfer of futures business to the Sydney, Australia, market. A table shows total London futures transactions in wooltops from 1963 to 1974 (volume of trading in 1,000 pound lots dropped from 233,550 in 1964 to 18,680 in 1973). A chart shows the monthly range of London spot wooltop prices from 1966 to early 1975.

Donnelly, Richard A. "Future in Wool? It's One Commodity That Almost Nobody Buys or Sells." *Barron's*, vol. 53, April 23, 1973, p. 5.

> Despite soaring wool prices in 1971-1972, volume of trading in wool futures on the New York Cotton Exchange remained very low. The reasons for this inactivity are said to be shrinking wool production in the United States and a resultant lack of hedging activity, as well as a shift of important wool trading to overseas markets.

Teweles, Richard J., and others. "Wool." In their *The Commodity Futures Game*, pp. 560–569. 1974.

    The authors consider price factors, information sources, supply, demand, government programs, and seasonal tendencies. Conditions in Australia are said to be important to wool traders.

Watling, T. F., and Morley, J. "Wool." In their *Successful Commodity Futures Trading*, pp. 193–195. 1974.

    The authors mention that two different wool futures contracts are traded on the London Commodity Exchange—one contract is for dry combed wooltops and the other is for greasy wool. Contract details are given, after which supply-demand factors are briefly discussed. Watling and Morley state that "Wool tends to be a very thin market and is often difficult to trade...."

BIBLIOGRAPHY

Angrist, Stanley W. *Sensible Speculating in Commodities, or How to Profit in the Bellies, Bushels and Bales Markets.* New York: Simon & Schuster, 1972. 223 pp. $7.95.

Arthur, Henry B. *Commodity Futures as a Business Management Tool.* Boston: Harvard University, Graduate School of Business Administration (Division of Research), 1971. 392 pp. $12.50.

Bache & Co., Inc. *Money Management Concepts for Commodity Traders.* New York: Bache & Co., no date. 10 pp. Free.

Belveal, L. Dee. *Charting Commodity Market Price Behavior.* Wilmette, Ill.: Commodities Press, 1969. 274 pp. $12.50.

Belveal, L. Dee. *Commodity Speculation with Profits in Mind.* Wilmette, Ill.: Commodities Press, 1969. 274 pp. $12.50.

Berlin, Bruce S. *Corporate Use of Commodity Futures.* New York: The Conference Board, 1972. 33 pp. $5.00 ($1.00 to Conference Board Associates and educational institutions).

Brealey, Richard A. and Pyle, Connie. *A Bibliography of Finance and Investment.* Cambridge, Mass.: MIT Press, 1973. 361 pp. $18.50.

Carabini, Louis E., ed. *Everything You Need to Know Now About Gold and Silver.* New Rochelle, N.Y.: Arlington House, 1974. 176 pp. $8.95.

Chicago Board of Trade. *Commodity Futures Trading: A Bibliography, 1967-1974.* Chicago: Chicago Board of Trade, 1975. 85 pp. Frequently updated. Apply.

Chicago Board of Trade. *Commodity Trading Manual.* Chicago: Chicago Board of Trade, 1973. 298 pp. $17.50.

Chicago Board of Trade. *Introduction to the Wheat Futures Market.* Chicago: Chicago Board of Trade, no date. 38 pp. Apply.

Commodities; the Magazine of Futures Trading. Investor Publications, Inc. Monthly, $34/yr., including May directory issue ("Reference Guide to Futures Markets"). May issue only, $6.

Commodity Journal. American Association of Commodity Traders. Bimonthly. $12/yr.

Commodity Year Book. New York: Commodity Research Bureau. Annual. $21.95.

Consensus. Consensus, Inc. Weekly. $195/yr.

Cowing, Cedric B. *Populists, Plungers, and Progressives; a Social History of Stock and Commodity Speculation, 1890-1936.* Princeton, N.J.: Princeton University Press, 1965. 299 pp. $11.

Cox, Houston A. *Concepts on Profits in Commodity Futures Trading.* New York: Reynolds Securities, Inc., 1972. 196 pp. Inquire as to availability and price.

Dobson, Edward D. *Commodity Spreads: A Historical Chart Perspective.* Greenville, S.C.: Dobson, 1975. 78 pp. $12.

Gardner, Robert L. *How to Make Money in the Commodity Market.* Englewood Cliffs, N.J.: Prentice-Hall, 1961. 194 pp. (Apparently out-of-print.)

Glick, Ira O. *A Social Psychological Study of Futures Trading.* Ph.D. Dissertation, Department of Sociology, University of Chicago, 1957. 267 pp. (Available on microfilm from the University of Chicago.)

Gold, Gerald. *Modern Commodity Futures Trading*, 6th ed. New York: Commodity Research Bureau, 1971. 262 pp. $10.

Goldberg, Ray A. *Agribusiness Coordination; A Systems Approach to the Wheat, Soybean, and Florida Orange Economies.* Boston: Harvard University, Graduate School of Business Administration, Division of Research, 1968. 256 pp. $12.

Goldberg, Ray A. *The Soybean Industry.* Minneapolis: University of Minnesota Press, 1952. 186 pp. $6.

Goss, B. A. *Theory of Futures Trading.* (Students Library of Economics) London and Boston: Routledge & Kegan Paul, 1972. 116 pp. $6.75.

Gould, Bruce G. *Dow Jones-Irwin Guide to Commodities Trading.* Homewood, Ill.: Dow Jones-Irwin, 1973. 357 pp. $14.95.

Granger, C. W. J., ed. *Getting Started in London Commodities*, 2nd ed. Cedar Falls, Iowa: Investor Publications, 1975. 117 pp. $4.95.

Gray, Roger W. *Trading in Plywood Futures.* Chicago: Chicago Board of Trade, 1972. 26 pp. Apply.

Green, Timothy. *How to Buy Gold.* New York: Walker and Co., 1975. 109 pp. $6.95.

Hammonds, T. M. *The Commodity Futures Market From an Agricultural Producer's Point of View.* New York: MSS Information Corp., 1972. 88 pp. $2.50.

Hayden, Jack J. *What Makes You a Winner or a Loser in the Stock and Commodity Markets?* Larchmont, N.Y.: Investors Intelligence, 1967. 64 pp. $2.95.

Heater, Nancy L. *Commodity Futures Trading, a Bibliography.* Urbana, Ill.: Department of Agricultural Economics, College of Agriculture, University of Illinois, 1966. unpaged (a list of 904 items). $2.60.

Hieronymus, Thomas A. *Economics of Futures Trading for Commercial and Personal Profit.* New York: Commodity Research Bureau, 1971. 338 pp. $12.95.

Houck, James P., Ryan, Mary E., and Subotnik, Abraham. *Soybeans and Their Products; Markets, Models, and Policy.* Minneapolis: University of Minnesota Press, 1972. 284 pp. $10.

International Monetary Market of the Chicago Mercantile Exchange, Inc. *Understanding Gold Futures Trading.* Chicago: 1974. 32 pp. Free.

Jiler, Harry and Parker, George B., eds. *Guide to Commodity Price Forecasting.* New York: Commodity Research Bureau, 1965. 275 pp. $17.50.

Jones, George A. *Trading in Corn Futures.* Chicago: Chicago Board of Trade, 1972. 42 pp. Apply.

Kallard, Thomas. *Make Money in Commodity Spreads! Limited-Risk and Dynamic Commodity Futures Trading Method for Bull and Bear Markets.* New York: Optosonic Press, 1974. 190 pp. $10.

Keltner, Chester W. *How to Make Money in Commodities.* Kansas City, Mo.: Keltner Statistical Service, 1960. 230 pp. $12.50.

Kroll, Stanley and Shishko, Irwin. *Commodity Futures Market Guide.* New York: Harper & Row, 1973. 370 pp. $15.

Kroll, Stanley. *The Professional Commodity Trader (Look Over My Shoulder).* New York: Harper & Row, 1974. 178 pp. $10.

Labys, Walter C. and Granger, C. W. J. *Speculation, Hedging and Commodity Price Forecasts.* Lexington, Mass.: D. C. Heath and Co., 1970. 320 pp. $15.

Liuzza, Vincent J. *Trading in Iced Broiler Futures.* Chicago: Chicago Board of Trade, 1972. 24 pp. Apply.

Longstreet, Roy W. *Viewpoints of a Commodity Trader.* New York: Frederick Fell, 1968. 147 pp. $5.95.

Love, J. S., and Associates. *Trading London Commodity Options.* New York: J. S. Love and Associates, 1974. 21 pp. Free.

Lowell, Fred R. *Profits in Soybeans.* Kansas City, Mo.: Keltner Statistical Service, 1966. 316 pp. $11.95.

Lowell, Fred R. *The Wheat Market.* Kansas City, Mo.: Keltner Statistical Service, 1968. 473 pp. $12.95.

Maxwell, Joseph R. *Commodity Futures Trading With Moving Averages.* Port Angeles, Washington: Speer Books, 1975. 76 pp. $8.

Merrill Lynch, Pierce, Fenner & Smith, Inc. *Do You Have What It Takes to be a Successful Commodity Futures Speculator?* New York: Merrill Lynch, no date. 4 pp. Free.

Merrill Lynch, Pierce, Fenner & Smith, Inc. *How to Buy and Sell Commodities.* New York: Merrill Lynch, 1972. 60 pp. Free.

Munn, Glenn G. *Encyclopedia of Banking and Finance,* 7th ed. Revised by F. L. Garcia. Boston: Bankers Publishing Co., 1973. 953 pp. $49.75.

194 BIBLIOGRAPHY

Powers, Mark J. *Getting Started in Commodity Futures Trading.* Cedar Falls, Iowa: Investor Publications, 1973. 208 pp. $4.95.

Reinach, Anthony M. *The Fastest Game in Town; Trading Commodity Futures.* New York: Random House, 1973. 175 pp. $15.

Rosen, Lawrence R. *When and How to Profit from Buying and Selling Gold.* Homewood, Ill.: Dow Jones-Irwin, 1975. 309 pp. $10.95.

Rukeyser, Louis. *How to Make Money in Wall Street.* Garden City, N.Y.: Doubleday, 1974. 271 pp. $7.95.

Sarnoff, Paul. *London Commodity Options Explained.* New York: Herzog & Co., Inc., no date. 2 pp. Free.

Shaw, John E. B. *A Professional Guide to Commodity Speculation.* West Nyack, N.Y.: Parker Publishing Co. (Prentice-Hall), 1972. 172 pp. $19.95.

Shulman, Morton. *Anyone Can Still Make a Million.* New York: Stein and Day, 1973. 189 pp. $6.95.

Smidt, Seymour. *Amateur Speculators; A Survey of Trading Styles, Information Sources, and Patterns of Entry Into and Exit From Commodity-Futures Markets by Non-Professional Speculators* (Cornell Studies in Policy and Administration). Ithaca, N.Y.: Cornell University, Graduate School of Business and Public Administration, 1965. 53 pp. Inquire.

Smyth, David and Stuntz, Laurance F. *The Speculator's Handbook.* Chicago: Henry Regnery, 1974. 284 pp. $12.95.

Sophisticated Investor. Select Information Exchange. Semiannual. $1.00 per copy. (This publication is also issued under the title *Investment Sources and Ideas.*)

Stewart, Blair. *An Analysis of Speculative Trading in Grain Futures* (U.S. Department of Agriculture Technical Bulletin No. 1001, October 1949). Commodity Exchange Authority. Washington, D.C.: U.S. Government Printing Office, 1949. 134 pp.

Stillman, Richard J. *Guide to Personal Finance; A Lifetime Program of Money Management.* Englewood, N.J.: Prentice-Hall, 1972. 356 pp. $7.50.

Teweles, Richard J., Harlow, Charles V., and Stone, Robert L. *The Commodity Futures Game; Who Wins? Who Loses? Why?* New York: McGraw-Hill, 1974. 638 pp. $16.95. (A complete revision of *Commodity Futures Trading Guide*, published in 1969.)

Train, John. *Dance of the Money Bees; A Professional Speaks Frankly on Investing.* New York: Harper & Row, 1974. 252 pp. $8.95.

Turner, Dennis and Blinn, Stephen H. *Trading Silver—Profitably.* New Rochelle, N.Y.: Arlington House, 1975. 190 pp. $14.95.

Watling, T. F. and Morley, J. *Successful Commodity Futures Trading; How You Can Make Money in Commodity Markets.* London: Business Books Ltd., 1974. 227 pp. $19.95. (Available from Beekman Publishers, Inc., 53 Park Place, New York, N.Y. 10007.)

Williams, Larry R. *How I made One Million Dollars in the Commodity Market Last Year.* Carmel Valley, Calif.: Conceptual Management, 1973. 130 pp. $25. (Available from Commodity Timing, 850 Munras No. 2, Monterey, Calif. 93940.)

Wyckoff, Peter. *International Stock and Commodity Exchange Directory.* Canaan, N.H.: Phoenix Publishing, 1974. 340 pp. $30.

Wyckoff, Peter. *The Language of Wall Street.* New York: Hopkinson and Blake, 1973. 247 pp. $6.50.

Zieg, Kermit C. and Zieg, Susannah H. *Commodity Options.* Larchmont, N.Y.: Investors Intelligence, 1974. 158 pp. $12.50.

GOVERNMENT REPORTS AND PERIODICALS OF INTEREST TO COMMODITY TRADERS

Agricultural Economics Research (Agriculture Department). U.S. Government Printing Office, Washington, D.C. 20402. Quarterly. $3.85/yr.

Agricultural Outlook. (Agriculture Department). U.S. Government Printing Office, Washington, D.C. 20402. Monthly. $19.50/yr.

Agricultural Outlook Digest. Economic Research Service, Agriculture Department, Washington, D.C. 20250. Monthly. Free.

Agricultural Prices. Crop Reporting Board, Agriculture Department, Washington, D.C. 20250. Monthly. Free.

Agricultural Situation; the Crop Reporters Magazine (Agriculture Department). U.S. Government Printing Office, Washington, D.C. 20402. Monthly. $3.30/yr.

Agricultural Supply and Demand Estimates. Outlook and Situation Board, Agriculture Department, Washington, D.C. 20250. Irregular. Free.

Average Monthly Weather Outlook (National Weather Service). U.S. Government Printing Office, Washington, D.C. 20402. Monthly. $7.50/yr.

Broiler Marketing Facts. Agricultural Marketing Service, Agriculture Department, Washington, D.C. 20250. Quarterly. Free.

Business Conditions Digest (Commerce Department). U.S. Government Printing Office, Washington, D.C. 20402. Monthly. $55.25/yr.

Cattle on Feed, Cattle Sold for Slaughter, Selected Markets. Crop Reporting Board, Agriculture Department, Washington, D.C. 20250. Monthly. Free.

Cold Storage Report. Crop Reporting Board, Agriculture Department, Washington, D.C. 20250. Monthly. Free.

Commitments of Traders in Commodity Futures, with Market Concentration Ratios. (Chicago edition: wheat, corn, oats, soybeans, soybean oil, soybean meal, coconut oil, crude palm oil, eggs, cattle, frozen pork bellies, live hogs.) Commodity Futures Trading Commission, 141 W. Jackson Blvd., Chicago, Ill. 60604. Monthly. Free.

Commitments of Traders in Commodity Futures, with Market Concentration Ratios. (New York edition: cotton, frozen concentrated orange juice, potatoes,

GOVERNMENT REPORTS AND PERIODICALS 197

wool, imported frozen fresh boneless beef.) Commodity Futures Trading Commission, 61 Broadway, New York, N.Y. 10006. Monthly. Free.

Confectionery. See *Current Industrial Reports (Confectionery) Construction Review* (Commerce Department). U.S. Government Printing Office, Washington, D.C. 20402. Monthly. $14.50/yr.

Copper Industry (Mineral Industry Survey). Mines Bureau, 4800 Forbes Ave., Pittsburgh, Pa. 15213. Monthly. Free.

Copper Production (Mineral Industry Survey). Mines Bureau, 4800 Forbes Ave., Pittsburgh, Pa. 15213. Monthly. Free.

Copper, Quarterly Report. (Commerce Department.) U.S. Government Printing Office, Washington, D.C. 20402. Quarterly. $3/yr.

Cotton and Wool Situation. Economic Research Service, Agriculture Department, Washington, D.C. 20250. Quarterly. Free.

Cotton Ginnings, Report on Cotton Ginnings. Census Bureau, Suitland, Maryland 20233. Irregular. 10¢ per report, by county or by state.

Cotton Price Statistics. Agricultural Marketing Service, P.O. Box 17723, Memphis, Tennessee 38117. Monthly, including annual for crop season. Free.

Crop Production. Crop Reporting Board, Agriculture Department, Washington, D.C. 20250. Monthly. Free.

Current Business Reports: Green Coffee Inventories, Imports, Roastings. Census Bureau, Suitland, Maryland 20233. Quarterly. $1/yr.

Current Industrial Reports (monthly). Census Bureau, Suitland, Maryland 20233. Price on application.
  Confectionery (Including Chocolate Products), Series M20C.
  Consumption on Woolen and Worsted Systems, Series M22D.
  Cotton . . . Consumption and Stocks and Spindle Activity, Series M22P.
  Fats and Oils, Oilseed Crushings, Series M20J.
  Fats and Oils, Production, Consumption, and Stock, Series M20K.
  Flour Milling Products, Series M20A.
  Inventories of Brass and Copper Wire Mill Shapes, Series M33K.

Current Industrial Reports (quarterly). Census Bureau, Suitland, Maryland 20233. Price on application.
  Copper Base Mill and Foundry Products, Series BDCF-84.
  Cotton Broadwoven Gray Goods, Series MQ-22T.1.
  Inventories of Brass and Copper Wire Mill Shapes, Series MQ-33K.
  Wool Broadwoven Goods, Series MQ-22T.3.

Daily Weather Maps, Weekly Series. (National Oceanic and Atmospheric Administration.) U.S. Government Printing Office, Washington, D.C. 20402. Weekly. $16.50/yr.

Demand and Price Situation. Economic Research Service, Agriculture Department, Washington, D.C. 20250. Quarterly. Free.

Economic Indicators. (Council of Economic Advisers.) U.S. Government Printing Office, Washington, D.C. 20402. Monthly. $10.10/yr.

198 GOVERNMENT REPORTS AND PERIODICALS

Egg Products; Liquid, Frozen, Dried Production Under Federal Inspection. Crop Reporting Board, Agriculture Department, Washington, D.C. 20250. Monthly. Free.

Eggs, Chickens and Turkeys. Crop Reporting Board, Agriculture Department, Washington, D.C. 20250. Monthly. Free.

Fats and Oils Situation. Economic Research Service, Agriculture Department, Washington, D.C. 20250. Five times a year. Free.

Feed Market News, Weekly Summary and Statistics. Agricultural Marketing Service, Agriculture Department, Washington, D.C. 20250. Weekly. Free.

Feed Situation. Economic Research Service, Agriculture Department, Washington, D.C. 20250. Quarterly. Free.

Foreign Agricultural Trade of the United States. Economic Research Service, Agriculture Department, Washington, D.C. 20250. Monthly. Free.

Foreign Agriculture. (Agriculture Department.) U.S. Government Printing Office, Washington, D.C. 20402. Weekly. $34.35/yr.

Foreign Agriculture Circulars. Foreign Agriculture Service, Agriculture Department, Washington, D.C. 20250. Irregular. Free. (Available to United States residents only.)
    Cocoa, Series FCB
    Coffee, Series FCOF
    Cotton, Series FC
    Grains, Series FG
    Livestock and Meat, Series FLM
    Oilseeds and Products, Series FOP (formerly *Fats and Oils*)
    Poultry and Eggs, Series FPE
    Sugar, Series FS
    Wool, Series FW

Fresh Fruit and Vegetable Market News, Weekly Summary, Shipments-Unloads. Agricultural Marketing Service, Agriculture Department, Washington, D.C. 20250. Weekly. Free.

Fruit Situation. Economic Research Service, Agrculture Department, Washington, D.C. 20250. Four times a year. Free.

Gold and Silver. (Mineral Industry Survey.) Mines Bureau, 4800 Forbes Avenue, Pittsburgh, Pa. 15213. Monthly. Free.

Grain Market News, Weekly Summary and Statistics. Grain Division, Agriculture Department, 310 West Lexington Street, Independence, Missouri 64050. Weekly. Free.

Grain Stocks. Crop Reporting Board, Agriculture Department, Washington, D.C. 20250. Quarterly. Free.

Hogs and Pigs. Crop Reporting Board, Agriculture Department, Washington, D.C. 20250. Quarterly. Free.

Livestock and Meat Situation. Economic Research Service, Agriculture Department, Washington, D.C. 20250. Six times/yr. Free.

GOVERNMENT REPORTS AND PERIODICALS 199

Livestock, Meat, Wool, Market News, Weekly Summary and Statistics. Agricultural Marketing Service, Agriculture Department, Washington, D.C. 20250. Weekly. Free.

Livestock Slaughter. Crop Reporting Board, Agriculture Department, Washington, D.C. 20250. Monthly. Free.

Long Staple Cotton Review. Cotton Division, Agricultural Marketing Service, Agriculture Department, 4841 Summer Avenue, Memphis, Tennessee 38122. Monthly. Free.

Monthly Cotton Linters Review. Cotton Division, Agricultural Marketing Service, Agriculture Department, 4841 Summer Avenue, Memphis, Tennessee 38122. Monthly. Free.

National Food Situation. Economic Research Service, Agriculture Department, Washington, D.C. 20250. Quarterly. Free.

On Call Positions in Spot Cotton Based on New York Cotton Futures Reported by Merchants in Special Account Status. Commodity Futures Trading Commission, 61 Broadway, New York, N.Y. 10006. Weekly. Free.

Platinum. (Mineral Industry Survey.) Mines Bureau, 4800 Forbes Avenue, Pittsburgh, Pa. 15213. Quarterly. Free.

Potato Stocks. Crop Reporting Board, Agriculture Department, Washington, D.C. 20250. Four times a year. Free.

Poultry and Egg Situation. Economic Research Service, Agriculture Department, Washington, D.C. 20250. Quarterly. Free.

Production, Prices, Employment, and Trade in Northwest Forest Industries. Forest Service, Agriculture Department, 319 SW Pine Street, Portland, Oregon 97204. Quarterly. Free.

Seed Crops (forecast report and field seed stocks report). Crop Reporting Board, Agriculture Department, Washington, D.C. 20250. Irregular. Free.

Stocks of Grain in Deliverable Positions for Chicago Board of Trade Futures Contracts in Exchange-Approved and/or Federally Licensed Warehouses, as Reported by Those Warehouses. Commodity Futures Trading Commission, 141 West Jackson Boulevard, Chicago, Ill. 60604. Weekly. Free.

Sugar and Sweetener Report. Economic Research Service, Agriculture Department, Washington, D.C. 20250. Monthly. Free.

Sugar Requirements and Area Quotas. Agricultural Stabilization and Conservation Service, Agriculture Department, Washington, D.C. 20250. Irregular. Free.

Survey of Current Business. (Commerce Department.) U.S. Government Printing Office, Washington, D.C. 20402. Monthly. $48.30/yr., including weekly supplement, *Business Statistics.*

Tuesday Spot Market Price Indexes and Prices. Bureau of Labor Statistics, Labor Department, Washington, D.C. 20210. Weekly. Free.

U.S. Export Sales. Foreign Agricultural Service, Agriculture Department, Washington, D.C. 20250. Weekly. Free.

Vegetable Situation. Economic Research Service, Agriculture Department, Washington, D.C. 20250. Quarterly. Free.

Vegetables, Fresh Market. Crop Reporting Board, Agriculture Department, Washington, D.C. 20250. Monthly. Free. (Acreage and estimated production of principal commercial crops.)

Weekly Cotton Market Review. Cotton Division, Agricultural Marketing Service, 4841 Summer Avenue, Memphis, Tennessee 38122. Weekly. Free.

Weekly Weather and Crop Bulletin. (National Weather Service.) Agricultural Climatology Service Office, South Building Mail Unit, Agriculture Department, Washington, D.C. 20250. Weekly. $5.00/yr. (Make checks payable to U.S. Department of Commerce; send orders and payments to Agriculture Department at above address.)

Wheat Situation. Economic Research Service, Agriculture Department, Washington, D.C. 20250. Quarterly. Free.

Wholesale Prices and Price Indexes. (Bureau of Labor Statistics.) U.S. Government Printing Office, Washington, D.C. 20402. Monthly. $23.75/yr.

DIRECTORY OF PUBLISHERS

American Association of Commodity Traders, 286 Fifth Ave., New York, N.Y. 10001

Arlington House, Inc., 165 Huguenot St., New Rochelle, N.Y. 10801

Bache & Company, 40 Wall St., New York, N.Y. 10005

Bankers Publishing Co., 210 South St., Boston, Mass. 02111

Chicago Board of Trade, 141 W. Jackson, Chicago, Ill. 60604

Commodities Press, 3100 Country Lane, Wilmette, Ill. 60091

Commodity Research Bureau, Inc., One Liberty Plaza, New York, N.Y. 10006

The Conference Board, Inc., 845 Third Ave., New York, N.Y. 10022

Consensus, Inc., 30 W. Pershing Rd., Kansas City, Mo. 64108

Cornell University, Graduate School of Business and Public Administration, Ithaca, N.Y. 14850

E. D. Dobson, P.O. Box 10344, Greenville, S.C. 29603

Doubleday & Company, 998 Franklin Ave., Garden City, N.Y. 11530

Dow Jones-Irwin, Inc., 1818 Ridge Rd., Homewood, Ill. 60430

Frederick Fell, Inc., 386 Park Ave., South, New York, N.Y. 10016

Harper & Row, Publishers, 10 E. 53 St., New York, N.Y. 10022

Harvard University, Graduate School of Business Administration, Division of Research, Boston, Mass. 02163

D. C. Heath & Company, 125 Spring St., Lexington, Mass. 02173

Henry Regnery Company, 180 N. Michigan Ave., Chicago, Ill. 60601

Herzog & Co., Inc., 170 Broadway, New York, N.Y. 10038

Hopkinson and Blake Publishing Co., 329 Fifth Ave., New York, N.Y. 10003

International Monetary Market, 444 Jackson Blvd. Chicago, Ill. 60606

Investor Publications, Inc., 219 Parkade, Cedar Falls, Iowa 50613

Investor Publications, Inc., 1000 Century Plaza, Columbia, Md. 21044

DIRECTORY OF PUBLISHERS

Investors Intelligence, Inc., Two East Ave., Larchmont, N.Y. 10538

Keltner Statistical Service, 1004 Baltimore Ave., Kansas City, Mo. 64105

J. S. Love and Associates, 641 Lexington Ave., New York, N.Y. 10022

McGraw-Hill, Inc., 1221 Avenue of the Americas, New York, N.Y. 10020

Merrill Lynch, Pierce, Fenner & Smith, Inc., One Liberty Plaza, New York, N.Y. 10006

MIT Press, 28 Carleton St., Cambridge, Mass. 02142

MSS Information Corp., 655 Madison Ave., New York, N.Y. 10021

Optosonic Press, P.O. Box 883, Ansonia Station, New York, N.Y. 10023

Phoenix Publishing, Canaan, N.H. 03741

Prentice-Hall, Englewood Cliffs, N.J. 07632

Princeton University Press, Princeton, N.J. 08540

Random House, Inc., 201 E. 50 St., New York, N.Y. 10022

Reynolds Securities, Inc., 120 Broadway, New York, N.Y. 10005

Routledge & Kegan Paul, 9 Park St., Boston, Mass. 02108

Select Information Exchange, 2095 Broadway, New York, N.Y. 10023

Simon & Schuster, Inc., 630 Fifth Ave., New York, N.Y.

Speer Books, First National Bank Bldg., Port Angeles, Wash. 98362

Stein and Day Publishers, Scarborough House, Briarcliff Manor, N.Y. 10510

U.S. Government Printing Office, Washington, D.C. 20402

University of Chicago, Chicago, Ill. 60637

University of Illinois, Department of Agricultural Economics, College of Agriculture, Urbana, Ill. 61801

University of Minnesota Press, 2037 University Ave. S.E., Minneapolis, Minn. 55455

Walker and Company, 720 Fifth Ave., New York, N.Y.

AUTHOR INDEX

Anderson, Hilding, 145
Angrist, Stanley W., 1, 2, 3, 16, 31, 52, 53, 57, 61, 66, 73, 76, 79, 85, 93, 99, 100, 106, 109, 119, 130, 133, 137, 139, 146, 152, 161, 165, 173, 185, 187
Arthur, Henry B., 8, 9, 15, 23, 24, 61, 66, 105, 141, 159, 180

Bache & Co., Inc., 89, 165
Bailey, Fred, 78
Baldwin, Gedney H., 187
Belveal, L. Dee, 7, 13, 17, 31, 57, 61, 67, 73, 80, 85, 100, 107, 110, 119, 124, 139, 147, 162, 165, 166, 176, 177, 179
Berlin, Bruce S., 67
Bernstein, Leonard S., 67
Beveridge, E. A., 67, 100
Biderman, Charles, 39
Brealey, Richard A., and Pyle, Connie, 10
Briloff, Abraham J., 160
Business Week, 68, 166

Carabini, Louis E., 10, 64, 111, 134
Cargill, Thomas F., and Rausser, Gordon C., 125
Chicago Board of Trade, 8, 10, 11, 15, 17, 24, 29, 31, 46, 47, 48, 50, 54, 57, 62, 68, 73, 76, 78, 83, 97, 105, 107, 112, 115, 117, 134, 135, 138, 140, 141, 147, 153, 156, 162, 167, 180, 188
Clifton, Frederick T., 8, 62, 68, 79, 90, 147, 148, 149, 162, 163, 186
Clough, Malcolm, 48
Commodities, 2, 11, 13, 18, 30, 32, 44, 111, 112
Commodity Journal, 111
Commodity Research Bureau, 50, 51, 62, 98, 118, 129, 130, 131, 144, 147, 154, 179, 183, 184
Consensus, 111
Conway, Vincent J., 64

Cornish, P. J., 40
Cowing, Cedric B., 74
Cox, Houston A., 8, 18, 23, 32, 52, 55, 57, 62, 74, 85, 90, 94, 101, 107, 110, 113, 158, 167, 173
Cramer, Scott E., 142

Davies, M. E. T., 24, 28, 157, 188
Dobson, Edward D., 149
Donchian, Richard D., 173
Donnelly, Richard A., 133, 188
Dunbar, Ernest A., 82

Elberty, Mary, 77, 115
Emery, Walter L., 48, 51, 138, 142, 157, 181

Feduniak, Robert, 18, 110
Figgis, T. S. E., 127
Fink, Robert, and Turner, Dennis, 44, 94, 131
Forbes, 3

Gardner, Robert L., 18, 23, 32, 62, 69, 74, 80, 101, 120, 149, 155, 167
Glick, Ira O., 120
Gold, Gerald, 19, 23, 32, 52, 53, 57, 61, 62, 66, 69, 74, 94, 102, 113, 149, 150, 153, 155, 158, 167, 174, 176, 177
Goldberg, Ray A., 11, 105, 142, 143, 181
Goss, B. A., 11, 33, 70
Gould, Bruce G., 3, 14, 19, 30, 33, 62, 70, 86, 90, 107, 108, 124, 125, 131, 153, 156, 163, 168
Granger, C. W. J., 30, 33, 62, 81
Gray, Roger W., 83
Green, Leslie, 105
Green, Timothy, 64
Greenberg, Stephen, 99, 145, 150, 184, 186, 187

Hammonds, T. M., 33, 62, 70, 168
Hart, John K., 19, 113
Hayden, Jack J., 19, 120
Heater, Nancy L., 11
Hershman, Arlene, 106

AUTHOR INDEX

Hieronymus, Thomas A., 3, 9, 29, 34, 49, 58, 70, 71, 74, 86, 91, 108, 121, 136, 138, 140, 143, 163, 168
Hill, G. Christian, 40
Houck, James P., and others, 136, 138, 143

Inkeles, David M., 54, 97, 117, 134, 157
International Monetary Market, 65

Jiler, Harry, and Parker, George B., 34
Jiler, Milton W., 62
Jiler, William L., 20, 102
Jones, George A., 49

Kallard, Thomas, 11, 63, 140, 150, 160
Keck, Robert T., 47
Keltner, Chester W., 1, 14, 20, 23, 34, 49, 53, 58, 63, 66, 71, 86, 87, 88, 94, 97, 98, 102, 108, 121, 128, 129, 131, 133, 143, 163, 169, 174, 175, 181, 183
Kiplinger Washington Editors, 35
Kroll, Stanley, 13, 35, 82, 169
Kroll, Stanley, and Shishko, Irwin, 4, 9, 12, 14, 21, 29, 35, 41, 44, 55, 59, 61, 66, 71, 75, 86, 88, 91, 95, 103, 113, 121, 151, 158, 163, 169, 170, 175, 178

Labys, Walter C., and Granger, C. W. J., 12, 75, 125, 154
Lessiter, Frank, 77
Leuthold, Raymond M., 126
Liuzza, Vincent J., 78
Loehwing, David A., 41
Longstreet, Roy W., 21, 59, 82, 110, 121, 133, 151
Love, J. S., and Associates, 41
Lowell, Fred R., 80, 144, 182, 183, 185
Lynch-Garbett, P., 91
Lynde, Harold W., 112

McHale, James E., 140
Maduff, Michael L., 115
Maxwell, Joseph R., 95
Merrill Lynch, Pierce, Fenner & Smith, Inc., 36, 63, 122, 132, 170, 182
Munn, Glenn G., 30, 63
Murray, Thomas J., 42

Nevans, Ronald, 160
Newsweek, 177
Nimrod, Vance L., and Bower, Richard S., 44

Olmedo, James P., 83
Oppenheimer, H. L., 15

Pappas, Vasil, 45
Parker, George B., 15, 16, 42, 81, 117, 129, 154
Powers, Mark J., 9, 13, 36, 59, 63, 72, 75, 103, 108, 126, 151, 153, 164
Prestbo, John A., 36

Radhakrishnan, P., 128
Reinach, Anthony M., 21, 37, 39, 60, 114, 159, 160, 175, 178

Roscow, James P., 4
Rosen, Lawrence R., 65
Rosenbaum, Clarence H., 106
Rukeyser, Louis, 4
Ryan, J. Patrick, 134

Sarnoff, Paul, 42
Sayers, W. B., 84
Schruben, Leonard W., and Clifton, Ruth E., 182, 184
Seim, Dick, 72, 82
Select Information Exchange, 2
Shakin, Bernard, 42
Shane, Arthur F., 136
Shaw, John E. B., 12, 21, 37, 45, 52, 53, 54, 63, 72, 77, 87, 88, 96, 104, 108, 114, 115, 132, 141, 152, 153, 160, 171, 178
Sherwood, Hugh C., 171
Shishko, Irwin, 21, 24, 60, 157
Shulman, Morton, 37, 43, 124, 171
Smidt, Seymour, 5
Smyth, David, and Stuntz, Laurance F., 5, 47, 65, 135
Snider, Thomas E., 72
Stern, William, 25
Stevenson, Richard A., and Bear, Robert M., 126
Stewart, Blair, 6
Stillman, Richard J., 37, 63
Stoken, Dick 115
Struning, William C., 28

Teweles, Richard J., and others, 6, 9, 12, 13, 16, 22, 25, 26, 27, 28, 37, 46, 47, 49, 51, 55, 56, 60, 73, 76, 77, 84, 87, 89, 91, 92, 96, 97, 99, 104, 106, 108, 109, 113, 116, 118, 122, 123, 127, 129, 132, 135, 137, 139, 141, 144, 145, 152, 154, 156, 157, 161, 164, 171, 172, 176, 178, 182, 186, 189
Thackray, John, 6, 172
Train, John, 7
Turner, Dennis, and Blinn, Stephen H., 135

Vannerson, Frank, 185

Warden, Paul S., 7
Watling, T. F., and Morley, J., 12, 25, 28, 30, 38, 43, 47, 63, 81, 123, 128, 135, 139, 154, 158, 172, 183, 189
Weymar, F. Helmut, 26
Wheelan, Alexander H., 114
Wideman, Frank L., 47
Williams, Larry R., 2, 14, 22, 37, 38, 60, 93, 96, 104, 118, 123
Wyckoff, Peter, 31, 63

Young, Clarke D., 79

Zieg, Kermit C., and Zieg, Susannah H., 12, 43

SUBJECT INDEX

Action and Reaction Theory, 1
Advisory Services, 1–2
Amateur Speculation, 3–7
Averaging Down, 7

Basis, 8–9
Bibliographies, 10–12
Brokers, 12–14

Cash Commodity, 14–16
Charts, 16–22
Clearinghouse, 22–23
Cocoa, 23–26
Cocoa—Seasonal Price Trend, 26–27
Coconut Oil, 27
Coffee, 27–29
Commissions, 29
Commodity Exchanges, 29–31
Commodity Futures (in General), 31–38
Commodity Futures as Inflation Hedges, 39
Commodity Options, 39–43
Computer Analysis, 44–45
Contrary Opinion, 46
Copper, 47
Corn, 48–49
Corn—Seasonal Price Trend, 50
Cotton, 50–51
Cotton—Seasonal Price Trend, 51
Cotton Spread, 51

Definitions, see Glossaries
Discretionary Accounts, 52
Double Tops and Bottoms, 53
Dow-Jones Commodity Futures Index, 53

Eggs, 54–55
Elliott Wave Principle, 55–56
Exchanges, see Commodity Exchanges

Fundamental Analysis, 56–60

Gaps, 61
Glossaries, 61–63
Gold, 64–65
Head-and-Shoulders Formation, 65–66
Hedging, 66–73
History of Futures Trading, 73–76
Hog-Corn Ratio, 76
Hogs (Live), 76–77

Iced Broilers, 78
Income Tax Considerations, see Tax Considerations
Institutional Investing, 79
Intermarket Wheat Spread, 79–80
Inverted Market, 80

Leverage, 80
London Commodity Markets, 81
Losses, 82
Lumber and Plywood, 83–84

Margin, 84–87
Mechanical Trading Systems, 87–89
Money Management, 89–93
Moon Cycles, 93
Moving Average, 93–96

News Events, 96

Oats, 97
Oats—Seasonal Price Trend, 98
Oats-Corn Spread, 98–99
Open interest, 100–104
Options, see Commodity Options
Orange Juice, 105–106
Orders to Brokers, 106–108
Oscillator Method, 109
Overtrading, 109–110

Periodicals, 111–112
Platinum and Palladium, 112–113
Point-and-Figure Charts, 113–114

205

SUBJECT INDEX

Pork Bellies, Frozen, 114–116
Pork Bellies Frozen—Seasonal Price Trend, 116
Potatoes, 117–118
Premium Market, 118
Presidential Election Years and Commodity Prices, 118
Psychology, 119–123
Pyramiding, 124

Random Walk Theory, 124–127
Rubber, 127–128
Rules for Trading, see Trading Rules
Rye, 128–129
Rye—Seasonal Price Trend, 129

Seasonal Price Trend, 130–132
Short Selling, 133
Silver, 133–135
Soybean Meal, 135–137
Soybean Meal Spread, 137
Soybean Oil, 138–139
Soybean Oil-Soybean Meal-Soybeans Spread, 139–141
Soybeans, 141–144
Soybeans—Seasonal Price Trend, 144–145
Soybeans Spread, 145
Spot Commodity, see Cash Commodity
Spreads, 146–152
Statistics Sources, 152–154

Statistics Sources (London Markets), 154
Statistics Sources (Soybeans), 154
Stock Prices and Commodity Prices, 154–155
Stop-loss Orders, 155–156
Straddles, see Spreads
Sugar, 156–158
Support and Resistance Levels, 158–159

Tax Considerations, 159–161
Technical Analysis, 161–164
Time Cycles, 164
Trading Rules, 165–172
Trend Following, 173–176
Triangles (Coils), 176

"The Voice From the Tomb," 176–177
Volume of Trading, 177–178

War and Commodity Prices, 179
Wave Theory, see Elliott Wave Principle
Weather Market, 179
Wheat, 180–183
Wheat—Seasonal Price Trend, 183–184
Wheat Spread, 184–185
Wheat-Corn Spread, 185–186
Wheat-Rye Spread, 186–187
Women as Commodity Traders, 187
Wool, 187–189